英语听力、口语技巧大全

Do you speak english?

王舒葳 著

北京理工大学出版社
BEIJING INSTITUTE OF TECHNOLOGY PRESS

使用说明 User's Guide

30堂英语特训课！
英语力速成！

本书规划了 10 个单元，共 30 堂课，另有 4 大练习单元。每一单元都由浅入深地讲解了各种最实用、最好用的听力、口语技巧。舒葳老师还整理出了每个单元的学习重点，让你时时保持课前预习的好习惯。

POINT 1
热身活动帮助你脑袋"开机"运转

每单元的第 1、第 3 堂课开始都会有热身练习题，是帮助你脑袋顺利"开机"运转、重新整理"死机"脑袋的最佳帮手！题目下面直接有答案，马上写马上对，一点都不会浪费时间。

POINT 2
一口流利地道的美式发音真容易

独家邀请专业美籍录音员详细录制书中各种发音。一次听不懂？重播 100 次直到听懂为止！清楚的咬字，详细地表达发音的细微不同之处。当发音细节都学会了，随时随地讲出流利地道的美式口音就不再是难事！

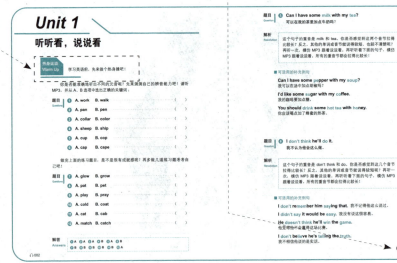

★ 录音内容包括题目、精选英语例句、英语词汇。
★ 本书附赠音频为MP3格式。
★ 音频编号即页码。

POINT 3

用心的实际演练解题技巧

热身的题目都不会做？放心！舒葳老师手把手，一题一题解析给你看！不怕你有问题，只怕你不愿学！每一道题解析下面还会补充从练习题里面整理出来的实用会话，帮助你更加熟悉老外的英语使用习惯。

舒葳老师详细解析

1 超级实用句型
舒葳老师精选的重要句型。

2 你也可以这么说
将出现过的重点句子进行整理。

3 可活用的补充句型
题目延伸的补充句子。

4 地道英语随便说
生活中能用到的句子，以及对话实例。

5 容易混淆的词汇
一般人容易混淆的词汇比较。

6 超级实用词汇
选取句子中最实用的词汇进行整理。

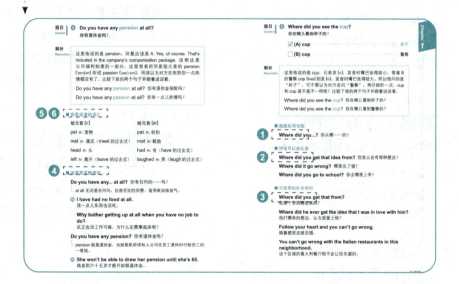

提醒便条纸，时时刻刻提醒你

如果还是抓不住重点的话，就来看看舒葳老师特别整理出来的经验分享以及篇章重点吧！当作是一张一张简单又易懂的便条纸时时刻刻提醒自己。

003

目录 Contents

- **Chapter 1**
  辨别发音相似的元音
  cap, cop, 还是 cup? / 001
  - Unit 1・听听看，说说看
  - Unit 2・自然发音
  - Unit 3・再听听看

- **Chapter 2**
  辨别发音相似的辅音
  sing, thing, 还是 thin? / 025
  - Unit 1・听听看，说说看
  - Unit 2・自然发音
  - Unit 3・再听听看

- **Chapter 3**
  词尾消失的规则
  You won't believe it! / 049
  - Unit 1・听听看，说说看
  - Unit 2・消失的辅音
  - Unit 3・再听听看

- **Chapter 4**
  掌握单词的重音
  compete, competition, competitive, competency / 067
  - Unit 1・听听看，说说看
  - Unit 2・单词的重音规则
  - Unit 3・标出重音节，并念念看

- **Chapter 5**
  句子的重音与节奏
  It's a beautiful day! / 087
  - Unit 1・听听看，说说看
  - Unit 2・句子重音与节奏的规则
  - Unit 3・再听听看

- **Chapter 6**
  非重点单词的弱化
  Let's rock'n roll! / 107
  - Unit 1・听听看，说说看
  - Unit 2・弱化的声音
  - Unit 3・再听听看

一步接着一步扎实地完成上课进度
30堂英语特训课让你立刻功力大增

● **Chapter 7**
连音变化
Tele ri mi ser. Tell her I miss her! / 123

- Unit 1・听听看，说说看
- Unit 2・连音规则
- Unit 3・再听听看

● **Chapter 8**
语调与弦外之音
What would you like? / 143

- Unit 1・听听看，说说看
- Unit 2・语调变化
- Unit 3・再听听看

● **Chapter 9**
语意单位及英语笔记
I don't think I know.
I don't think. I know. / 167

- Unit 1・听听看，说说看
- Unit 2・语意单位
- Unit 3・再听听看

● **Chapter 10**
成语、惯用语及短语 / 187

- Unit 1・听听看，说说看
- Unit 2・成语、惯用语及短语
- Unit 3・再听听看

Goal

目录 Contents

上完课之后立即验收成果!
牛刀小试。

Practice 1 听力实战练习1

Conversational Exchange
常见表达用语及对话模式 / 223

- Unit 1・必备日常用语
- Unit 2・赞美与回应
- Unit 3・同意与反对
- Unit 4・告知坏消息

Practice 2 听力实战练习2

Daily Conversations
生活会话 / 235

- Unit 1・短篇对话
- Unit 2・长篇对话

Practice 3 听力实战练习3

Announcement and TV / Radio Commercials
广播与广告 / 265

- Unit 1・公共场合的广播
- Unit 2・电视及广播的广告

Practice 4 听力实战练习4

News and Weather Reports
新闻与天气预报 / 311

- Unit 1・新闻与天气预报

学习表 Study Schedule

记录填下完成日期，确认复习次数，让学习滴水不漏。

第 1 堂	第 2 堂	第 3 堂	第 4 堂
／ ／	／ ／	／ ／	／ ／
check □□□□	check □□□□	check □□□□	check □□□□
第 5 堂	第 6 堂	第 7 堂	第 8 堂
／ ／	／ ／	／ ／	／ ／
check □□□□	check □□□□	check □□□□	check □□□□
第 9 堂	第 10 堂	第 11 堂	第 12 堂
／ ／	／ ／	／ ／	／ ／
check □□□□	check □□□□	check □□□□	check □□□□
第 13 堂	第 14 堂	第 15 堂	第 16 堂
／ ／	／ ／	／ ／	／ ／
check □□□□	check □□□□	check □□□□	check □□□□
第 17 堂	第 18 堂	第 19 堂	第 20 堂
／ ／	／ ／	／ ／	／ ／
check □□□□	check □□□□	check □□□□	check □□□□
第 21 堂	第 22 堂	第 23 堂	第 24 堂
／ ／	／ ／	／ ／	／ ／
check □□□□	check □□□□	check □□□□	check □□□□
第 25 堂	第 26 堂	第 27 堂	第 28 堂
／ ／	／ ／	／ ／	／ ／
check □□□□	check □□□□	check □□□□	check □□□□
第 29 堂	第 30 堂		
／ ／	／ ／		
check □□□□	check □□□□		

听力实战练习 1	听力实战练习 2	听力实战练习 3	听力实战练习 4
／ ／	／ ／	／ ／	／ ／
check □□□□	check □□□□	check □□□□	check □□□□

Chapter 1

辨别发音相似的元音
cap, cop, 还是 cup？

听力 Listening
口语 Speaking

Unit 1 听听看，说说看

Unit 2 自然发音

Unit 3 再听听看

学习重点
Main Point

cap, cop, 还是 cup？这三个单词你说得对、分得清吗？

可能从来没有人告诉过你，想要轻松听懂老外说英语，或要老外听懂我们说什么，第一件要做的事其实是正音。因为发音相似的英语元音，是造成我们说得不对，也听不懂老外说什么的原因之一。如果我们能分辨这些发音的不同，并且自己也能说清楚，一定有助于听力的改善！

本课我们学习容易混淆的元音，并全方位练习，帮助同学检测自己的发音和辨音能力，进而打下良好听力的基础！

Unit 1

听听看，说说看

热身活动 Warm Up 学习英语前，先来做个热身操吧！

你是否能准确地听出不同的元音呢？先来测测自己的辨音能力吧！请听 MP3，并从 A、B 选项中选出正确的关键词：

题目 Questions

1. A. work   B. walk   (   )
2. A. pan   B. pen   (   )
3. A. collar B. color   (   )
4. A. sheep   B. ship   (   )
5. A. cup   B. cop   (   )
6. A. cap   B. cape   (   )

做完上面的练习题目，是不是很有成就感呢？再多做几道练习题考考自己吧！

题目 Questions

7. A. glow   B. grow   (   )
8. A. pat   B. pet   (   )
9. A. play   B. pray   (   )
10. A. cold   B. coat   (   )
11. A. cat   B. cab   (   )
12. A. match B. catch   (   )

解答 Answers

1 A   2 A   3 A   4 B   5 A   6 B
7 B   8 B   9 B   10 B 11 B 12 A

Unit 1 听听看，说说看

实际演练 Explanation 通过认真的解题练习打下扎实的基础。

题目 Question

❶ Why are you working in the dark?
你为什么在黑暗中工作？

☑ (A) work ……………………………………… 工作
☐ (B) walk ……………………………………… 散步

解析 Resolution

这里他说的是 working，元音发 [ɜ]，有卷舌。答案 B 的 walking，元音则发 [ɔ]，没有卷舌，嘴形张开。所以他问的是你为什么在黑暗中工作，而不是你为什么在黑暗中散步。再仔细听一次，working 和 walking 是不是不一样呢？比较下面的两个句子并跟着说说看。

Why are you working in the dark? 你为什么在黑暗中工作？
Why are you walking in the dark? 你为什么在黑暗中散步？

■ 超级实用句型

Why are you...? 你为什么要……？

in the dark 在黑暗中；在暗处

■ 你也可以这么说

Why are they sitting in the dark?
他们为什么坐在黑暗中？

Why are you dancing in the dark?
你们为什么在黑暗中跳舞？

■ 可活用的补充例句

I'm afraid of the darkness. 我怕黑。

She couldn't see anything in the dark.
她在黑暗中什么也看不见。

I was kept in the dark.
我（那时）被蒙在鼓里。

题目 Question ❷ **Could you pass me that pan over there, please?**
可以请你把那个平底锅递给我吗？

☑ **(A) pan** ·· 平底锅

☐ **(B) pen** ··· 钢笔

解析 Resolution

这里他说的是 pan，元音发 [æ]，发音时嘴巴张得较开而扁。答案 B 的 pen，元音则发 [e]，发音时嘴巴比较含蓄。如果我们不知道 [æ] 和 [e] 在发音上的差别，就很容易误以为他说的是 pen [pen]，而误递"钢笔"给他了。再仔细听一次，pan 和 pen 是不是不一样呢？比较下面的两个句子并跟着说说看。

Could you pass me that pan over there, please?
可以请你把那个平底锅递给我吗？

Could you pass me that pen over there, please?
可以请你把那支钢笔递给我吗？

■ **超级实用句型**

Could you pass me the...? 可以请你把……递给我吗？

■ **你也可以这么说**

Could you pass me the salt? 可以请你把盐递给我吗？

Could you pass me the bread? 可以请你把面包递给我吗？

■ **可活用的补充例句**

Most people in China eat too much salt.
在中国，大多数人都吃太多盐了。

Please slice a loaf of bread for me.
请帮我切一片面包。

I can't miss another day of work. That's my bread and butter.
我不能再缺勤了，那可是我的饭碗啊。

小贴士 Tip

bread and butter 是"面包与奶油"的意思，也可以引申为"赖以为生的方式"。

题目 Question

3 **I think the collar of this shirt would suit you better.**
我想这件衬衫的领子应该会比较适合你。

- ☑ **(A) collar** ……………………………………………… 领子
- ☐ **(B) color** ………………………………………………… 颜色

解析 Resolution

这里他说的是 collar，元音发 [ɑː]，发音时嘴巴张得较大。答案 B 的 color，元音则发 [ʌ]，发音时嘴巴张得较小，音也发得稍短。所以他说的是那件衬衫的"领子"而非它的"颜色"。再仔细听一次，collar 和 color 是不是不一样呢？比较下面的两个句子并跟着说说看。

I think the collar of this shirt would suit you better.
我想这件衬衫的领子应该会比较适合你。

I think the color of this shirt would suit you better.
我想这件衬衫的颜色应该会比较适合你。

■ 你也可以这么说

He suits you well. 他很适合你。

That suits me fine. 那很适合我。

That color doesn't suit you at all. 那个颜色一点也不适合你。

Suit yourself. 随便你。

■ 可活用的补充例句

Red is your color. 红色适合你。

小贴士 Tip

听到 ... suit(s) you，或是 ... is your color 就表示对方在 compliment（赞美）你。这时候可以回应对方的赞美，说声：

It's nice of you to say so. Thank you!
你这么说真好，谢谢！

而如果对方说的是 It doesn't suit you.，你可能便要反问：

You think so? 你这么觉得吗？

What's wrong with it? 什么地方不对吗？

题目 ④ Look! What a huge ship!
看！好大的一艘船啊！

- ☐ (A) sheep ……………………………………………… 绵羊
- ☑ (B) ship ………………………………………………… 船

解析 Resolution

这里他说的是 ship，元音发短音 [ɪ]。答案 A 的 sheep，元音则发长音 [i]。所以他指的是好大的"船"，而非好大的"绵羊"。再仔细听一次，sheep 是不是声音拉得比较长，而 ship 比较短呢？比较下面的两个句子并跟着说说看。

Look! What a huge sheep! 看！好大的一只绵羊啊！

Look! What a huge ship! 看！好大的一艘船啊！

■ 超级实用句型

What a(n) + ...! 真是个……啊！

小贴士 Tip

听到 What a(n)...!，就知道对方要对某人、事、物的感觉表达他的看法，可以是正面的也可以是负面的。如果后面的名词为不可数名词，则不加冠词"a / an"。

■ 可活用的补充例句

How amazing! 多神奇啊！

How ugly that building is! 那栋建筑物真丑！

小贴士 Tip

上面的 What a(n) + ...! 是 What 后面接名词，表达对某件事物的赞叹或不好的感觉。这里的 How + ...! 也是类似的用法，只是加的是形容词。

回应对方的句子，如果你赞同，便说：

It surely is! 的确是！

不赞同则可以说：

Well, I think it's OK. 这个嘛，我觉得还可以。

Well, I quite like it. 这个嘛，我倒是蛮喜欢的。

Unit 1 听听看，说说看

题目 **⑤** **Where did you see the cup?**
Question
你在哪儿看到杯子的？

☑ **(A) cup** ··· 杯子

☐ **(B) cop** ··· 警察

解析
Resolution

这里他说的是 cup，元音发 [ʌ]，发音时嘴巴张得较小。答案 B 的 cop，元音则发 [ɑ]，发音时嘴巴张得较大。所以他问的是"杯子"，可不要以为对方在问"警察"。再仔细听一次，cup 和 cop 是不是不一样呢？比较下面的两个句子并跟着说说看。

Where did you see the cup? 你在哪儿看到杯子的？
Where did you see the cop? 你在哪儿看到警察的？

■ 超级实用句型

Where did you...? 你从哪儿……的？

■ 你也可以这么说

Where did you get that idea from? 你怎么会有那种想法？
Where did it go wrong? 哪里出了错？
Where did you go to school? 你去哪里上学？

■ 可活用的补充例句

Where did you get that from?
那个东西哪里来的？

Where did he ever get the idea that I was in love with him?
他怎么会认为我爱上了他？

Follow your heart and you can't go wrong.
跟着感觉走就没错。

You can't go wrong with the Italian restaurants in this neighborhood.
这个街区的意大利餐厅绝不会让你失望的。

题目 Question

6 **Who is that woman wearing a cape?**
穿着斗篷的那个女人是谁？

☐ **(A) cap** .... 帽子

☑ **(B) cape** .... 斗篷

解析 Resolution

这里他说的是 cape，元音发 [e]，声音要拉长。答案 A 的 cap，元音则发 [æ]，是嘴形扁而开的短音。所以他问的是"穿着斗篷的那个女人"而不是"戴着帽子的那个女人"。再仔细听一次，cape 是不是声音拉得比较长，而 cap 的声音比较短呢？比较下面的两个句子并跟着说说看。

Who is that woman wearing a cap?
戴着帽子的那个女人是谁？

Who is that woman wearing a cape?
穿着斗篷的那个女人是谁？

■ 超级实用句型

Who is that... wearing...? 穿……的那个……是谁？

小贴士 Tip
问某人是谁时，常以他的穿着来说明指的是谁。这里我们也可以说：Who is... in / with...。

■ 你也可以这么说

Who is that woman wearing a yellow dress?
穿黄色连衣裙的那个女人是谁？

Who is that girl in yellow?
穿黄色衣服的那个女人是谁？

Who is that man with a beard and a moustache?
留胡须的那个男人是谁？

小贴士 Tip
beard 指的是长在下巴上的络腮胡，moustache 则是指嘴巴上方的胡子。

Unit 1 听听看，说说看

提醒便条纸
Reminder

舒葳老师的小叮咛，提枪上阵也不怕。

上面的练习你都做对了吗？在日常生活中，我们听不懂或听错老外的意思，常常是因为混淆了发音相似的单词。因为很多单词我们自己都念不正确，听到时自然也就分辨不出，或误以为是别的单词。所以培养良好听力的第一步便是把元音发得正确，之后自然也就听得轻松了！

MEMO

Listening & Speaking

Unit 2

自然发音

课前准备 Preparation　准备充足的话，必能事半功倍。

英语的字母和音标有紧密的关联性，我们只要掌握一些原则，大半的单词看到就会念，会念就会拼。念得准了，也就听得懂了。下面我们就一起来看看发音和拼单词间的关系。

英语用 26 个字母来组成单词，却用另一套音标来标注这些字母。以第一个字母 a 来说，它的读音用音标来表示是 [e]。反过来我们也可以说，音标 [e] 的发音就如同字母 a。这样的规则，对我们来说反而是学正确发音的好方法。26 个字母中的五个元音字母 a、e、i、o、u 的读音用音标标示，分别如下表：

字母	Aa	Ee	Ii	Oo	Uu
读音（音标）	[e]	[i]	[aɪ]	[o]	[ju]

从上表我们得知音标 [e] 如同字母 Aa，[i] 如同 Ee，以下类推。这五个音标是元音，而且是长元音。另外这五个元音字母还可以发成短元音，我们看下表：

字母	Aa	Ee	Ii	Oo	Uu
长元音	[e]	[i]	[aɪ]	[o]	[ju]
短元音	[æ]	[ɛ]	[ɪ]	[ɑ], [ɔ]	[ʌ]

Unit 2 自然发音

至于五个元音字母 a、e、i、o、u 分别在何种情况下读长元音，在何种情况下读短元音，则有规则可循：

■ **短元音**
Rule：单音节或重音节里的单一元音字母发短元音

a [æ] ———— ax n. 斧　　　　　　　bat n. 球棒
　　　　　　　rapid a. 快速的　　　batman n. 蝙蝠侠

e [ɛ] ———— egg n. 蛋　　　　　　　pet n. 宠物
　　　　　　　setup n. / v. 安排　　rental n. 出租；a. 出租的

i [ɪ] ———— ink n. 墨水　　　　　　trip n. 旅途
　　　　　　　riddle n. 谜语　　　　tickle v. 搔痒；n. 痒的感觉

o [ɑ] ———— ox n. 公牛　　　　　　mop v. 拖地；n. 拖把
　[ɔ]　　　　problem n. 问题　　　Boston n. 波士顿
（o 短元音有时发 [ɑ]，有时发 [ɔ]。）

u [ʌ] ———— bus n. 公交车　　　　cut v. 切；n. 割伤
　　　　　　　butter n. 黄油　　　　umbrella n. 雨伞

■ **长元音**
Rule 1：元音字母 + 辅音字母 + e 的组合，元音字母发长元音

a [e] ———— make v. 做　　　　　　rate n. 比率
　　　　　　　fake v. 伪造；n. 赝品　classmate n. 同学

e [i] ———— gene n. 基因　　　　　scene n. 场景、背景
　　　　　　　theme n. 主题　　　　mete v. 分配

i [aɪ] ———— rice n. 米　　　　　　　hike v. 爬山
　　　　　　　spine n. 脊椎　　　　　file n. 档案；v. 归档

o [o] ———— hope n. / v. 希望　　　globe n. 地球；地球仪
　　　　　　　Pope n. 教皇　　　　　cone n. 圆锥体

u [ju] ———— cute a. 可爱的　　　　　mute a. 沉默的
　[u]　　　　crude a. 粗糙的；粗野的　flute n. 长笛

■ 长元音
Rule 2：两个元音字母组合，发前面元音字母的长元音

字母	音标	例词
ai ay	[e]	rain n. 雨；v. 下雨　　mail n. 邮件；v. 寄信 play v. 玩乐　　halfway a. 中途的
ee ea ei	[i]	fee n. 费用　　heel n. 脚后跟；鞋跟 flea n. 跳蚤　　realize v. 明白；了解 ceiling n. 天花板　　either a. （两者之中）任何一个
igh ie	[aɪ]	sigh n. / v. 叹气　　delight n. 欣喜；v. 使高兴 necktie n. 领带　　lie v. 说谎；n. 谎言
oa oe	[o]	coat n. 大衣　　loan n. / v. 贷款 toe n. 脚趾头　　foe n. 仇敌
ue ui	[u]	true a. 真实的　　clue n. 线索 suit n. 套装　　cruise v. / n. 巡航；巡游

音标中除了以上列举的元音之外，还有其他元音，而这些元音也与字母有着一定的联系，且有规则可循：

■ 长元音
Rule 3：双元音

字母	音标	例词
au aw	[ɔ]	fault n. 错误　　naughty a. 顽皮的 law n. 法律　　raw a. 生的；未加工的
ou ow	[aʊ]	cloud n. 云　　bounce v. / n. 跳跃 clown n. 小丑　　town n. 城镇 （注意：ow 也可以发 [o]，如：snow 雪 n.；glow 发光 v.；光辉 n. 等。）
ew	[ju] [u]	few a. 少的　　stew v. 炖煮；焖煮；n. 炖菜 crew n. 工作人员
oo	[u] [u]	moon n. 月亮　　fool n. 笨蛋 cook v. 做菜；n. 厨师　　foot n. 脚
oi oy	[ɔɪ]	avoid v. 避免　　moisture n. / v. 湿润 toy n. 玩具　　loyal a. 忠诚的

Unit 2 自然发音

■ 长元音
Rule 4：加 "r" 的元音

ar [ɑr] —— hard a. 难的；硬的　garden n. 花园
March n. 三月
arch n. 拱门；v. 拱起；形成弧形

or [ɔr] —— fork n. 叉子　　　　morning n. 早晨
lord n. 君主；上帝　sort n. 种类；分类；v. 整理

er ir ur [ɜ] —— clerk n. 办事员　　herd n. 畜群；v. 放牧
shirt n. 衬衫　　　flirt n. / v. 调情
hurry v. 赶快；n. 急忙
burden n. 负担；v. 加负担于……

air are ear [ɛr] —— fair a. 公平的、皮肤白皙的；n. 博览会
stair n. 楼梯
fare n. 票价　　　dare v. 敢；n. 果敢行为
wear v. 穿　　　　pear n. 梨

ear [ɪr] —— year n. 年
clear a. 清楚的；晴朗的；v. 清除、使清楚
dear a. 亲爱的；n. 亲爱的人
fear v. / n. 害怕

（注意：ear 可以发 [ɪə]，也可以发 [ɪr]。）

收尾练习 Exercise

上完课是不是头昏脑涨了？来做做收尾练习吧！

依照自然发音的原则写下你听到的单词：

题目 Questions

1. _____
2. _____
3. _____
4. _____
5. _____
6. _____
7. _____
8. _____

现在请听 MP3，比较下面单词发音的不同，并跟着说说看。

- fill v. 填满 — feel n. / v. 感觉
- fail v. 失败 — fell v. 掉落（fall 的过去式）
- chip n. 炸薯条（片）；晶片 — cheap a. 便宜的 — chop v. / n. 砍；n. 肋排
- eel n. 鳗鱼 — ill a. 生病的、不好的
- bowl n. 碗 — boil v. 煮沸 — ball n. 球
- draw v. 画；拖；领取 — drew v. 画；拖；领取（draw 的过去式）
- saw v. 看（see 的过去式）— soul n. 灵魂
- four n. 四 — fall n. 秋天

解答 Answers

1. fill 2. fell 3. chip 4. ill 5. boil
6. draw 7. soul 8. four

Unit 2 自然发音

提醒便条纸
Reminder

舒葳老师的小叮咛，提枪上阵也不怕。

我们在前面介绍的这些规则可以帮助你抓住英语拼单词与发音之间的关系，也就是说听到声音你便能准确判断对方说的是什么单词。

要特别说明的是，我们在这里介绍的是大方向的原则，有些较琐碎的规则，我们在这里暂不介绍。虽然英语单词发音不乏不符合规则的例外，但只要熟悉了大方向，抓住了发音的基本原则，就能为你将来的听说能力打下扎实的基础！

MEMO Listening & Speaking

Unit 3

再听听看

热身活动 Warm Up 学习英语前，先来个热身活动吧！

在学会了自然发音后，现在你是否能准确地听出不同的元音了呢？请听 MP3，并从 A、B 选项中选出适当的回复：

题目 Questions

1. A. He was our neighbor from 1992 to 1998.
   B. About half an hour ago.
   ……………………………………………………………………… (　)

2. A. Sure. Would you like the salt too?
   B. Sure. And you have a pen there, don't you?
   ……………………………………………………………………… (　)

3. A. Oh, no! I left it on the dock.
   B. Oh, no! I left it on the baseball court.
   ……………………………………………………………………… (　)

4. A. Yes, of course. That's included in the company's compensation package.
   B. Give me a break. I'm just having a bad day, OK?
   ……………………………………………………………………… (　)

5. A. Do you think so? I thought it was a bit too sour.
   B. It sure was. He's one of the best players I have ever seen.
   ……………………………………………………………………… (　)

6. A. Yeah, especially if we want to finish this project in time.
   B. Yes, but we need to get the material ready first.
   ……………………………………………………………………… (　)

解答 Answers ① B ② A ③ A ④ A ⑤ B ⑥ A

Unit 3 再听听看

实际演练 Explanation 通过认真的解题练习打下扎实的基础。

题目 Question

① **When did he leave here?**
他什么时候离开这里的?

解析 Resolution

这里他问的是何时离开,因此恰当的回答应该是 B。这里如果没有注意,长短音分辨不清楚,很容易把 leave 误以为是 live,而完全误解了对方的问题。比较下面的两个句子并跟着说说看。

When did he leave here? 他什么时候离开这里的?
When did he live here? 他什么时候住在这里的?

■ 容易混淆的词汇

长元音 [iː]

sheep n. 绵羊
sheet n. 一片;一张
heat n. 高温;热度
lead n. 铅
least a. 最少的

短元音 [ɪ]

ship n. 船
shit n. 屎
hit n. 打;打击 v. 打击;袭击
lid n. 盖子
list n. 名单

■ 地道英语随便说

The train leaves at a quarter to the hour.
火车在每个整点过 45 分钟时发车。
└ a quarter (of a year) 三个月,也就是一年的四分之一。

例 **There was a fall in unemployment in the third quarter of the year.**
今年第三季度的失业率有所下降。

I get an electricity bill every quarter.
我每个季度都会收到一次电费账单。

题目 Question ❷ Can you pass me the pepper, please?
可以请你把胡椒递给我吗？

解析 Resolution

> 这里他说的是 pepper，当然回复应该是答应后再问需要盐吗。因此恰当的回答是 A。这里容易犯的错，是把 [ɛ] 和 [e] 混淆，把 pepper 听成了 paper。比较下面的两个句子并跟着说说看。
>
> Can you pass me the pepper, please?
> 可以请你把胡椒递给我吗？
>
> Can you pass me the paper, please?
> 可以请你把纸递给我吗？

■ 容易混淆的词汇

短元音 [ɛ]

let v. 让

bet v. 赌

tell v. 说

fell v. 摔倒（fall 的过去式）

长元音 [e]

late a. 晚的；迟的

bait n. 诱饵

tale n. 故事

fail n. 不及格 vi. 失败；缺乏
vt. 不及格；使失重

■ 地道英语随便说

bell pepper 甜椒类（包含绿青椒、红色与黄色的甜椒）

chili pepper 辣椒

chili pepper sauce (= hot pepper sauce)
辣椒酱（液状，如墨西哥辣椒酱）

hot pepper paste 辣椒糊（较浓稠，如韩国辣椒酱）

例 The **Hot Pepper Challenge** is a popular dare game involving eating extremely hot peppers, normally the ghost pepper.
"辣椒挑战"是一种很受欢迎的挑战游戏，参赛者比赛吃非常辣的辣椒，而且通常是吃"魔鬼辣椒"。

题目 Question

③ Where did you put the bait?
你把鱼饵放哪儿了?

解析 Resolution

这里他说的是 bait，比较恰当的回复应该是 A，表示留在码头了。这里容易犯的错是把 [e] 和 [æ] 混淆，把 bait 听成了 bat。比较下面的两个句子并跟着说说看。

Where did you put the bait? 你把鱼饵放哪儿了?

Where did you put the bat? 你把球棒放哪儿了?

■ 容易混淆的词汇

长元音 [e]　　　　　　　　短元音 [æ]

rate n. 比率　　　　　　　rat n. 老鼠

pace n. 速度　　　　　　　pass v. 经过

tape n. 带子　　　　　　　tap n. 轻敲；水龙头 v. 轻敲；轻打

main a. 主要的　　　　　　man n. 男人

■ 地道英语随便说

When the fisherman reeled in the line, all of the bait was gone.
渔夫把钓线收回来时，鱼饵已经消失了。

例 **It was a bait to lure me in.**
那是个引诱我上当的诱饵（那是个套路）。

题目 **❹ Do you have any pension at all?**
Question
你有退休金吗？

解析
Resolution

这里他说的是 pension，回复应该是 A，说明这是公司福利制度的一部分。这里容易把同是短元音的 pension ['pɛnʃən] 听成 passion ['pæʃ(ə)n]，而误以为对方在抱怨你一点热情都没有。比较下面的两个句子并跟着说说看。

Do you have any pension at all? 你有退休金吗？
Do you have any passion at all? 你有一点儿热情吗？

■ **容易混淆的词汇**

短元音 [ɛ]   短元音 [æ]

pet n. 宠物   pat n. 轻拍

met v. 遇见（meet 的过去式）   mat n. 鞋垫

head n. 头   had v. 有（have 的过去式）

left v. 离开（leave 的过去式）   laugh v. 笑

■ **地道英语随便说**

Do you have any... at all? 你有任何的……吗？
└ at all 无论是在问句中，还是在否定的回答句中，皆用来加强语气。

⑩ **I had no food at all.**
我一点儿东西也没吃。

Why bother getting up at all when you have no job to do?
反正也没工作可做，为什么还费事起床呢？

Do you have any pension? 你有退休金吗？
└ pension 就是退休金，也就是政府或私人公司在员工退休时付给员工的一笔钱。

⑩ **She won't be able to draw her pension until she's 65.**
她直到六十五岁才能开始领退休金。

题目 Question

⑤ That was a great pitch!
这个球投得真好！

解析 Resolution

> 这里他说的是 pitch，适当的回复应该是针对投球这件事做回应，也就是 B。这里容易出现的状况和第一题相同，长元音 [i] 和短元音 [I] 不分，把 pitch 听成了 peach，还以为对方在称赞桃子呢。比较下面的两个句子并跟着说说看。
>
> That was a great pitch! 这个球投得真好！
>
> That was a great peach! 这个桃子真好！

■ 容易混淆的词汇

短元音 [I]	长元音 [i]
knit v. 编织	neat a. 整齐的
sit v. 坐	seat n. 座位
bit n. 一点	beat v. 打击
bid n. 出价	bead n. 珠子

■ 地道英语随便说

What a great pitch! 这个球投得真好！
└ pitch 在这里指的是棒球里，投手投球给打击手。

例 **Who will be pitching first this evening?**
今晚谁是先发投手？

She has a high-pitched voice. 她的嗓门很高。
└ pitch 也指音调的高低。

例 **How can I stop this high-pitched noise from the speakers?**
我怎么能让这些扩音器停止发出刺耳的噪声呢？

题目 Question ❻ **We need to make a plan.**
我们必须做个计划。

解析 Resolution

> 这里他说的是 plan，回复应该是与计划有关，也就是 A。很多人常常会把 plan 和 plane 的发音发得一样，原因和第二题是相同的，短元音 [æ] 和长元音 [e] 不分，于是听老外说话时，便搞不清楚到底是 plan 还是 plane。对方说的是要做计划，结果我们竟然去买了卡纸、糨糊，准备做飞机了。比较下面的两个句子并跟着说说看。
>
> We need to make a plan. 我们必须做个计划。
>
> We need to make a plane. 我们必须做架飞机。

■ 容易混淆的词汇

短元音 [æ]

pants n. 裤子

lack n. 缺乏

fat a. 胖的

rap n. 饶舌乐

长元音 [e]

paints n. 颜料

lake n. 湖

fate n. 命运

rape n. 掠夺

■ 地道英语随便说

What's your plan?
你有什么计划？

A goal without a plan is just a wish.
没有计划的目标，充其量只能称之为愿望。

Unit 3 再听听看

提醒便条纸 Reminder

舒葳老师的小叮咛，提枪上阵也不怕。

- 大致了解拼单词与发音之间的关系，可以帮助自己准确地发音。
- 元音的发音正确，或至少对元音的发音有正确的认识，才有可能听懂老外用的单词。
- 学任何新单词时，要大声念出来，模仿老外的发音。千万不要只眼睛认得，耳朵却听不懂。
- 当声音内化成你的一部分时，听力自然会进步！

MEMO   Listening & Speaking

MEMO

Listening & Speaking

Chapter 2

辨别发音相似的辅音
sing, thing, 还是 thin?

听力 Listening
口语 Speaking

Unit 1 听听看，说说看
Unit 2 自然发音
Unit 3 再听听看

学习重点 Main Point

sing, thing, 还是 thin？这三个单词的差别，你听得出吗？

发音相似的英语辅音，也同样是我们听错、听不懂的原因。今天，我们将一起来学习这些容易混淆的辅音的辨音及发音，让你听得轻松，说得漂亮！

Unit 1

听听看，说说看

热身活动 Warm Up 学习英语前，先来做个热身吧！

你是否能准确地听出不同的辅音呢？先来测测自己的辨音能力吧！
请听 MP3，并从 A、B 选项中选出正确的关键词：

题目 Questions

① A. think　　B. sink　　　　　　（　　）
② A. say　　　B. save　　　　　　（　　）
③ A. same　　B. sane　　　　　　（　　）
④ A. three　　B. tree　　　　　　（　　）
⑤ A. ships　　B. chips　　　　　　（　　）
⑥ A. roll　　　B. rope　　　　　　（　　）

做完上面的练习题目，是不是很有成就感呢？再多做几道练习题考考自己吧！

题目 Questions

⑦ A. crab　　B. grab　　　　　　（　　）
⑧ A. right　　B. write　　　　　　（　　）
⑨ A. fine　　B. find　　　　　　（　　）
⑩ A. wine　　B. wipe　　　　　　（　　）
⑪ A. felt　　　B. fail　　　　　　（　　）
⑫ A. wear　　B. weird　　　　　　（　　）

解答 Answers
① B　② B　③ A　④ B　⑤ B　⑥ A
⑦ A　⑧ B　⑨ A　⑩ A　⑪ A　⑫ B

Unit 1 听听看，说说看

| 实际演练 Explanation | 通过认真的解题练习打下扎实的基础。 |

题目 Question ❶ **The old man was sinking fast.**
老人快速地沉没到海中。

☐ (A) think ·· 思考

☑ (B) sink ·· 沉没

解析 Resolution

这里说的是 sinking fast "下沉得很快"，而不是 thinking fast "思考得很快"。sink 开头的发音 [s] 和 thinking 的 [θ] 相似，学生常发音不正确，因此在听的时候也很容易混淆。想想看，如果有人告诉塔台人员 "We are sinking."（我们正快速地下沉。），向他求救，他却回问："What are you thinking about?"（你们在想什么？）闹笑话事小，误了人命，事可就大了。比较下面的两个句子并跟着说说看。

The old man was sinking fast. 老人快速地沉没到海中。

The old man was thinking fast. 老人快速地思考。

■ 超级实用句型

We're sinking!
我们正在往下沉！

We're sinking in a sea of information.
我们沉浸在信息的海洋里。
└ sink 是沉没、下沉的意思。

■ 你也可以这么说

The ship sank. 船沉了。

The country's image is sinking fast.
这个国家的形象在迅速下降。

He sank back into a chair.
他瘫倒在椅子上。

题目 ❷ **What did you save that for?**
Question
你为什么储存它？

☐ **(A) say** .... 说

☑ **(B) save** .... 储存

解析 这里他说的是 save，最后面的 v 因为是辅音，下一个单词 that
Resolution 又以辅音起始，所以这个"v"的声音会弱化到你几乎听不见，但
即便如此，你会发现说话者还是会"做动作"，表示要发"v"
这个音，因此会有一些停顿，再继续发下一个音 that。再仔细听
一次，是不是这样呢？比较下面的两个句子，第一个句子在 that
之前有停顿，第二个句子则没有。

What did you save that for? 你为什么储存它？

What did you say that for? 你为什么那么说？

■ **超级实用句型**

What did you save...for? 你为什么储存……？

What... for? ……是做什么用的？

小贴士 What... for? 意思和 why 相同。听到对方这么说时，表示他不
Tip 清楚某事物的用途或目的，或对某事物的存在不以为然。

■ **你也可以这么说**

What is the party for? 为什么要开这个晚会？

What did you do that for? 你为什么这么做？

小贴士 以上两句均有不以为然的意思。
Tip
出其不意地送人礼物时，对方可能会这么回答，表示客气：
What is this for? 这是做什么用的？

当某人受朋友帮助，表达感谢后，我们常常会听到的回应就
是：What are friends for? 朋友是拿来做什么的？表示朋友就
是应该互相帮助的。

Unit 1 听听看，说说看

题目 **③** **We have the same attitude towards this subject.**
Question 我们对这件事持有相同的态度。

☑ **(A) same** ……………………………………………… 一样的

☐ **(B) sane** ……………………………………… 理智的；合乎情理的

解析
Resolution

这里他说的是 the same，same 后面的"m"和 sane 的"n"听起来很相似，我们很容易把 same 和 sane 混淆。"m"字尾的"m"说的时候嘴巴要闭，因此听得出来说话者在说下一个单词 attitude 之前，嘴巴是闭起来的；而"n"则嘴巴不闭，而且会听得到"n"的鼻音。再仔细听一次，是不是这样呢？学生也常因"m"和"n"不分，使得老外不理解你在说什么。另外，a 和 the 在说得快的时候，听起来也会很相似。比较下面的两个句子并跟着说说看。

We have the **same** attitude towards this subject.
我们对这件事持有相同的态度。

We have a **sane** attitude towards this subject.
我们对这件事持有理智的态度。

■ 超级实用句型

... have a... attitude towards... ……对……有……的态度

小贴士
Tip

在上面的句型，我们可以应用特定的说法：the same attitude 一样的态度；a sane attitude 理智（合乎情理）的态度。

■ 你也可以这么说

It's important to have a positive attitude towards life.
对生活持有积极的态度是很重要的。

How do you keep sane in the insane world?
在这个没有理智的社会里要如何保持清醒？

■ 可活用的补充例句

Attitude is everything.
态度决定一切。

029

题目 ❹

The tree houses are located in a protected rainforest area.

这些树屋位于雨林保护区。

☐ (A) three houses —————————— 三栋房屋

☑ (B) tree houses —————————— 树屋

解析

这里他说的是 tree houses，而不是 three houses。tree 开头 tr 的发音和 three 开头 thr 的发音相似，我们很容易混淆。比较下面的两个句子并跟着说说看。

The tree houses are located in a protected rainforest area.
这些树屋位于雨林保护区。

The three houses are located in a protected rainforest area.
这三栋房屋位于雨林保护区。

■ 超级实用句型

... are located... ……位于……

■ 你也可以这么说

The hotel is located at top of the hill. 旅馆位于山顶上。

Our international headquarters are located in Amsterdam, the Netherlands and Singapore.
我们的国际总部位于荷兰的阿姆斯特丹和新加坡。

■ 可活用的补充例句

Our headquarters is based in Frankfurt.
我们的总部位于法兰克福。

I am a PhD student based in Hong Kong.
我在香港读博士。

小贴士 Tip

be based in... 是"住在……""在……工作或读书"的意思；当用在商业公司时，指的就是"总部设在……"。

Unit 1 听听看，说说看

题目 **⑤** **Chips are my favorite!**
Question 我最喜欢薯片了！

☐ (A) ships ———————————————— 船

☑ (B) chips ———————————————— 薯片

解析 这里他说的是 chips，而不是 ships。chips 开头 ch 的发音和
Resolution ships 的开头 sh 的发音相似，我们很容易混淆。再仔细听一次，
是不是这样呢？比较下面的两个句子并跟着说说看。

Ships are my favorite! 我最喜欢船了！

Chips are my favorite! 我最喜欢薯片了！

■ 超级实用句型

... are my favorite. 我最喜欢……了。

■ 你也可以这么说

How sweet of you to buy me those chocolate chip cookies. They're my favorite.
你真贴心，给我买巧克力饼干，那是我最喜欢的。

■ 可活用的补充例句

That is my favorite flavor of ice cream. I'd eat it daily if I could. 这是我最爱的冰淇淋口味。如果可以的话，我愿意每天都吃。

What are your top 10 favorite movies of all time?
你最喜欢的十部电影是哪些？

This is my personal favorite Chinese restaurant in London. 这是我在伦敦最爱的中国餐厅。

This song has very powerful lyrics, and is my personal favorite. 这首歌的歌词很有震撼力，是我个人的最爱。

小贴士 my favorite... 是 "我最喜欢的……" 的意思。of all time 有 "有
Tip 史以来" 的意思。

031

题目 **6** Let's roll the wheels to the bike.
让我们把这些轮胎滚动到自行车那里吧。

☑ (A) roll .... 滚动

☐ (B) rope .... 用绳索绑在一起

解析

这里他说的是 roll，答案 B 则是 rope。roll 词尾发音 [l] 和 rope 词尾发音 [p] 都很容易被忽略，因此也容易相互混淆。[l] 的发音舌尖必须顶到上颚牙齿后方。[p] 则是发音较轻的清辅音。再仔细听一次，是不是这样呢？比较下面的两个句子并跟着说说看。

Let's roll the wheels to the bike.
让我们把这些轮胎滚动到自行车那里吧。

Let's rope the wheels to the bike.
让我们把这些轮胎和自行车用绳索绑在一起吧。

■ 超级实用句型

Let's... 让我们……吧。

小贴士 听到 Let's... 就知道对方在提议做某事。

■ 可活用的补充例句

She was on a roll. 她近来运气很好。

His business is on the ropes. 他的生意濒临失败。

They are on a roll. 他们近来很顺利。

They are on the ropes. 他们处境艰难。

小贴士 on a roll 是短语，表示最近这一段时间很成功，运气很好。

另一个听起来很相似的短语是 on the ropes，但有完全不同的意思，是用来表示事情做得不好且濒临失败。

Unit 1 听听看,说说看

提醒便条纸 Reminder

舒葳老师的小叮咛,提枪上阵也不怕。

发音相似的英语辅音如 m - n、th - s、p - b 等,都是学生常常说不正确的发音。而一旦错误的发音说久了,便会误以为自己说的就是正确的发音,结果是当老外说出正确的发音时,学生反而听不懂。这也是为什么有时候我们听中国人说英语反而比听老外说英语更明白的原因了!因此,我们要赶紧纠正自己辅音的发音,进而培养有效的听力、加强沟通!

MEMO Listening & Speaking

Unit 2

自然发音

课前准备 Preparation 准备充足的话，必能事半功倍。

英语里的辅音，字母与音标有一大半是一致的，不一致的也有规律可循。下表是字母与音标的对照：

浊辅音							
字母	b	g	v	z	th	s / su	j / ge	d
音标	[b]	[g]	[v]	[z]	[ð]	[ʒ]	[dʒ]	[d]
例	boy cab	pig game	vine live	zoo zip	those bathe	vision pleasure	John George large	day date
字母	l	m	n	ng	r	y	w	
音标	[l]	[m]	[n]	[ŋ]	[r]	[j]	[w]	
例	kill like	come man	nice ten	sing king	poor rope	yes yet you	we weather	

清辅音							
字母	p	k / c / ck / ch	t	f / gh / ph	s / c / ce	th	sh	ch / tch	h
音标	[p]	[k]	[t]	[f]	[s]	[θ]	[ʃ]	[tʃ]	[h]
例	pen lap	cook school check	sent take	fish enough phone	star center nice	think bath	wash she	church watch	how hill

加上我们在 Chapter 1 对元音字母与音标间的关系的认识，我们应该知道了英语的字母和音标有紧密的关联性，我们只要熟悉这些规则，大部分的单词看了就会念，会念就会拼。也就是说，我们看到 bed 就会念 [bɛd]，会念 [bɛd] 就会拼 b-e-d。

下面我们就来看看同学们常会发得不正确的辅音：

字母	词首		词尾	
	浊辅音	清辅音	浊辅音	清辅音
b - p	back	pack	hob	hop
g - c	gang	can	bag	back
d - t	doe	toe	feed	feet
v - f	vine	fine	save	safe
z - s	zip	sip	buzz	bus
th - th	then	thin	breathe	breath
dr - tr	drip	trip		
j - ch	joke	choke		

字母	词首		词尾	
th - s	thank	sank	path	pass
sh - ch	shop	chop	cash	catch
m - n	map	nap	Sam	sun
l - r	lice	rice	pool	poor
n - ng			thin	thing

在发音上，词尾音也是学生最难发得正确的部分，常常会念得太重，所谓的"中式英语"也因之而生。而发音的不正确，直接影响了我们的听力。

清辅音只送气流，声带不振动，听的时候要注意听才听得到，因此念的时候也不要念得太用力。浊辅音则注意不要念太长，切忌把辅音音节化，无中生有地在辅音后面加上一个元音。

看完上一页的字母与音标对照表以及辅音对照表，有没有对于辅音在词尾发音有更多的了解呢？

辅音词尾通常会被轻轻带过，稍稍不留意就没听到了，不注意听清楚的话，就会跟相似的词汇混淆。因此要特别留意！如果还不是很懂，也没关系，再翻回上一页的表格反复多看、多念几次吧！

下面列举出容易混淆的词汇，请打开 MP3 并跟着说说看。

■ **容易混淆的词汇**
词首相似，长元音 + 辅音词尾

sue v. 控告   suit n. 西装；v. 适合；适当

bar n. 酒吧   bark v. / n. 狗叫

play v. 玩耍；表演   plate n. 盘子

lie v. 躺   light n. 光亮；a. 明亮的

we pron. 我们   weak a. 虚弱的

why ad. 为什么   white a. 白色的

sea n. 海洋   seat n. 座位

fee n. 费用；v. 付费   feet n. 脚（foot 的复数）

而当词尾是清辅音时，常因发音很小声，或说得很快，很容易就被听者忽略了。所以听的时候要特别留意词尾。

不过事实上，这里还有一个秘诀！如果比较上面两栏，你会发现，虽然两栏的字母音的发音都是一样的，看起来好像唯一的不同就是词尾的辅音，但如果你再仔细听听看，你会发现左栏的元音念起来的时候发音稍长，而右栏的元音念起来发音稍短。这是因为当词尾有辅音时，说话者要赶着去发词尾的辅音，就只好把长元音念得稍微快一些。

Unit 2 自然发音

再听一次，熟悉它们不同的发音，并跟着说说看。

■ 容易混淆的词汇
词首相似

did v. 做（do 的过去式）   didn't v. 没做（do 的过去式）

swim n. / v. 游泳   swing v. / n. 摇摆

fake a. 假的   fade v. 褪色；消退

sit up 坐起来   sit down 坐下来

fun a. 有趣的   fund n. 资助；基金

feed v. 喂食   fit v. / n. / a. 适合

respectively ad. 分别地   respectfully ad. 恭敬地

wind v. 上发条   wine n. 红酒

supplies n. 供给（supply 的复数）   surprise n. / v. 惊喜

■ 容易混淆的词汇
词尾相似

hand n. 手   brand n. 品牌

cab n. 出租车   tab v. / n. 标牌

large a. 大的   charge v. / n. 索价

place n. 地方   pace v. / n. 速度

grain n. 谷类   drain v. / n. 排水

rest n. / v. 休息   guest n. 客人

dine v. 吃饭   fine a. 好的

date n. / v. 约会   rate n. / v. 比率

crazy a. 疯狂的   lazy a. 懒惰的

inferior a. 较差的   superior a. 优越的

interior a. 内部的 n. 内部   exterior a. 外部的 n. 外部

037

收尾练习 Exercise

上完课是不是头昏脑涨了？来做做收尾练习吧！

请写下你听到的句子。

题目 Questions

1. _____
2. _____
3. _____
4. _____
5. _____
6. _____
7. _____

现在请听 MP3，比较下面单词发音的不同，并跟着说说看。

- Come along. 一起来吧。
  Come alone. 独自一个人来。

- She ran. 她跑了。（run 的过去式）
  She rang. 她打电话。（ring 的过去式）

- Nice place. 好地方。
  Nice play. 打得好（球）。

- It's a pleasure. 那是个享受。
  It's a pressure. 那是个压力。

- It's a beautiful word. 这是个很美的单词。
  It's a beautiful world. 这是个美丽的世界。

- She laughs. 她笑了。
  She's alive. 她活着。

- He's tan. 他是棕褐色的。
  He's Dane. 他是丹麦人。

解答 Answers

❶ Come along. ❷ She rang. ❸ Nice place. ❹ It's a pressure.
❺ It's a beautiful word. ❻ She laughs. ❼ He's tan.

Unit 2 自然发音

提醒便条纸
Reminder 舒葳老师的小叮咛，提枪上阵也不怕。

有些英语单词在速度较慢、念得清楚时，声音并不见得相似，但当老外以自然速度说话时，因速度较快，若同学原本就不太熟悉这些单词的用法，便很容易听不清楚而误以为对方说的是另一个单词而无法理解。以上这些单词是舒葳老师针对常见的听力问题整理给大家的练习。平时同学在学单词时也可以自己归纳发音类似的单词，自己多念多做练习。

MEMO

Listening & Speaking

Unit 3

再听听看

热身活动 Warm Up 学习英语前，先来做个热身操吧！

请听 MP3 中的句子，并选择出正确的回应：

题目 Questions

① A. I thought the plot was great.
B. It has a beautiful floral design which I like very much.
....( )

② A. Yeah, it was really yummy.
B. No, sorry. It's still wet.
....( )

③ A. Yeah, it's a real bargain.
B. Actually, I was hoping to get something better.
....( )

④ A. Sure. Any specific brand or color?
B. Sure. I'll call right away.
....( )

⑤ A. Especially on the green grass.
B. Especially in the summer lake.
....( )

⑥ A. You're joking. How can I miss it?
B. Don't worry. I'll do that in a minute.
....( )

⑦ A. Don't worry. I have no intention to cut my feet.
B. OK. I will walk on the pavement.
....( )

解答 Answers ①A ②A ③B ④B ⑤B ⑥B ⑦A

实际演练 Explanation

通过认真的解题练习打下扎实的基础。

题目 Question

① How did you like the play?
你觉得那部剧如何？

- ☑ (A) I thought the plot was great. ……… 我觉得剧情很棒。
- ☐ (B) It has a beautiful floral design which I like very much. ……… 它有很漂亮的花样设计，我非常喜欢。

解析 Resolution

这里他说的是：How did you like the play? 因此回应应该是 A。
plot 是"情节；故事架构"的意思。

play 和 plate 发音相似，容易混淆。play 中的 ay 发音拉长，因为词尾没有辅音。plate 词尾的 t 是清辅音，念起来并不会被清楚地听见声音。而且你会发现 play 的元音较长，plate 的元音念得较短。比较下面的两个句子并跟着说说看。

How did you like the play? 你觉得那部剧如何？
How did you like the plate? 你觉得那个盘子如何？

■ 容易混淆的词汇

词尾为元音长音	词尾为清辅音
May n. 五月	mate n. 伙伴
hay n. 干草	hate v. 恨
sigh n. / v. 叹气	sight n. 视力；景象
tie n. 领带；v. 绑	tight a. 紧的

■ 可活用的补充例句

How was the play? 你觉得那部剧如何？
How did you find the play? 你觉得那部剧如何？

题目 Question ❷ **Did you try that?**
你尝试过那个了吗？

☑ **(A) Yeah, it was really yummy.** ……… 是啊，很好吃。

☐ **(B) No, sorry. It's still wet.** …… 没有，抱歉。它还是湿的。

解析 Resolution

> 这里他说的是：Did you try that? try 是"尝试"的意思，也可以当"试吃"讲。try 的词首 tr 因为和 dry 的 dr 发音相似，我们很容易把 try 和 dry 混淆。在这里，tr 的发音是清辅音，dr 的发音则是浊辅音。比较下面的两个句子并跟着说说看。
>
> Did you try that? 你尝试过那个了吗？
>
> Did you dry that? 你有烘干那个吗？

■ 容易混淆的词汇

词首为 tr	词首为 dr
trunk n. 树干；行李箱	drunk a. 喝醉的
trip n. 旅途	drip n. / v. 滴下
trill n. / v. 颤动；颤音	drill n. / v. 钻；训练

■ 你也可以这么说

Did you hear that?
你听到了吗？

Did you see that? 你看到了吗？

■ 可活用的补充例句

Give it a try. 试试看。

Why don't you give it a shot? 为何不试试看呢？

小贴士 Tip

> "Give it a try"或是"Give it a shot（go）"都可以用来鼓励别人鼓起勇气尝试看看。

Unit 3 再听听看

题目 Question

③ It's a good prize, isn't it?
这个奖项很好，不是吗？

☐ (A) Yeah, it's a real bargain. .... 是啊，真是赚到了。

☑ (B) Actually, I was hoping to get something better.
.... 事实上，我本来希望拿到更好的东西。

解析 Resolution

这里他说的是：It's a good prize, isn't it? 所以回复应与拿奖有关。这里容易把 prize 听成 price，而误以为对方说的是价格很合适了。prize 的尾音是浊辅音 [z]，price 的尾音则是清辅音 [s]。比较下面的两个句子并跟着说说看。

It's a good prize, isn't it? 这个奖项很好，不是吗？

It's a good price, isn't it? 这个价格很合适，不是吗？

■ 容易混淆的词汇

词尾为清辅音 [s]	词尾为浊辅音 [z]
peace n. 和平	peas n. 豌豆（pea 的复数）
ice n. 冰	eyes n. 双眼
rice n. 米饭	rise n. / v. 上升；上涨
face n. 脸	phase n. 阶段；时期

■ 你也可以这么说

In the days before the wedding, I was hoping that the weather would be good.
婚礼前，我一直期盼天气会很好。

I was hoping you could lend me some money.
我希望你可以借我点钱。

小贴士 Tip

I was hoping... 可以用来客气地请求他人的帮助。"I was hoping you could lend me some money" 比 "Can you lend me some money?" 客气。我们常使用过去时态来正式且客气地向别人提出要求、询问或建议。

题目 Question

④ Could you get me a cab, please?
请帮我叫辆出租车好吗？

☐ **(A) Sure. Any specific brand or color?**
    好的，你有任何特定的牌子或颜色要求吗？

☑ **(B) Sure. I'll call right away.** ……… 好的，我马上打电话。

解析 Resolution

这里他说的是：Could you get me a cab, please? 因此回应是：Sure. I'll call right away. 表示他马上打电话叫车。cab 词尾的 b 因为和 cap 的 p 发音相似，我们很容易把 cab 和 cap 混淆。在这里，b 是浊辅音，但是因为在词尾，我们反而常会听不见 b 的声音。而 p 则是清辅音，只听得到"气的声音"。再仔细听一次，是不是这样呢？比较下面的两个句子并跟着说看。在会话中，老外对句尾的辅音常会做势而不发。当你真的听不出是 cab 或 cap 时，只得从上下文去体会了。

Could you get me a cap, please? 请帮我找顶帽子好吗？
Could you get me a cab, please? 请帮我叫辆出租车好吗？

■ **容易混淆的词汇**

词尾为清辅音 [p]

mop n. 拖把；v. 拖地

tap n. / v. 轻拍；n. 水龙头

rip n. / v. 撕；扯

词尾为浊辅音 [b]

mob n. 暴民；v. 聚众滋事

tab n. / v. 标签

rib n. 排骨；肋骨

■ **你也可以这么说**

Could you get me another cup of coffee?
你可以再帮我买 / 拿杯咖啡吗？

Can I get you something to drink?
我可以请你喝点什么吗？／我可以为你准备点喝的吗？

小贴士 Tip

get 在这里可以是买的意思；视情境而定，也可以当作去拿的意思。

题目 Question ❺ Boys like to row.
男孩喜欢划船。

☐ (A) Especially on the green grass.
尤其在绿绿的草地上。

☑ (B) Especially in the summer lake.
尤其在夏天的湖里。

解析 Resolution

这里他说的是 row，指的是划船。这里 row 无辅音词尾，很容易与词尾音不是那么明显的 roll 混淆。roll 的词尾音是 l，发音时舌尖要顶到上颚，学生一般发音时都没有确实做到，听的时候也往往就忽略了这个 l 音造成的声音以及字意上差别。比较下面的两个句子，第二个句子句尾会听到舌尖要顶到上颚的 l 音。

Boys like to row. 男孩喜欢划船。
Boys like to roll. 男孩喜欢打滚。

■ 容易混淆的词汇

词尾为 [o] 或 [ɔ]

tow v. / n. 拖吊
mow v. / n. 除草
saw v. 看见（see 的过去式）
four n. 四

词尾为 [ol] 或 [ɔl]

toll n. 损失；死伤人数
mall n. 购物中心
soul n. 灵魂
fall v. / n. 掉落

■ 可活用的补充例句

I disliked them all, especially Sylvia.
他们几个我一个都不喜欢，尤其是西维亚。

I like all the children, Tom especially.
我喜欢全部的小朋友，尤其是汤姆。

Sleep is especially important for growing children.
睡眠对正在成长的儿童尤其重要。

题目 Question ❻ Are you going to wash that?
你要去洗那个吗？

☐ **(A) You're joking. How can I miss it?**
……你开玩笑，我怎么能错过它？

☑ **(B) Don't worry. I'll do that in a minute.**
……别担心，我马上就做。

解析 Resolution

这里他说的是 wash，指的是洗。这里 wash 字尾的 sh [ʃ] 和 watch 的 tch [tʃ] 相似，很容易混淆。要注意听，否则还以为对方在问你要看什么节目呢。

比较下面的两个句子并跟着说说看。

Are you going to watch that? 你会看那个吗？
Are you going to wash that? 你要去洗那个吗？

■ 容易混淆的词汇

词尾或词首为 [ʃ]	词尾或词首为 [tʃ]
wish v. 希望	witch n. 女巫
mush n. 软块	much a. 多
cash n. 现金	catch v. 赶上
share v. 分享	chair n. 椅子
sheep n. 绵羊	cheap a. 便宜的
shop v. 购物	chop v. 切；砍

■ 可活用的补充例句

I'll be back in a minute.
我马上就回来。

Haven't heard anything from you in a while. How are you?
有一阵子没有你的任何消息了。你过得如何呢？

Unit 3 再听听看

题目 **❼ Be careful. Don't step on the glass.**
Question
小心。不要踩到玻璃了。

☑ **(A) Don't worry. I have no intention to cut my feet.**
别担心,我一点也不想割伤我的脚。

☐ **(B) OK. I will walk on the pavement.**
好,我会走在人行道上。

解析
Resolution

这里他说的是 glass,指的是玻璃。答案的 have no intention to 是 "无意" 的意思。这里 glass 字首的 gl 很容易与 grass 的 gr 混淆。gr 有轻微的卷舌音,gl 则没有。这也是一般学生在发音时容易忽略的,从而直接影响到听的结果。比较下面的两个句子并跟着说说看。

Be careful. Don't step on the glass.
小心,不要踩到玻璃了。

Be careful. Don't step on the grass.
小心,不要踩到草皮上了。

■ 容易混淆的词汇

词首为 [gl] [kl] 或 [pl]	词首为 [gr] [kr] 或 [pr]
glow v. / n. 发光	grow v. 种植
clash v. / n. 不合;冲突	crash v. / n. 冲撞;坠毁
pleasant a. 愉悦的	present n. 礼物
play v. / n. 玩耍	pray v. / n. 祈祷
clown n. 小丑	crown n. 皇冠

■ 可活用的补充例句

What was your intention?
你究竟想做什么? / 你有什么企图?

It was not my intention to offend anyone.
我无意冒犯任何人。

047

提醒便条纸
Reminder

舒葳老师的小叮咛，提枪上阵也不怕。

- 辅音的发音正确与否同样会影响自你对英语发音的认知，进而影响你的听力。
- 熟悉本章容易混淆的发音和词汇，多加练习。将来听老外说话时能有更迅速、正确的反应。
- 平时练习听力时若有将一个单词听成另一个单词的情形，一定要找出这两个单词的正确发音并反复练习。

MEMO　　　　　　　　　　　　　　　　　Listening & Speaking

Chapter 3

词尾消失的规则
You won't believe it!

听力 Listening
口语 Speaking

Unit 1 听听看，说说看

Unit 2 消失的辅音

Unit 3 再听听看

学习重点
Main Point

请先念念这里的标题，再听听 MP3 怎么说。你有没有发现 won't 的 t 不会说出来，it 的 t 也只有气的声音呢？事实上，在英语里，t 在词尾都是不会大声念出来的。同学们如果不熟悉这个词尾音消失的规则，自然就会产生听力上的障碍！

今天我们就来学习英语词尾消失的规则吧。多听，多念，以后听到老外说这类单词的时候才能正确反应！

Unit 1

听听看，说说看

热身活动 Warm Up 学习英语前，先来做个热身吧！

你是否能准确地听出 MP3 在说什么呢？
请听 MP3，并写下你听到的句子：

题目 Questions

1. _____.
2. _____.
3. _____.
4. _____.
5. _____.
6. _____.
7. _____.
8. _____.

解答 Answers

1. You can't beat that.
2. Let him do it.
3. I have a date tonight.
4. Put my hat back.
5. What's that look on your face?
6. Shall we leave a tip?
7. Can you find that shop on the map?
8. Didn't he bring his backpack?

Unit 1 听听看，说说看

实际演练 Explanation

通过认真的解题练习打下扎实的基础。

题目 Question ❶ **You can't bea*t* that.**
这已经是最便宜的了。

解析 Resolution

这句话乍听起来像"You can be that"，但事实上，他说的是"You can't beat that"。这句话字面上的意思是"你没办法打败这个了"。也就是说，当客人在讨价还价时，老板可以说："You can't beat that." 表示"这已经是最便宜的了"的意思。

要注意的是，虽然 can't 和 beat 的 t 消音了，在说话的时候还是会留下短暂的停留时间，只是不会把 t 发出来而已。再听一次，练习跟着说说看。

■ 可活用的补充例句

That's my best offer. 那是我可以给的最好的价钱了。

题目 Question ❷ **Le*t* him do i*t*.**
让他做吧。

解析 Resolution

Let 中的 t 消音，it 中的 t 则发气音，说得快时也可能消音，因此如果不熟悉这个规则，乍听之下就不知道对方在说什么。要注意的是，虽然 t 消音了，在说话的时候还是会留下短暂的停留时间，只是不会把 t 发出来而已。再听一次，练习跟着说说看。

■ 可活用的补充例句

I'm going to give him an offer that he can't refuse.
我要开一个他无法拒绝的条件。

I went for an interview, and now they have made me an offer. 我去面试了，现在他们已经同意给我这份工作。

题目 ❸ **I have a da_t_e tonigh_t_.**
我今晚有约会。

解析
date 中的 t 消音，tonight 中的 t 在这里发 [t]，说得快时也可能消音。date 在这里是约会的意思，但乍听之下，你可能以为他说的是：I have a day tonight. 所以摸不着头脑了。date 也可以当约会对象用。再听一次，练习跟着说说看。

■ 可活用的补充例句

My friend set me up on a blind date.
我朋友替我安排了一次相亲。

How was your date?
你的约会顺利吗？

Will you be my date?
你愿意当我的女／男伴吗？

题目 ❹ **Pu_t_ my ha_t_ back.**
把我的帽子放回去。

解析
put 中的 t 和 hat 中的 t 都消音，不只如此，back 中的 ck 也消音喔。虽然我们前面听到的例子都是 t 消音，但事实上，字尾发 [p] 或 [k] 时也会有消音的现象。要注意的是，[p] 或 [k] 在发音时，嘴巴都要做到动作，只是声音不用发出来。再听一次，练习跟着说说看。

■ 可活用的补充例句

Put back the book when you have finished with it.
看完时请把书放回去。

Put it back where it belongs.
物归原位。

Unit 1 听听看，说说看

题目 **⑤ What's that look on your face?**
Question 你那是什么表情？

解析
Resolution

that 中的 t 消音，look 中的 k 也消音。如果你第一次听的时候没有听懂，有可能是你不了解消音的现象，也有可能是你不熟悉这个句型。发 [k] 的时候嘴巴要做出动作，只是不要把声音发出来，所以听的时候会觉得中间有短暂的停顿。再听一次，练习跟着说说看。

■ 可活用的补充例句

Don't give me that look.
不要给我那种表情。

Don't look at me like that.
不要那样看我。

Why the long face?
为什么拉长着脸？

题目 **⑥ Shall we leave a tip?**
Question 我们要不要给个小费？

解析
Resolution

tip 的 p 会发消音，leave a tip 是"给小费"的意思。Shall we...? 表示"我们要不要……？"是问对方意见的意思。再听一次，练习跟着说说看。

■ 可活用的补充例句

Do we leave a tip?
我们该给小费吗？

Don't forget to leave a tip for the server.
别忘了给服务生小费。

053

题目 Question

❼ Can you find that shop on the map?
你可以在地图上找到那家商店吗？

解析 Resolution

在这句话里，that 中的 t，shop 中的 p 和 map 中的 p 都发气音，说得快的时候则会消音。如果我们自己平时不懂得这样发音，也不熟悉这些发音变化，很容易就听不懂了。再听一次，模仿他的方法自己说说看。

■ 可活用的补充例句

Put the map on the mat.
把地图放在地毯上。

题目 Question

❽ Didn't he bring his backpack?
他没有带背包吗？

解析 Resolution

在这句话里，didn't 中的 t，和 backpack 中的两个 ck，都发气音，说得快的时候则会消音。消音的时候，声音与声音中间会留下短暂的停顿，仔细再听一次，并模仿他的方法说说看。pack lunch 指的是外出时带的午餐，如三明治、水果、干粮等。

■ 可活用的补充例句

I didn't bring my pack lunch.
我没有带午餐便当。

Unit 1 听听看，说说看

提醒便条纸
Reminder

舒葳老师的小叮咛，提枪上阵也不怕。

上面的练习你都做对了吗？我们在这课学到了词尾的 [t]、[p] 和 [k] 在英语中是会消音的，了解这个现象后，便能帮助你的听力更进一步！然而 [t] 的声音在英语中相当特别，除了在词尾消音，还有一些其他的变化。下面我们就针对 [t] 的消音规则做更进一步的分析与练习，同时也介绍另一个消音规则——[h] 的消音。

MEMO   Listening & Speaking

Unit 2

消失的辅音

课前准备 Preparation 准备充足的话，必能事半功倍。

■ 消失的 t
Rule 1：t 词尾消音

Si**t** down. 坐下。

Le**t** me see. 让我看看。

He wen**t** the nex**t** day. 他隔天去了。

Wha**t** migh**t** happen? 可能会发生什么事？

Pa**t** was qui**t**e righ**t**, wasn'**t** she? 帕特是正确的，不是吗？

Wha**t**? Pu**t** my ha**t** back! 什么？把我的帽子放回去！

Sorry, bu**t** you can'**t** sit at tha**t** chair.
抱歉，但你不能坐在那张椅子上。

Wha**t** is the name of tha**t** fa**t** cat on the ma**t**?
那个在垫子上的胖猫叫什么名字？

■ 消失的 t
Rule 2：[t] 和 [d] 在 [n] 之前消音

The hikers wen**t** in the moun**t**ains. 登山者进了山。

She's cer**t**ain that he has wri**tt**en it. 她确定他已经写了。

The co**tt**on cur**t**ain is not in the foun**t**ain. 那条棉窗帘不在喷泉里。

The frigh**t**ened wi**t**ness had forgo**tt**en the impor**t**ant wri**tt**en message. 惊吓过度的目击者已忘了这个重要的文字信息。

Stu**d**ents study La**t**in in Bri**t**ain. 学生们在英国学拉丁文。

I coul**d**n't do it. 我做不下去。

■ 消失的 t
Rule 3：[t] 在 [n] 之后也消音

He had a great int**erview.** 他的面试很顺利。

Sorry to int**errupt.** 抱歉打断你。

She's at the int**ernational center.** 她在国际中心。

Don't **take advan**t**age of her.** 不要占她便宜。

There are twent**y of them.** 他们有二十个人。

Try to ent**er the information.** 试着输入这些信息。

Here's a list of the top 10 online vint**age shops.**
这些是最佳线上古董商店的前十名。

Ent**er the in**t**ersection while the light is green or yellow.**
绿灯或黄灯的时候进入十字路口。

■ 消失的 t
Rule 4：want to 讲成 wanna，going to 讲成 gonna

I wanna **go. (= I want to go.)**
我要去。

I wanna **see it. (= I want to see it.)**
我要看。

Don't you wanna **try? (= Don't you want to try?)**
你不想试试看吗？

I'm gonna **go. (= I am going to go.)**
我会去。

He's gonna **love it. (= He's going to love it.)**
他会爱死这个。

What're you gonna **do? (= What are you going to do?)**
你要怎么办？

We're gonna **miss you. (= We're going to miss you.)**
我们会想你的。

■ 消失的 t

Rule 5：t 在两个母音之间时发 [D]

在这里，[D] 是"弹舌音"的意思，跟 [d] 的发音类似。听 MP3，跟着说说看。

Here's your le*tt*er. 这是你的信。

She had a li*tt*le bo*tt*le. 她有一个小瓶子。

Be*tt*y bought some bu*tt*er. 贝蒂买了点黄油。

Ge*t* a be*tt*er wa*t*er hea*t*er. 买一个好一点的热水器。

Pu*t* all the da*t*a in the compu*t*er. 把所有的资料放在电脑里。

Inser*t* a quar*t*er in the me*t*er. 把一个二十五分的硬币放进收费器里。

注意，后三句的 get 与 a，put 与 a，和 insert 与 a，虽然都是分开的两个单词，但是因为 [t] 仍是处于两个元音之中，因此也发弹舌音 [D]。

■ 消失的 h

在英语口语中，说话说得快的时候要发 [h] 这个音会较吃力，因此在句子中的 [h] 也消音。

Give *h*er a break. 放她一马吧。

Did *h*e go? 他去了吗？

I'll tell *h*im. 我会告诉他。

Give *h*er the message. 给他这个信息。

Is *h*is work good? 他的工作怎么样？

Did you take *h*er pen? 你拿了她的笔吗？

He won't let *h*er. 他不让她（做这件事）。

上面的这几个句子也包含了连音的声音规则在内，连音我们在 **Chapter 7** 会进一步介绍。

Unit 2 消失的辅音

收尾练习 Exercise

上完课是不是头昏脑涨了？来做做收尾练习吧！

听听看下面的短文，留意 t 的发音，并跟着说说看。

I'm studying this Pronunciation and Listening course. There's a lot to learn, but I find it very enjoyable. I think I will find it easier and easier to listen to native speakers speaking English, but the only way to really improve is to practice all of the time.

Now I can distinguish different vowels and consonants that sound similar, and I also pay more attention to stresses when I listen than I used to. I have been talking to a lot of native speakers of English lately and they tell me that I'm easier to understand. Anyway, I could go on and on, but the important thing is to listen well and sound good. And I hope I'm getting better and better!

提醒便条纸 Reminder

舒葳老师的小叮咛，提枪上阵也不怕。

我们一直强调，对英语发音的正确了解是提升听力的第一步。希望学到这里，你对英语发音已有更进一步的认识！认识了发音的规则后，还需要充分的练习，才能把这些知识"内化"，在未来说英语或听英语时才能自然地加以使用！

Unit 3

再听听看

热身活动 Warm Up 学习英语前，先来做个热身吧！

请听 MP3 中的句子，并选择出正确回应。

题目 Questions

① A. Sure. Come with me.
B. So why didn't you?
( )

② A. No, he isn't.
B. No, she isn't.
( )

③ A. Don't worry. I won't bother her anymore.
B. Don't worry. I won't bother him anymore.
( )

④ A. Oh, really? Why are you leaving so early?
B. OK. I hope you'll enjoy it.
( )

⑤ A. It was awful.
B. Don't forget your umbrella.
( )

⑥ A. Yes, Mom. It sure is cold.
B. Yes, Mom. It is quite hot.
( )

解答 Answers ① A ② A ③ B ④ A ⑤ B ⑥ A

实际演练 Explanation

通过认真的解题练习打下扎实的基础。

题目 Question

① I wan**na** go.
我想去。

☑ (A) Sure. Come with me. ················ 当然，跟我一起来。

☐ (B) So why didn't you? ················ 那么你为什么没去呢？

解析 Resolution

这里他说 "I wanna go" 就是 "I want to go" 的意思。所以你恰当的回应应该是：Sure. Come with me. 请比较练习下面两个句子，在第二句的 "I wanted to go" 中，t 发弹舌音。

I wanna go. 我想去。

I wanted to go. 我本来想去的。

■ 超级实用句型

I wanna sleep. 我想睡觉。

■ 你也可以这么说

I wanna be with you. 我想跟你在一起。

I wanna be the guy. 我想成为那个人（Mr. Right）。

I just wanna say thank you. 我只想跟你道谢。

■ 可活用的补充例句

Why don't you join us? 你为什么不一起来？

Will you join us for dinner? 你要跟我们一起去吃晚餐吗？

Can I join you? 我可以加入你们吗？

题目 ❷ Is he the one?
Question
他就是那个人吗？

☑ (A) No, he isn't. ······ 不，他不是。

☐ (B) No, she isn't. ······ 不，她不是。

解析
Resolution

> 这里他说"Is he the one?"其中 h 消音。你恰当的回应应该是：No, he isn't. 请比较练习下面两个句子：
> Is he the one? 他就是那个人吗？
> Is she the one? 她就是那个人吗？

■ 你也可以这么说

Is this the end? 结束了吗？／这就是结局吗？

Is that it? 就这样吗？／这样就好了吗？

Is that the case? 是这样的吗？

Is that the best we can do? 我们只能做到这样吗？

■ 可活用的补充例句

Good weather brings out the best in me.
好天气使我展现出最好的一面。

You bring out the best in me.
你成就了最好的我。

Some people bring out the worst in you; others bring out the best.
有些人能让你展现最糟的一面，还有些人则能让你展现最好的一面。

Unit 3 再听听看

题目 **③** **Leave him alone.**
Question 不要烦他。

☐ **(A) Don't worry. I won't bother her anymore.**
　　　　　　　　　　　　　不用担心，我再也不会打扰她了。

☑ **(B) Don't worry. I won't bother him anymore.**
　　　　　　　　　　　　　不用担心，我再也不会打扰他了。

解析 这里他说"Leave him alone"，其中 h 消音。你恰当的回应应
Resolution 该是：Don't worry. I won't bother him anymore. 请比较练习下面两个句子：

Leave her alone. 不要烦她。

Leave him alone. 不要烦他。

■ 超级实用句型

Leave me alone. 不要烦我。

■ 你也可以这么说

Leave it. 不用管它。

Leave it as it is. 这样就好。／顺其自然。

Leave it where it is. 不要拿它。／把它留在原位。

■ 可活用的补充例句

Take it or leave it. 不要就拉倒。

Leave it to me. 我来处理。

题目 **④** I got to go.
我得走了。

☑ **(A)** Oh, really? Why are you leaving so early?
哦，真的吗？你为什么这么早就要离开？

☐ **(B)** OK. I hope you'll enjoy it.
好的，希望你玩得愉快。

解析

这里他说"I got to go"，其中第一个 t 消音，第二个 t 便可以视为介于两个母音 o 的中间，因此发弹舌音 [D]。"I got to go"就是"I have to go"，是"我得走了"的意思。因此，你恰当的回应应该是：Oh, really? Why are you leaving so early? 请比较练习下面两个句子：

I got to go. 我得走了。

I'm gonna go. 我会去。

■ **超级实用句型**

I gotta get back. 我得回去了。

■ **你也可以这么说**

I gotta say this. 我得说一件事。

I gotta find him. 我得找到他。

■ **可活用的补充例句**

Enjoy it while it lasts.
在还能享受时，尽量享受它吧。

Time is like a balloon, you'd better enjoy it while it lasts.
时光稍纵即逝，享受须及时。

题目 Question ❺ It's gonna rain.
要下雨了。

☐ **(A) It was awful.** ……………（之前）真是太糟了。

☑ **(B) Don't forget your umbrella.** ………… 不要忘记带伞。

解析 Resolution

这里他说的是"It's gonna rain",也就是"It's going to rain"的意思。因此,恰当的回应应该是:Don't forget your umbrella. 请比较练习下面两个句子:

It's gonna rain. 要下雨了。

It rained. 下雨了。

■ 可活用的补充例句

It's gonna be alright. 一切都会没问题的。

题目 Question ❻ Pu<u>t</u> your ha<u>t</u> on.
戴上你的帽子。

☑ **(A) Yes, Mom. It surely is cold.** 好的,妈妈。真的很冷。

☐ **(B) Yes, Mom. It is quite hot.** 好的,妈妈。还挺热的。

解析 Resolution

这句话中,put 的 t 和 your 会连音,发 [t] 的声音,hat 的 t 和 on 会连音,发弹舌音 [D]。连音的规则我们在第七章会正式介绍。现在,请先比较练习下面两句:

Put your hat on. 把帽子戴起来。

Take your hat off. 把帽子脱下来。

■ 可活用的补充例句

Put on the show! 开始表演吧!

提醒便条纸 Reminder 舒葳老师的小叮咛，提枪上阵也不怕。

- 英语中有许多消音的现象，了解消音规则，可以帮助自己发音准确。
- 把消音规则融入自己平时的发音中，听老外说英语时才较能迅速反应。
- 养成常听英语的习惯，嘴巴跟着说，长期培养对声音的正确认知。
- 当声音内化成你的一部分时，听力自然会进步！

Chapter 4

掌握单词的重音
compete, competition, competitive, competency

听力
Listening
口语
Speaking

Unit 1 听听看，说说看

Unit 2 单词的重音规则

Unit 3 标出重音节，并念念看

学习重点
Main Point

在英语单词里，重音是不可分割的一部分。重音也帮助我们辨识听到的是什么单词。有时候我们明明学过一个单词，看也看得懂，但经老外的口中说出就听不懂了。这常常是因为我们把重音放错了位置，听到正确的发音反而听不懂。

那么我们该如何掌握单词的重音呢？其实重音的位置也是有规则的，现在就让我们来看看这些规则吧！

Unit 1

听听看，说说看

热身活动 Warm Up 　学习英语前，先来做个热身吧！

你是否能准确地读出不同重音的单词呢？先来测测自己对重音的认识是否正确吧！请读出下列各组的单词。

题目 Question

1. extreme
   extremely

2. famous
   infamous

3. equal
   equality

4. admire
   admirable
   admiration

5. economy
   economic
   economical

6. compete
   competitive
   competitor
   competition
   competence

现在听 MP3，你念得正确吗？

Unit 1 听听看，说说看

实际演练 Explanation
通过认真的解题练习打下扎实的根基。

题目 Question

① extreme adj. 极端的、极度的；n. 极端
extremely adv. 极端地、极度地

解析 Resolution

这两个单词，一个是形容词，一个是副词，重音都在同一个位置。许多多音节的单词，形容词与副词重音都在同一个位置，如：

incredible adj. 不可思议的 和 **incredibly** adv. 不可思议地
amazing adj. 令人惊艳的 和 **amazingly** adv. 令人惊艳地
fabulous adj. 非常棒的 和 **fabulously** adv. 非常棒地

■ 可活用的补充例句

You gave me extreme joy.
你带给我极大的快乐。

We should avoid extremes.
我们应该避免走极端。

We get on extremely well.
我们相处得极好。

We got on extremely well.
我们之前相处得非常好。

I'm never an eloquent person and I can be extremely quiet sometimes.
我从来不是个能言善辩的人，而且有的时候可以非常安静。

I don't understand why people enjoy extreme sports.
我不懂为什么有人会喜欢极限运动。

题目 Question

❷ **fa**mous a. 有名的

infamous a. 声名狼藉的；臭名昭著的

解析 Resolution

infamous 和 famous 一样，都是"有名的"的意思，但是 infamous 是因不好的名声而有名，也就是"臭名昭著"的意思。

由于 infamous 由 famous 延伸而来，因此很多同学会理所当然地把重音放在 fa，但这是不正确的。当你的重音念错时，老外就会较难理解你说的话，你也听不懂老外说什么了。

■ 可活用的补充例句

I want to be famous. 我想成名。

The restaurant is famous for its seafood.
这家餐厅的海鲜很有名。

The infamous murderer was sentenced to death.
臭名昭著的谋杀者被判了死刑。

He wrote an essay on the infamous Watergate scandal.
他写了一篇关于不光彩的水门事件的文章。

Which Hollywood stars have a reputation for being good to work with?
哪些好莱坞明星有容易一起工作的好名声？

小贴士 Tip

have a good reputation for... 意思是"享有……的好名声"，意思近似于 be famous for，但是更强调其"好"的名声；be notorious for 则是"因为……而臭名昭著"，意思近似于 be infamous for。

A small firm's good reputation is one of its most important assets.
对小公司而言，好的名声是最重要的资产之一。

James is notorious for his volcanic temper.
詹姆士的火暴脾气是出了名的。

He is notorious for dirty tricks.
他的诡计多端是出了名的。

Unit 1 听听看，说说看

题目 **❸** equal　a. 平等的
Question　　unequal　a. 不平等的
　　　　　　equality　n. 平等
　　　　　　inequality　n. 不平等

解析
Resolution

> equality 是 equal 的名词，如果你以为 equality 的重音也在第一个音节可就错了。equality 和 inequality 的重音都在 qua，练习说说看。
>
> 另外，equal 也可以当名词使用，表示地位相同的人、事、物。
>
> 想想看，你有没有认识一些单词词尾是 ty 的呢？这些单词的重音在哪里，是否有共同点？关于词尾是 ty 的字的重音规则，我们会在下一个章节正式介绍。

■ 可活用的补充例句

All men are created equal.
人生而平等。

Men and women had unequal education opportunities in the old days.
在古时候，男性和女性没有平等的受教育机会。

Everybody had an equal chance. 每个人都有均等的机会。

Income inequality in our society is continuously increasing.
我们社会的贫富差距持续拉大。

Your beauty has no equal on this earth.
你的美无与伦比。

There's an unequal distribution of wealth here.
这里的财富分配不平均。

To ensure equality of educational opportunity has been the challenge.
确保教育机会的平等是很大的挑战。

There is an increase in social and economic inequality.
社会经济的不平等加重了。

题目 Question ❹ ad**mi**re　v. 仰慕；钦佩
admirable　a. 令人仰慕；令人钦佩的
ad**mi**ration　n. 仰慕；钦佩

解析 Resolution

admirable 是 admire 的形容词，因此很多同学会以为 admirable 的重音也在 mi。从听力的角度来说，因为 admirable 的重音在第一个音节，听起来跟 admire 不像，所以造成了同学就算认识 admire 这个单词，在听到老外说 admirable 时，也完全反应不过来，不知道其实就是 admire 的词性变化而已，还以为是从来没听过的新单词呢！另外，admiration 是名词，重音在 ra，也要特别注意。

■ 可活用的补充例句

I admire him for his courage.
我钦佩他的勇气。

His honesty is admirable.
他的诚实令人钦佩。

I have a lot of admiration and respect for him.
我对他有非常多的仰慕和尊敬。

I admire people who have been through a lot but still keep their heads up.
我欣赏经过许多挫折后仍抬头挺胸面对人生的人。

I admire your writing very much.
我非常欣赏你的写作。

My admiration for her increased when I discovered she had learned English only since coming to the U.S.
当我发现她来到美国才开始学英语之后，对她更加钦佩了。

Ella looked at her boyfriend in admiration as he talked about his dream of becoming an artist.
当艾拉的男友述说着他想成为艺术家的梦想时，艾拉崇拜地看着他。

That was an absolutely admirable performance.
那场表演真是太精彩了。

题目 Question ⑤

economy n. 经济
economic a. 经济的
economical a. 节约的
economics n. 经济学

解析 Resolution

economy 是经济的意思，重音在 co。economic 是经济的形容词，而 economical 则是在使用资源上很经济的，也就是很节省、很省钱的意思。两个形容词的重音都在 no。另外，economics 是名词，是经济学的意思，重音也在 no。

想想看，你有没有认识词尾是 y，ic，或是 cal 的单词呢？这些单词的重音在哪里，是否有共同点呢？关于词尾是 y，ic，或是 cal 的重音规则，我们会在下一个章节正式介绍！

■ 可活用的补充例句

The world economy is going down.
世界经济正在下滑。

Why is China's economy slowing down?
中国经济发展为什么趋缓？

What's the most economical way of traveling around Taiwan?
台湾环岛旅行最经济的方式是什么？

She studied economics at college.
她在大学读经济学。

Should I fly economy or business?
我应该坐经济舱还是商务舱？

They chose to live in this area for economic reasons.
他们选择住在这个区域是出于经济上的考虑。

This car is economical to run because it doesn't use much fuel.
这辆车很经济，因为它很省油。

How can we avoid the next economic crisis?
我们如何能避免下一次的经济危机呢？

题目 ❻

com**pe**te　v. 竞争
com**pe**titive　a. 好竞争的；有竞争力的
com**pe**titor　n. 竞争对手
compe**ti**tion　n. 竞争者；竞赛
competent　a. 有能力的；能胜任的
competence　n. 能力；胜任

解析

compete 是竞争的意思，延伸出数个词类变化。注意各个词类变化的重音，练习说说看。

想想看，你有没有认识词尾是 tive 或是 tion 的单词呢？这些单词的重音在哪里，是否有共同点呢？关于词尾是 tive 或是 tion 的单词的重音规则，我们会在下一个章节正式介绍。

■ 可活用的补充例句

You need good language ability to compete in the job market.
你需要好的语言能力才能在职场上与人竞争。

Mary is a very competitive person.
玛莉是个很好胜的人。

City Café has become Starbucks' competitor.
城市咖啡已经成了星巴克的竞争对手。

We are in a market with no competition.
我们处在一个没有竞争者的市场。

He entered a singing competition and finished second.
他参加了一个歌唱比赛并且得了第二名。

Workers who are incompetent can get fired.
能力不强的人会被炒鱿鱼。

Managers who hire people at work look for people with competence.
雇用员工的经理要找的是有能力的人。

Unit 1 听听看，说说看

提醒便条纸
Reminder

舒葳老师的小叮咛，提枪上阵也不怕。

英语单词的词类变化常会有不同的重音，因此常会有听得懂一个单词的动词却听不懂它的名词或形容词的状况。要克服这个问题、听懂不同重音的词类变化，可是有小贴士的！下一课就让我们来学习重音变化的基本规则吧。

MEMO

Listening & Speaking

Unit 2

单词的重音规则

行前准备 Preparation 准备充足的话，必能事半功倍。

单词的重音变化是有规则可循的。虽然不是所有的单词都符合以下的规则，但是了解这些基本规则仍可以帮助你掌握重音的原则，改善发音及听力！

■ **Rule 1**：两个音节的名词，通常重音在第一个音节

present n. 礼物　permit n. 许可证　product n. 产品　butter n. 奶油
curtain n. 窗帘　album n. 相册　novel n. 小说　liquor n. 酒

■ **Rule 2**：两个音节的形容词，通常重音在第一个音节

pretty a. 漂亮的　　　　　　fancy a. 花哨的
ugly a. 丑的　　　　　　　shining a. 发光的
shocking a. 令人震惊的　　　tempting a. 有诱惑力的
peaceful a. 和平的　　　　　perfect a. 完美的

■ **Rule 3**：两个音节的动词，通常重音在第二个音节

present v. 呈现　permit v. 许可　produce v. 制造　seduce v. 引诱
combine v. 合并　create v. 创造　inhale v. 吸气　replace v. 取代

（注意，请比较这部分的前三个动词及 Rule 1 的前三个名词。）

■ **Rule 4**：以 tion，sion，cian 结尾的单词，通常重音在倒数第二个音节
　　　　　（tion，sion，cian 前一个音节）

solution n. 解决方案　　information n. 资讯　　operation n. 运作
decision n. 决定　　　　permission n. 允许　　precision n. 明确性；精确度
physician n. 内科医生　　Christian n. 基督教徒　magician n. 魔术师

Unit 2 单词的重音规则

■ **Rule 5**：以 **ic**，**ical** 结尾的单词，通常重音在倒数第三个音节
（**ic**，**ical** 前一个音节）

rea**lis**tic a. 现实的   ae**ro**bic a. 有氧的   stra**te**gic a. 策略性的
critical a. 批判的   eco**no**mical a. 节约的   **co**mical a. 喜剧的
po**li**tical a. 政治的   **cu**bical a. 立方体的   **ra**dical a. 激进的

■ **Rule 6**：以 **ious**，**eous** 结尾的单词，通常重音在倒数第三个音节
（**ious**，**eous** 前一个音节）

curious a. 好奇的   no**to**rious a. 臭名昭著的
furious a. 火冒三丈的   **dan**gerous a. 危险的
instan**ta**neous a. 即时的   ou**tra**geous a. 无法无天的、可憎的

■ **Rule7**：以 **cy**，**ty**，**phy**，**gy** 结尾的单词，通常重音在倒数第三个音节
（**cy**，**ty**，**phy**，**gy** 前两个音节）

de**mo**cracy n. 民主   **po**licy n. 政策   bu**reau**cracy n. 官僚制度
pos**si**bility n. 可能性   perso**na**lity n. 个性   crea**ti**vity n. 创造力
phi**lo**sophy n. 哲学   pho**to**graphy n. 摄影   ge**o**graphy n. 地理
tech**no**logy n. 科技   bi**o**logy n. 生物学   psy**cho**logy n. 心理学

■ **Rule 8**：复合单词
如果两个英语单词合起来成了一个独立的新单词，它就是复合单词。复合单词无论连起来写成一个单词，或分成两个单词，都是一个意思。

1. 复合名词，通常重音在第一部分
greenhouse n. 温室   **rain**coat n. 雨衣   **smo**king room n. 吸烟室
phone book n. 电话簿   **high** school n. 高中   **rice** cooker n. 电锅

2. 复合形容词，通常两个部分皆为重音
bad-tempered a. 脾气坏的   old-**fa**shioned a. 过时的
well-designed a. 设计良好的   well-**man**nered a. 有教养的；有礼貌的
poorly-made a. 做得粗糙的   ill-**fit**ting a. 不适宜的；不合的

3. 复合动词，通常重音在第二部分的原重音
under**stand** v. 了解   under**es**timate v. 低估
over**look** v. 忽视   over**em**phasize v. 过度强调

077

提醒便条纸
Reminding 舒葳老师的小叮咛,提枪上阵也不怕。

如前所说,这些规则提供了我们英语单词重音的基本原则,但是你可能也会发现,还有许多单词是无法套用这些规则的。碰到了重音不确定的单词,最好的方式是查字典,务必在新学一个单词时就掌握它正确的发音。如此一来,才能在刚开始就养成正确的发音习惯,也才能听得正确!

MEMO Listening & Speaking

Unit 3

标出重音节，并念念看

热身运动 Warm Up 学习英语前，先来做个热身操吧！

请将下列各组单词标出重音节，并念念看。
然后听 MP3，比较一下与老外的发音。

题目 Questions

1. suspect
   suspect
   suspicious
   suspicion

2. character
   characteristic
   characterization

3. technology
   technological
   technician

4. subscribe
   subscriber
   subscription

5. courage
   discourage
   courageous

6. a turnoff
   to turn off

实际演练 Explanation

通过认真的解题练习打下扎实的根基。

题目 Question ❶
- sus**pect** n. 嫌疑犯
- sus**pect** v. 怀疑
- sus**pi**cious a. 疑心的
- sus**pi**cion n. 疑心

解析 Resolution

suspect 可以是名词，嫌疑犯，重音在前面（见本章 Unit 2 Rule 1）；也可以是动词，怀疑，重音在后面（见本章 Unit 2 Rule 3）。

■ 可活用的补充例句

The prime suspect in the case committed suicide.
这件案子的主要嫌疑犯自杀了。

Who do you suspect stole the car?
你怀疑是谁偷了这辆车？

I have a suspicion that he asked me out simply because you asked him to.
我怀疑他约我出去只是因为你叫他这么做。

Don't be so suspicious.
不要疑心病这么重。

I suspect his motives.
我怀疑他的动机。

Who do you suspect?
你怀疑谁？

I believe there is something suspicious going on.
我相信事有蹊跷。

Your suspicion is unfortunately correct.
很不幸，你的怀疑是正确的。

Unit 3 标出重音节，并念念看

题目 Question ❷ **cha**racter n. 性格

characte**ris**tic a. / n. 特性

characteri**za**tion n. 具有……的特性；电影或小说的人物塑造

解析 Resolution

character 是名词，重音在第一音节；characteristic 因词尾是 ic，重音节在 ic 的前一个音节（见本章 Unit 2 Rule 5）；characterization 词尾是 tion，重音节在 tion 的前一个音节（见本章 Unit 2 Rule 4）。

想想看，你有没有认识词尾是 ic 或是 tion 的单词呢？是否符合相同的规则呢？

■ 可活用的补充例句

It would be very out of character for her to lie.
她如果说谎就太不像她的个性了。

She dealt with it with characteristic dignity.
她以一贯的尊严处理这件事。

A big nose is a family characteristic.
大鼻子是一个家族特征。

Who's the main character in the novel?
这本小说的主角是谁？

She has a strong character.
她性格坚毅。

I just heard my friend's characteristic laugh.
我刚听到我朋友极具个性的笑声。

Red and gold are the characteristic colors of autumn.
红色和金色是秋天的经典颜色。

What would you say are some characteristics of a great leader?
你觉得一个好的领导应该具有什么样的特质？

题目 ③

tech**no**logy n. 科技
techno**lo**gical a. 科技的
tech**ni**cian n. 技师

解析

technology 词尾是 gy，重音在 gy 的前两个音节（见本章 Unit 2 Rule 7）；technological 词尾是 ical，重音节在 ical 的前一个音节（见本章 Unit 2 Rule 5）；technician 词尾是 cian，重音节在 cian 的前一个音节（见本章 Unit 2 Rule 4）。

■ 可活用的补充例句

Modern technology is simply amazing.
现代科技令人赞叹。

We've seen tremendous technological changes over the last 20 years.
过去的二十年我们看到了科技急剧的变化。

He works as a lab technician.
他是实验室的工程师。

We must rethink education in the age of technology.
在这个科技时代，我们必须重新审视一下教育。

The company is on the cutting edge of technology.
这家公司走在科技的尖端。

How can we apply this new technology to our everyday lives?
这个新科技要如何应用在日常生活中？

Our company has just hired a technician to help maintain the office's computers.
我们公司刚雇用了一位工程师，协助维护办公室的电脑。

Mary is the lighting technician for the play.
玛丽是这部戏剧的灯光师。

题目 Question

④ subscr**ibe** v. 订阅
subscr**iber** n. 订阅者
subscr**iption** n. 订阅

解析 Resolution

subscribe 是双音节的动词，重音在第二个音节（见本章 Unit 2 Rule 3）；subscriber 是 subscribe 的名词，重音节仍在 scri；subscription 是指订阅的这件事、这个动作，词尾是 tion，重音节在 tion 的前一个音节（见本章 Unit 2 Rule 4）。

■ 可活用的补充例句

To subscribe to our newsletter, simply fill out this form here.
如果你要订阅我们的通讯报，只要填这个表格就好了。

I am a subscriber of *National Geographic Magazine*.
我是《国家地理》杂志的订阅者。

You can pay your subscription fee online.
你可以在线支付订阅费用。

You'll receive a user name and password when you subscribe.
你下单时会收到账号及密码。

I subscribe to your opinion.
我完全赞同你的看法。

Henry was unwilling to subscribe to the agreement.
亨利不愿意签署同意书。

I have been a subscriber to this magazine for many years.
我成为这本杂志的订阅户已经很多年了。

You can become a member by paying the yearly subscription.
订阅一年期的杂志就可以成为我们的会员。

题目 **❺** **cour**age n. 勇气
Question
　　　　　dis**cour**age v. 使泄气、阻止

　　　　　cou**ra**geous a. 有勇气的

解析
Resolution

> courage 是双音节的名词，重音在第一个音节（见本章 Unit 2 Rule 1）；discourage 前面加 dis 是否定的意思，重音节仍在 cour；courageous 的词尾是 eous，重音节在 eous 的前一个音节（见本章 Unit 2 Rule 6）。

■ 可活用的补充例句

I didn't have the courage to tell the truth.
我（那时）没有勇气说实话。

I was discouraged by what he said.
他说的话使我气馁。

That was a very courageous thing to do.
那么做需要非常大的勇气。

It takes courage to stand up for your rights.
为自己的权益挺身而出是需要勇气的。

What gave you the courage to leave?
是什么给你离开的勇气？

Karen is a courageous woman.
凯伦是一位有勇气的女人。

Try not to let losing discourage you.
试着不要让失败打击你。

The area's dry climate discourages agriculture.
这个区域的干燥气候不利于发展农业。

题目 Question

6 a **turn**off phr. 令人失去兴趣的事
to turn off phr. 关掉

解析 Resolution

这里 to turn off 是短语，是"关掉"的意思，turn 和 off 两个单词都是重音。a turnoff 中，turnoff 是复合名词，如果有个人或事把你"关起来"了，就表示这个人或这件事是"令你失去兴趣、令你倒胃的人、事、物"，重音在第一部分（见本章 Unit 2 的 Rule 8）。

■ 可活用的补充例句

Could you turn that light off, please?
可以请你把那盏灯关掉吗？

His bad habits were a real turnoff.
他的坏习惯着实让我对他失去兴趣。

I turned the water off.
我把水关了。

Jack really turns me off.
杰克真的很令我倒胃口。

Would you turn on the TV?
你可以开电视吗？

My aunt turned me on to jazz.
我阿姨带我进入爵士音乐的世界。

My sister turned on to surfing last summer.
我姐姐从去年夏天开始对冲浪很感兴趣。

They turned and walked away.
他们转身离开了。

提醒便条纸
Reminder

舒葳老师的小叮咛，提枪上阵也不怕。

- 学习单词时，务必确实找出正确的重音位置。
- 找到正确重音位置后，反复大声念出正确的读音能帮助你熟悉这个单词的发音。
- 有时候我们并不一定能确实听清楚对方说的每个音节，但重音节能帮助你掌握一个单词大致听起来的音调，帮助你判断出听到的是什么单词。

MEMO

Listening & Speaking

Chapter 5

句子的重音与节奏
It's a beautiful day!

听力 Listening
口语 Speaking

Unit 1 听听看，说说看

Unit 2 句子重音与节奏的规则

Unit 3 再听听看

学习重点 Main Point

当同学们在听老外说英语时，常会希望听清楚每一个单词、每一个音，而一旦听不清楚某几个单词，便开始惊慌失措，更加无法专心理解对方在说什么了。但是你可能不知道，听老外说英语时，其实并不需要听懂每一个单词！今天，舒葳老师就要带同学来学习如何通过句子重音和节奏听出老外所要表达的重点。

Unit 1

听听看，说说看

热身活动 Warm Up　学习英语前，先来做个热身吧！

请听 MP3，标出他说得最大声、最清楚的音节 / 单词：

题目 Questions

1. Excellent!
2. It's a beautiful day!
3. It's hard to tell.
4. He's planning to resign.
5. Can I have some milk with my tea?
6. I don't think he'll do it.

做完上面的解题题目，是不是很有成就感呢？再多做几题练习题考考自己吧！

题目 Questions

7. That's simply amazing!
8. Your girls are absolutely adorable!
9. I had an awful weekend.
10. The cake turned out beautifully.
11. My hotel room has a wonderful view of the harbor.
12. I'm going to meet up with my best friend this weekend.

Unit 1 听听看，说说看

实际演练 Explanation
通过认真的解题练习打下扎实的基础。

题目 Question ❶ **Ex**cellent!
太好了！

解析 Resolution
这个单词的重音是 ex，除了重音之外，你是否感觉到这个重音节也拉得特别长，而第二和第三个音节相对而言就说得较短呢？再听听下面的句子，模仿 MP3 跟着说说看。所有的重音节都应拉得比较长！

■ 可活用的补充例句

It's ri**di**culous! 太荒唐了！

It's unbe**lie**vable! 真不敢相信！

That's a**ma**zing! 真是太惊人了！

He's a **man** of determi**na**tion. 他是个坚定的人。

题目 Question ❷ It's a **beau**tiful **day**!
天气真好！

解析 Resolution
这个句子的重音是 beautiful 的 beau 和 day。你是否感觉到这两个音节拉得比较长，而其他的单词或音节就说得较短呢？再听一次，模仿 MP3 跟着说说看。再听听下面的句子，模仿 MP3 跟着说说看。所有的重音节都应拉得比较长！

■ 可活用的补充例句

It's a **won**derful **thought**! 这是个很棒的想法！

That's a **bri**lliant i**dea**! 那是个好主意！

It's a de**pre**ssing **day**. 真是令人沮丧的一天。

That's a **te**rrible **joke**. 那个笑话一点也不好笑。

题目 ③ It's **hard** to **tell**.
很难说 / 很难分辨出来。

解析 / Resolution

这个句子的重音是 hard 和 tell。你是否感觉到这两个音节拉得比较长，而其他的单词或音节就说得较短也较不清楚呢？再听一次，模仿 MP3 跟着说说看。再听听下面的句子，模仿 MP3 跟着说说看。所有的重音节都应拉得比较长！

■ 可活用的补充例句

It's **hard** to be**lie**ve. 很难相信。

It's im**po**ssible to **tell**. 这是不可能预测的。

It's **like**ly to **ha**ppen. 这很有可能发生。

It's a **stu**pid **que**stion to **ask**. 那是个很愚蠢的问题。

题目 ④ He's **plan**ning to re**sign**.
他正计划辞职。

解析 / Resolution

这个句子的重音是 planning 的 plan 和 resign 的 sign。你是否感觉到这两个音节拉得比较长，而其他的单词或音节就说得较短也较不清楚呢？再听一次，模仿 MP3 跟着说说看。再听听下面的句子，模仿 MP3 跟着说说看。所有的重音节都应拉得比较长！

■ 可活用的补充例句

I'm **go**ing to pro**pose**. 我会求婚。

He's **go**ing to pre**sent**. 他要做简报。

I'm **plan**ning to **stu**dy Engi**nee**ring. 我计划读工程学。

I'm **ha**ppy to **help**. 我很乐意帮忙。

I've been **mea**ning to **tell** you. 我一直想告诉你。

Unit 1 听听看，说说看

题目
Question

❺ Can I have some milk with my tea?
可以在我的茶里加点牛奶吗？

解析
Resolution

这个句子的重音是 milk 和 tea。你是否感觉到这两个音节被拉得比较长，而其他的单词或音节就说得较短也较不清楚呢？再听一次，模仿 MP3 跟着说说看。再听听下面的句子，模仿 MP3 跟着说说看。所有的重音节都应拉得比较长！

■ 可活用的补充例句

Can I have some pepper with my soup?
我可以在汤中加点胡椒吗？

I'd like some sugar with my coffee.
我的咖啡要加点糖。

You should drink some hot tea with honey.
你应该喝点加了蜂蜜的热茶。

题目
Question

❻ I don't think he'll do it.
我不认为他会这么做。

解析
Resolution

这个句子的重音是 don't think 和 do。你是否感觉到这几个音节被拉得比较长，而其他的单词或音节就说得较短呢？再听一次，模仿 MP3 跟着说说看。再听听看下面的句子，模仿 MP3 跟着说说看。所有的重音节都应拉得比较长！

■ 可活用的补充例句

I don't remember him saying that. 我不记得他这么说过。

I didn't say it would be easy. 我没有说这很容易。

He doesn't think he'll win the game.
他觉得他不会赢得这场比赛。

I don't believe he's telling the truth.
我不相信他说的是实话。

提醒便条纸 Reminder 舒葳老师的小叮咛，提枪上阵也不怕。

　　老外在说英语的时候并不是每个单词都说得一样重，因此同学在听不清楚说得较轻的单词通常会很紧张、会慌，所以不能听懂对方说的话。事实上，老外加重或加长的单词就是句子的重点，听到了这些单词，其实也就足够了！下面我们就来了解英语句子重音的变化和如何能利用这些规则帮助我们听得更轻松吧！

Unit 2

句子重音与节奏的规则

> **课前准备 Preparation** 准备充足的话，必能事半功倍。

一个句子会强调的重音，一定是特别重要、需要对方听清楚的单词。而加重的音，也自然都会被拉得比较长，令对方比较容易听得清楚！因此，我们在听老外说话时，只要能掌握这些重且长的音，基本的意思也就能抓到了。这节课我们就来看看在一般的英语言谈中，哪些类别的单词特别容易因强调而拉长。

■ 内容词与架构词

英语句子中的单词可以分成"内容词"和"架构词"两类。"内容词"为带有"意义"，也就是主导句子含义的单词，包括：名词、动词、否定助动词、副词、形容词、疑问词等。因为是整个句子所要传达信息的重点所在，这些单词通常也是句子的重音所在，帮助我们听到重要的信息。

反之，"架构词"便不具有这么丰富的意义，包括：代词、介词、冠词、be 动词、连词。这些单词的功能只是保持句子的语法正确而已，因此就算没听见，通常也不会影响我们的理解，因此不带重音，说话时也是快速带过。

内容词

名词	动词	否定助动词	副词	形容词	疑问代词
meeting book bike	talk read go	don't can't won't	now later quickly	happy beautiful horrible	who what where when why how

架构词

代词	介词	连词	冠词	be 动词
he she it	in of to	and but because	a an the	is am are

实际演练 Explanation

通过认真的解题练习打下扎实的基础。

题目 Questions ①

This is my cat `n.` .
What `pron.` does it eat `v.` ?
Please `interj.` do `v.` it quickly `ad.` .
You did `v.` an excellent `a.` job `n.` .
Why `pron.` did you ask `v.` that question `n.` ?
Why `pron.` didn't `aux.v` you write `v.` that letter `n.` ?
What `pron.` does it eat `v.` ?

解析 Resolution

你是否发现上面的句子中右边标注了词性的单词不仅说得比较大声，花的时间也较其他单词长呢？

现在，请不要看书，再听一次。把注意力放在重音即可，感受你是否能从重音及句子节奏中抓到所要表达信息的重点。

题目 Questions ②

What `pron.` does it eat `v.` ?
He is my brother `n.` .
What `pron.` does he do `v.` ?
Please `interj.` ask `v.` him to come `v.` over `a.` .
He painted `v.` an amazing `a.` painting `n.` .
Why `pron.` did he go `v.` to the hospital `n.` ?
Why `pron.` didn't `aux.v` he call `v.` you?

解析 Resolution

你是否发现上面句子中右边标注了词性的单词不仅说得比较大声，花的时间也较其他字长呢？

现在，请不要看书，再听一次。把注意力放在重音即可，感受你是否能从重音及句子节奏中抓到所要表达信息的重点。

Unit 2 句子重音与节奏的规则

题目 Questions ❸ Men like online games.
Men like the online games.
The men might like the online games.
Some of the men might have liked the online games here.
Some of the men might have liked some of the online games here.

解析 Resolution

注意，上面的从第一句延伸出来的各个句子，虽然句子越来越长，但加进去的都是架构词，因此句子的重音也未改变，节奏也都与第一句 Men like online games. 大致相同。这里 might 加重音是因为 might 是"情态助动词"强调"可能"的意思，是"内容词"。除此之外，其他的单词都快快带过，听不清楚对意思的理解也影响不大。

现在，请不要看书、再听一次。把注意力放在重音即可，感受你是否能从重音及句子节奏中抓到所要表达信息的重点。

题目 Questions ❹ Women like clothes.
The women like beautiful clothes.
The women like to dress themselves with beautiful clothes.
The women don't like to dress themselves with beautiful clothes.
Why don't the women like to dress themselves with beautiful clothes?

解析 Resolution

注意上面从第一句延伸出来的句子。后面加的单词有内容词也有架构词，因此当句子变长，句子的重音节奏也有了变化。所有的标颜色的单词都会说得清楚且大声。反之，未标颜色单词部分听不清楚并无大碍。

现在，请不要看书、再听一次。把注意力放在重音即可，感受你是否能从重音及句子节奏中抓到所要表达信息的重点。

收尾练习 Exercise

上完课是不是头昏脑涨了？来做做收尾练习吧！

听听看下面的短文，并模仿 MP3 跟着说说看。再听一次，练习把注意力放在重音即可。

I'm studying this Pronunciation and Listening course. There's a lot to learn, but I find it very enjoyable. I think I will find it easier and easier to listen to native speakers speaking in English, but the only way to really improve is to practice all of the time.

Now I can distinguish different vowels and consonants that sound similar, and I also pay more attention to stresses when I listen than I used to. I have been talking to a lot of native speakers of English lately and they tell me I'm easier to understand. Anyway, I could go on and on, but the important thing is to listen well and sound good. And I hope I'm getting better and better!

提醒便条纸 Reminder

舒葳老师的小叮咛，提枪上阵也不怕。

英语句子中并不是每个单词都说得一样重、一样久的。影响句子意义的重要单词会说得长、说得重，而只有语法功能，不影响意义传达的单词自然不需要太花力气去强调。在这节课我们介绍了英语句子重音与节奏的基本规则，只要能掌握这些句子中的重音、长音，我们在听老外说话的时候，就不需因为漏听了几个单词而慌张了。也就是说，听力变得轻松多了，只要听到重音就等于听到全貌了。

Unit 3

再听听看

热身活动 Warm Up 学习英语前，先来做个热身吧！

听 MP3，写下听到的句子，标出他说得最大声、最清楚的音节 / 单词：

题目 Questions

1. _____.
2. _____.
3. _____.
4. _____.
5. _____.
6. _____.
7. _____.
8. _____.

解答 Answers

1. **Thanks** for in**vit**ing me.
2. **Sorry** but I **can't** make it on **Mon**day because I'm **work**ing **late**.
3. Do you **like** the **pain**tings in the **con**ference **room**?
4. Uni**ver**sity students **pay** a **lot** of **mo**ney for their **books**.
5. How **long** have you been **do**ing this **sort** of **work**?
6. Do you **think** it's **harder** to **speak** or to under**stand** English?
7. That was a **real**ly **awe**some i**dea**!
8. Can you **send** me your **most up**dated **month**ly re**port**?

097

实际演练 Explanation

通过认真的解题练习打下扎实的基础。

题目 Question ① **Thanks for in**vi**ting me.**
谢谢你邀请我。

解析 Resolution

这个句子的重音是 thanks 和 inviting，其中 inviting 的重音又在 vi。除了要养成听重音的习惯，我们也要确保耳朵听到句子中的 inviting 这个单词。为什么这么说呢？因为我们即使眼睛认识 inviting 这个单词，在听对方说话时，却常因为对方说话速度快，我们只听到 vi 的重音而一时听不出对方说的是 inviting。当重音在非第一音节的时候尤其不容易听出来，这也是造成听力困难的常见原因之一。

听听看下面的几个句子，先不要看书，专注听重音，你听得出来他在说什么吗？多听几次，模仿 MP3 跟着说说看。

■ 超级实用句型

Thanks for sharing. 谢谢你的分享。

Thanks for your attention. 谢谢你的聆听。

■ 你也可以这么说

Thanks for your coopera**tion.**
谢谢你的合作。

We need your confirmation **as** soon **as** po**ssible.**
我们需要你尽快确认。

Sandy has a degree **in busi**ness administra**tion.**
Sandy 拥有商业管理学位。

■ 可活用的补充例句

This soup **is de**li**cious.** 这汤真美味。

He's so **irres**pon**sible.** 他真不负责任。

Turn left **at the** next **inter**sec**tion.** 下个十字路口左转。

Unit 3 再听听看

题目 **❷** **Sorry** but I **can't make** it on **Mon**day because I'm **work**ing **late**.
抱歉我星期一不能去，因为我得加班。

解析

这个句子的重音是 sorry，can't make，Monday，working 和 late。其中 Monday 的重音在 mon，working 的重音在 work。make it 是"做得到，去得了，赶得到"的意思。如果你刚才在做练习题时写下了这些单词，是否就能抓到要告诉你的信息了呢？

听听看下面的几个句子，先不要看书，专注听重音，你听得出来在说什么吗？多听几次，模仿 MP3 跟着说说看。

■ 超级实用句型

Sorry, I can't make it to work today.
抱歉我今天没办法去公司。

Sorry, I can't make it to your party.
抱歉我不能参加你的派对。

■ 你也可以这么说

I don't think I can make it to the end.
我觉得我撑不到最后。

I can't do it alone.
我没办法独立完成。

■ 可活用的补充例句

I didn't make it to the meeting last Friday.
我上周五没赶得及参加会议。

Do you think you'll make it to the party tonight?
你觉得你今晚能参加派对吗？

I couldn't have it done without you.
没有你，这件事我是不可能做到的。

题目 ❸ **Do you like the paintings in the conference room?**
你喜欢在会议室的画吗？

解析

这个句子的重音是 like，paintings，conference 和 room。其中 paintings 的重音在 paint，conference 的重音在 con。conference room 是 "会议室" 的意思。如果你刚才在做练习题时写下了这些单词，应该就能抓到他要告诉你的信息了。

听听看下面的几个句子，先不要看书，专注听重音，你听得出来在说什么吗？多听几次，模仿 MP3 跟着说说看。

■ 你也可以这么说

Did you enjoy your first day back to school?
回到学校的第一天你开心吗？

Did you like the present that we got you for your birthday?
你喜欢我们送你的生日礼物吗？

Have you ever thought about giving up all your technology and stripping your life back to the bare essentials?
你曾经想过放弃所有的科技，回到最原始、基本的生活方式吗？

■ 可活用的补充例句

What did you like or dislike about your previous job?
上一份工作的哪些地方是你喜欢或不喜欢的？

Have you met the new assistant in the payroll department?
你见过薪资部门那个新来的助理了吗？

Did you see the notice they put up the other day about postponing the meeting?
你看到他们那天张贴关于会议延期的通知了吗？

Unit 3 再听听看

题目 Question ❹ **University students pay a lot of money for their books.**
大学生花很多钱在买书上。

解析 Resolution

这个句子的重音是 university，students，pay，lot，money 和 books。其中 university 的重音在 ver，你可能会觉得 uni 听起来也像是重音，那是因为句首的第一个单词如果是"内容词"时，听起来会比较高昂。student 的重音在 tu，money 的重音在 mon。如果你刚才在做练习题时写下了这些单词，应该就能抓到要告诉你的信息了。

听听看下面的几个句子，先不要看书，专注听重音，你听得出来在说什么吗？多听几次，模仿 MP3 跟着说说看。

■ 超级实用句型

My parents pay a lot of money for my tuition.
我父母为我的学费花了很多钱。

Women spend a lot of money on shoes and clothes.
女人花很多钱在买鞋子和衣服上。

■ 你也可以这么说

Many of us dream of earning money without having to do a lot of extra work.
许多人梦想着不用做很多额外工作就能赚钱。

■ 可活用的补充例句

He spends a lot of time online.
他花很多时间上网。

I know I spend a lot of time thinking about trying to save money.
我知道我花了很多时间思考如何可以省钱。

Many of us dream of having thousands and thousands of dollars to spend on anything we desire.
我们很多人都梦想拥有成百上千万的钱来买我们想要的任何东西。

题目 ❺ How long have you been doing this sort of work?
你做这类工作多久了？

解析

这个句子的重音是 how, long, doing, sort 和 work。其中 doing 的重音在 ing。如果你刚才在做练习题时写下了这些单词，应该就能抓到他要告诉你的信息了。

听听看下面的几个句子，先不要看书，专注听重音，你听得出来他在说什么吗？多听几次，模仿 MP3 跟着说说看。

■ 超级实用句型

How long have you been driving?
你开车有多久了？

■ 你也可以这么说

How long have you been married?
你结婚有多久了？

How long have you lived in your apartment?
你住在你的公寓有多久了？

How often do you call your mother?
你多久打一次电话给你妈妈？

■ 可活用的补充例句

How long has he been the CEO of the company?
他当这个公司的执行总裁有多久了？

How often do you go to this sort of place?
你多久去一次这类的场所？

I wouldn't normally do this kind of thing.
我通常不会做这种事情。

Unit 3 再听听看

题目 **6** Which do you **think** is **har**der? To **speak** or to under**stand** **Eng**lish?

你觉得说英语和（听）懂英语哪一个更难？

解析

这个句子的重音是 think，harder，speak，understand 和 English。其中 harder 的重音在 hard，understand 的重音在 stand。如果你刚才在做练习题时写下了这些单词，应该就能抓到要告诉你的信息了。

听听看下面的几个句子，先不要看书，你听得出来在说什么吗？多听几次，模仿 MP3 跟着说说看。

■ 超级实用句型

Do you **think** it's **be**tter to **live** in **Ca**nada or **Eng**land?
你觉得住在加拿大或英国是不是会更好？

Do you **think** it's **more fun** be**ing** the **old**est or **young**est **si**bling?
你觉得当家里最大或最小的孩子会不会更有趣？

■ 你也可以这么说

Which is **be**tter, i**Phone** or An**dro**id?
哪一个比较好，苹果手机还是安卓手机？

Do you **think** it's **be**tter to **tell** a **small lie** than to de**liv**er a **pain**ful **truth**?
你觉得撒个小谎是否比说出一个令人痛苦的真相更好？

■ 可活用的补充例句

Which do you **think** it's **bet**ter? By **plane** or by **train**?
你觉得坐飞机还是坐火车去比较好？

Which is **ea**sier, to **learn bass** or e**lec**tric gui**tar**?
学贝斯或电吉他，哪一个比较容易？

> **想想看 Thinking**
> 学习疲乏了吗？现在，静下心来安静地想想。

题目 Question ❼ **That was a really awesome idea!**
那是个很棒的主意！

解析 Resolution

这个句子的重音是 really，awesome 和 idea，其中 really 的重音在 rea，awesome 的重音在 awe，idea 的重音在 de。

另外，因为这句话强调是的 really awesome，idea 并不是句子最需要强调的元素，因此虽然 idea 也是重音，idea 的 de 并不会说得特别大声。

■ 可活用的补充例句

That was incredibly nice of him to say that.
他这么说真是太仁慈了。

We sell a wide range of cosmetics and at a very reasonable price.
我们以非常合理的价格出售各式各样的化妆品。

题目 Question ❽ **Can you send me your most updated monthly report?**
你可以发给我最新的月报表吗？

解析 Resolution

这个句子的重音是 send，most，updated，monthly 和 report，其中 updated 的重音在 da，monthly 的重音在 month，report 的重音在 port。

■ 可活用的补充例句

We will have to adopt a more scientific approach in the future.
未来，我们必须采取一个更为科学化的方式。

The special effects were so realistic.
这些特效真逼真。

Unit 3 再听听看

提醒便条纸 Reminder

舒葳老师的小叮咛,提枪上阵也不怕。

- 不要尝试听到或听懂每一个单词,因为这是非常难以达成的目标,更会为我们带来不必要的挫折感。
- 每一个人在说话时,都会自然地把希望对方听到的重要信息说得比较大声、比较长、比较清楚。这些也是我们需要专注地去听的信息。
- 把注意力放在抓重音单词,根据你能听懂的数个重音单词,便能快速拼凑对方要表达信息的全貌。利用英语句子的重音与节奏能帮助你听得更轻松。
- 如果听见了重音仍不能理解,便可能是单词或常用语不足的问题,要尽快积累这些不会的单词或惯用语。
- 自己平时说英语也应该利用重音与节奏,让老外也能理解你的英语。久而久之,你便能将自然的英语声音内化,听说能力都会得到提高。

MEMO
Listening & Speaking

MEMO

Listening & Speaking

Chapter 6

非重点单词的弱化
Let's rock'n roll!

听力 Listening
口语 Speaking

Unit 1 听听看,说说看

Unit 2 弱化的声音

Unit 3 再听听看

学习重点
Main Point

在 Chapter 5 我带同学们一起练习听英语句子的重音,也就是所谓的"关键词"或句子的重点。今天我们来看看那些非重音的单词在老外的口中会起什么样的变化。一旦我们了解了平时为什么不容易听懂这些单词,我们便能更进一步突破自己听力上的障碍!

在熟悉老外说话的习惯后,不仅你的听力会进步,你的发音和口语表达也会更容易让老外听懂了!

Unit 1

听听看，说说看

热身活动 Warm Up 学习英语前，先来做个热身吧！

请练习说说下面的句子。然后听 MP3，比较你的发音跟 MP3 中老外的发音有何不同。

题目 Questions

1. I have bread and butter for breakfast.
2. I don't like any of them.
3. What do you mean?
4. Who's to blame?
5. More or less.
6. I've had enough of her.

做完上面的解题题目，是不是很有成就感呢？再多做几道练习题考考自己吧！

题目 Questions

7. Come and see me.
8. Two and two equals four.
9. I have a lot to do today.
10. They went to lunch.
11. They'll arrive in five or six days.
12. It's one of the best movies of this year.

Unit 1 听听看，说说看

实际演练 Explanation
通过认真的解题练习打下扎实的基础。

题目 Question ❶ I have bread and butter for breakfast.
我早餐吃面包涂奶油。

解析 Resolution
> 这个句子的重音单词是 have，bread，butter 和 breakfast。除了这几个重音之外，你是否注意到其他的单词相对而言就说得较短，元音也发得不够清晰呢？再听听下面的句子，模仿 MP3 跟着说说看。重音单词需要拉得比较长，轻音单词的元音则要弱化，念得又快又短。

■ 可活用的补充例句

I had toast and jam for breakfast.
我今天早餐吃了吐司和果酱。

I'll have cream and sugar with my coffee.
我的咖啡要加奶精和糖。

题目 Question ❷ I don't like any of them.
那些我都不喜欢。

解析 Resolution
> 这个句子的重音是 don't，like 和 any。除了这几个重音之外，你是否注意到其他的单词相对而言就说得较短，元音也发得不够清晰呢？再听听下面的句子，模仿 MP3 跟着说说看。重音单词在念时需要拉得比较长，轻音单词的元音则要弱化，念得又快又短。

■ 可活用的补充例句

I only know one of them.
我只认识他们中的一个。

I really enjoy working with some of my colleagues.
我真的很喜欢跟一些同事共事。

题目 **❸ What do you mean?**
Question 你是什么意思？

解析 这个句子的重音是 what 和 mean。除了这几个重音之外，你是
Resolution 否注意到其他的单词相对而言就说得较短，元音也发得不够清晰
呢？再听听下面的句子，模仿 MP3 说说看。重音词在念时需要
拉得比较长，轻音单词的元音则要弱化，念得又快又短。

■ 可活用的补充例句

Where did you go?
你去了哪里？

Which one do you like?
你喜欢哪一个？

题目 **❹ Who's to blame?**
Question 谁该为此负责？／这件事该怪谁？

解析 这个句子的重音是 who 和 blame。除了这几个重音之外，你是
Resolution 否注意到其他单词相对而言就说得较短，元音也发得不够清晰
呢？再听听下面的句子，模仿 MP3 跟着说说看。重音单词在念
时需要拉得比较长，轻音单词的元音则要弱化，念得又快又短。

■ 可活用的补充例句

Who's to blame for the financial crisis?
谁该为财务危机负责？

We're all to blame.
我们都有责任。

I have no one to blame.
我不能责怪任何人。

Unit 1 听听看，说说看

题目 | ❺ **More** or **less**.
Question | 差不多吧。

解析 | 这个句子的重音是 more 和 less。除了这两个重音之外，你是否注意到 or 这个单词相对而言就说得较短，元音也发得不够清晰呢？再听听下面的句子，模仿 MP3 着说说看。重音单词在念时需要拉得比较长，轻音单词的元音则要弱化，念得又快又短。

■ 可活用的补充例句

Are you talking about John or Mary?
你在说的是约翰还是玛莉？

It's now or never.
现在不做就再也没机会了。

题目 | ❻ **I've had enough of her.**
Question | 我受够她了。

解析 | 这个句子的重音是 had 和 enough。除了这两个重音单词之外，你是否注意到其他的单词相对而言就说得较短，元音也发得不够清晰呢？再听听看下面的句子，模仿 MP3 说说看。重音单词在念时需要拉得比较长，轻音单词的元音则要弱化，念得又快又短。

■ 可活用的补充例句

Have you had enough to eat?
你吃饱了吗？

He isn't good enough for you.
他配不上你。

Stop yelling at me. I've had enough.
别再对我大吼大叫。我受够了。

| 提醒便条纸 Reminder | 舒葳老师的小叮咛，提枪上阵也不怕。|

老外在说英语的时候并不是每个单词都说得一样重，重要的单词讲得大声，不重要的单词会相对弱化，同学们常会因为听不清楚或听不懂这些说得较轻的单词而紧张慌乱。但是现在我们已经知道，原来我们常听不清楚这些单词，有很大的原因是老外在说这类单词的时候发音弱化了，和我们原本想象的发音不同，也难怪我们会听不懂。下面我们就来进一步了解，到底这些轻音的单词老外是怎么发音的吧！

MEMO   **Listening & Speaking**

Unit 2

弱化的声音

学前准备 Preparation 准备充足的话，必能事半功倍。

一个句子中不需强调的轻音单词会弱化，因为对方是否听得清楚都不是很重要，因此就会说得较快、较轻、较短，从而产生了弱化的现象。这些弱化的声音都会发[ə]的声音。这节课我们就来练习弱化音的发音，让自己听得更懂、说得也更标准。请注意，以下均使用淡化的套色字表示弱化的音节。

■ 单词弱音节的弱化音
Rule：在单词中，弱音节弱化

banana

Europe

woman

surface

addition

economics

■ 句子弱音、单词的弱化
Rule 1：重音单词的轻音节或轻音字母音皆弱化

As usual.

Look at this.

Which one do you want?

There are as many as two thousand.

You are the sunshine of my life.

Leave them at the door.

■ 句子弱音、单词的弱化
Rule 2：常听见的弱化单词

to

See you tonight. 今晚见。
He went to work. 他去工作了。
Don't jump to conclusions. 不要妄下结论。
You've got to pay to get it. 要付费才能使用。
Let's go to lunch. 去吃午餐吧。
So to speak. 比如说。

and

ham and eggs 火腿蛋
gold and jewelry 黄金和珠宝
Coffee? With cream and sugar? 咖啡？加糖和奶精吗？
They watched it again and again. 他们看了一次又一次。
They kept going back and forth. 他们不停地来来回回。
We learned by trials and errors. 我们从尝试与错误中学习。

or

Soup or salad? 汤还是沙拉？
One or two? 一个或两个？
Now or later? 现在还是等会？
More or less. 多多少少。
For here or to go? 在这儿吃还是带走？
Are you going up or down?（电梯中）你往上还是往下？

can

I can do it. 我能够做。
Can it wait? 可以等一下吗？
No one can fix it. 没有人能修得好。
What can I do? 我能怎么办？
They can afford the house. 他们买得起这栋房子。
I don't think you can open the cans. 我觉得你打不开这些罐头。

Unit 2 弱化的声音

of

all of them 他们全部

the rest of it 剩下的

That's the best of all! 那真是最好的！

As a matter of fact, ... 事实上，……

Get out of here. 滚出去。

What's the name of the game? 这个游戏叫什么？

are

What are you doing? 你在做什么？

Where are you going? 你要去哪里？

What are you planning on doing? 你打算怎么做？

Those are no good. 那些不好。

How are you doing? 你好吗？

They are all back. 他们都回来了。

■ 缩音

你读到的是……	你听到的是……	你读到的是……	你听到的是……
I am	I'm	I do not I cannot I will I will not I will not	I don't I can't I'll I'll not I won't
he is that is there is he is not he has he has not	he's that's there's he isn't he's he hasn't	I have we have they have I had	I've we've they've I'd
I would I should I would not I would not	I'd I'd I'd not I wouldn't	I would have I wouldn't have I should have I shouldn't have I could have I couldn't have I might have	I'd've I wouldn't've I should've I shouldn't've I could've I couldn't've I might've

收尾练习 Exercise

上完课是不是头昏脑涨了？来做做收尾练习吧！

再听听看下面的短文，注意弱化音的发音，并跟着说说看。

I'm studying this Pronunciation and Listening course. There's a lot to learn, but I find it very enjoyable. I think I will find it easier and easier to listen to native speakers speaking in English, but the only way to really improve is to practice all of the time.

Now I can distinguish different vowels and consonants that sound similar, and I also pay more attention to stresses when I listen than I used to. I have been talking to a lot of native speakers of English lately and they tell me I'm easier to understand. Anyway, I could go on and on, but the important thing is to listen well and sound good. And I hope I'm getting better and better!

提醒便条纸 Reminder

舒葳老师的小叮咛，提枪上阵也不怕。

英语句子中并不是每个单词都说得一样大声、一样久的。影响句子意义的重要单词会说得长、说得重，而只有语法功能不影响意义传达的单词自然不需要太花力气去强调。这节课我带同学们一起发现与体会了老外在弱音单词的发音方式，只要能掌握这些句子中的重音与弱音分别是如何说的，我们在听老外说话的时候，就更容易听懂对方说的话了！

Unit 3

再听听看

热身活动 Warm Up 学习英语前，先来做个热身吧！

写出你听到的句子。

题目 Questions

1. _____.
2. _____.
3. _____.
4. _____.
5. _____.
6. _____.
7. _____.
8. _____.

解答 Answers

1. You should've told her.
2. I wouldn't've done it without you.
3. I'd've come if I'd known.
4. I've cut the bread.
5. They've gone.
6. We've eaten.
7. I could've been there.
8. I would've liked to see that movie.

实际演练 Explanation

通过认真的解题练习打下扎实的基础。

题目 Question ❶ You should've told her.
你应该告诉她的。

解析 Resolution

"You should have told her"会说成"You should've told her"，意思是说"你应该告诉她的（你却没告诉她）"。请比较下面的句子并练习跟着说说看。

You should've told her. 你应该告诉她的。

You shouldn't've told her. 你不该告诉她的。

■ 可活用的补充例句

You should've known better. 你应该更了解的。

题目 Question ❷ I wouldn't have done it without you.
没有你我是不可能做到的。

解析 Resolution

"I wouldn't have done it without you."会说成"I wouldn't've done it without you."。这整句话的意思是说"没有你我是不可能做得到的（但是因为有你的帮忙，所以做到了）"。请比较下面的句子并练习跟着说说看。

I would've done it. 我本来应该做得到的。

I wouldn't've done it. 我本来是做不到的。

■ 可活用的补充例句

We wouldn't've done anything differently.
如果是我们，也会这么做。

I wouldn't have done it if I didn't think I could.
如果我不相信自己做得到，一定无法办到。

Unit 3 再听听看

题目 Question ❸ **I'd've come if I'd known.**
早知道我就来了。

解析 Resolution

"I would have come if I had known" 会说成 "I'd've come if I'd known"，是"我要是早知道，我就会来了（但是我不知道，所以也没来）"的意思。请比较下面的句子并练习跟着说说看。

I'd've come if I'd known.
早知道我就来了。

I wouldn't've come if I'd known.
早知道我就不来了。

■ 可活用的补充例句

They should've warned you.
他们应该警告你的。

You should've said no.
你应该拒绝的。

题目 Question ❹ **I've cut the bread.**
我已经切好面包了。

解析 Resolution

"I have cut the bread" 会说成 "I've cut the bread"。请比较下面的句子并练习跟着说说看。

I've cut the bread. 我已经切好面包了。

I'll cut the bread. 我要切面包了。

■ 可活用的补充例句

I've been thinking about it.
我一直在考虑这件事。

I've been there.
我也经历过。

🎧 119

题目 ⑤ They've gone.
他们已经走了。

解析

"They have gone"会说成"They've gone"。这里的重点是要熟悉 gone 是 go 的过去分词。请比较下面的句子并练习跟着说说看。

They've gone. 他们已经走了。

They'll go. 他们会去。

■ 可活用的补充例句

He's long gone. 他离开很久了。

My watch is gone. 我手表不见了。

题目 ⑥ We've eaten.
我们吃过了。

解析

"We have eaten"会说成"We've eaten"。这里的重点是要熟悉 eaten 是 eat 的过去分词。另外,你是否发现,eaten 中的 t 消音了呢?请比较下面的句子并练习跟着说说看。

We've eaten. 我们吃过了。

We'll eat. 我们要去吃饭。

■ 可活用的补充例句

Have you had dinner?
你吃过晚餐了吗?

Have you ever tried fortune cookies before?
你吃过幸运饼干吗?

题目 Question ❼ I could've been there.
我本来可以去的。

解析 Resolution

"I could have been there" 会说成 "I could've been there"，意思是说 "要不是因为（某个我无法改变的因素），我本来是可以去的"。could have 用来表示某事之所以没有完成是因为一个其他的因素，而非当事人的错。

■ 可活用的补充例句

We could've bought the car if the salesman had respected the deal.
如果汽车销售员尊重我们的协议，我们本已买了这辆车了。

题目 Question ❽ I would've liked to see that movie.
我本来想看那部电影来着。

解析 Resolution

"I would have liked to see that movie" 会说成 "I would've liked to see that movie"，意思是说 "我本来想看那部电影来着"。would have 用来表示某事因为某个因素而没有完成。

■ 可活用的补充例句

We would've bought the car if we had the money.
我们如果有钱就买了这辆车。

提醒便条纸
Reminder 舒葳老师的小叮咛，提枪上阵也不怕。

- 老外说话时，会把重点放在重要的内容词。而不那么重要的单词，也就是架构词，便会自然地弱化。
- 在口语中，弱化单词的元音皆会发 [ə] 的音，和我们单独念那个单词本身的时候是有些不同的。
- 熟悉弱化单词的发音方式会帮助我们听得更明白。
- 自己平时说英语也应该学习老外说话的方式，强化内容词、弱化架构词。当你的说话方式更接近老外的说话方式时，他们也就更能理解你的英语了。

MEMO　　　　　　　　　　　　　　　　　　　**Listening & Speaking**

Chapter 7

连音变化
Tele ri mi ser.
Tell her I miss her!

听力
Listening
口语
Speaking

Unit 1 听听看，说说看

Unit 2 连音规则

Unit 3 再听听看

学习重点
Main Point

我们先看看这章的标题。你知道"Tell her I miss her."在老外口中，听起来像是"Tele ri mi ser."吗？为什么会这样呢？

事实上，不只是这句话，很多时候老外说的话会令我们摸不着头脑，都是因为在一般英语口语中，话一说得快，便会产生所谓的"连音"现象。原本是分开的单词声音连在了一起，也难怪我们会听不懂了。

今天，我们就来看看各种连音的现象。了解了英语连音变化的规则后，听力自然会进步！

Unit 1

听听看，说说看

热身活动 Warm Up 学习英语前，先来做个热身吧！

请听 MP3，写出你听到的句子。

题目 Questions

1. _____.
2. _____.
3. _____.
4. _____.
5. _____.
6. _____.
7. _____.
8. _____.

解答 Answers

1. I'm sick of it.
2. Here's a bag of candy.
3. We agree.
4. I'll deal with it.
5. We have a deep pot.
6. As soon as you can.
7. Please share your ideas with us.
8. Describe the process in a paragraph or two.

Unit 1 听听看，说说看

> **实际演练**
> **Explanation**
> 通过认真的解题练习打下扎实的基础。

题目 Question ❶ **I'm sick of it.**
我烦透了。

解析 Resolution
"I'm sick of it" 听起来像是 "I'm si cko fit"，最后的 t 会消音或只发气音。再听听看下面的句子，模仿 MP3 说说看。

■ 可活用的补充例句

I'm tired of it. 我烦透了。

I'm sure of it. 我很确定。

题目 Question ❷ **Here's a bag of candy.**
这里是一袋糖。

解析 Resolution
"Here's a bag of candy." 听起来像是 "Here'sa bagof candy."。再听听看下面的句子，模仿 MP3 说说看。

■ 可活用的补充例句

Can you get me a pack of cigarettes?
你可以帮我买一包烟吗？

There is a carton of milk in the fridge.
冰箱里有一盒牛奶。

125

题目 ❸ We agree.
我们同意。

解析 "We agree" 听起来像是 "Wea gree"。再听听看下面的句子，模仿 MP3 说说看。

■ 可活用的补充例句

We oppose it. 我们反对这件事。

He enjoyed it. 他很喜欢它。

题目 ❹ I'll deal with it.
我会处理这件事。

解析 "I'll deal with it" 听起来像是 "I'll deal withit"，最后的 t 会消音。再听听看下面的句子，模仿 MP3 说说看。

■ 可活用的补充例句

I can't cope with it. 我无法承受。

Can you manage it? 你处理得来吗？

Unit 1 听听看，说说看

题目 **⑤** **We have a deep pot.**
Question
我们有一只较深的罐子。

解析
Resolution
"We have a deep pot" 听起来像是 "We have a deepot"，句中 have 的 e 不发音，最后的 t 也会消音。再听听看下面的句子，模仿 MP3 说说看。

■ 可活用的补充例句

Stop pushing me around.
不要一直指使我做这个做那个。

I have a black cat.
我有一只黑猫。

题目 **⑥** **As soon as you can.**
Question
尽快。

解析
Resolution
"As soon as you can" 听起来像是 "A ssoonasyou can"。再听听看下面的句子，模仿 MP3 说说看。

■ 可活用的补充例句

We'll go as soon as he comes.
他一来我们就走。

I'll come back as soon as possible.
我会尽快回来。

题目 Question ❼ Please share your ideas with us.
请跟我们分享你的想法。

解析 Resolution

"Please share your ideas with us" 听起来像是 "Plea share youri deas withus"。please 的尾音和 share 的词首，因为发音的位置相近，说话时会连在一起。

■ 可活用的补充例句

Please shut up. 请闭嘴。

Please stand up. 请起立。

题目 Question ❽ Describe the process in a paragraph or two.
用一到两段文字形容这个过程。

解析 Resolution

"Describe the process in a paragraph or two" 听起来像是 "Describe the processi na paragraphor two"。再听听下面的句子，模仿 MP3 说说看。

■ 可活用的补充例句

Could you summarize that in a couple of sentences?
你可以用一两句话做个摘要吗？

They walked a couple of miles in silence.
他们一言不发地走了一两英里。

Unit 1 听听看，说说看

提醒便条纸
Reminder

舒葳老师的小叮咛，提枪上阵也不怕。

  英语的连音是造成同学听不懂老外说话的原因之一。但我们在学校学英语时，却很少有老师会特别教我们连音的规则。事实上，连音的道理很简单，话说得快了，音也自然就连在一块了！但我们如果不了解连音形成的方式，就是想说快也快不了。长久以来，我们说英语的习惯便与老外不同，听到老外说话也就不容易反应过来了。因此，有系统地学习连音的方式和规则对我们的发音和听力都会有很大的帮助！

MEMO　　　　　　　　　　　　　　　　　　　　**Listening & Speaking**

Unit 2

连音规则

学前准备 Preparation 准备充足的话，必能事半功倍。

老外在说话时，可不是每一个单词都是独立分开的。反之，单词与单词之间会自然连贯在一起。英语的连音可以分为三大类：辅音与元音的连音，元音与元音的连音，以及辅音与辅音的连音。我们现在就分别来看看这三类连音的规则吧！

■ **Rule 1：Consonant-to-Vowel 辅音接元音的连音**

当前一个单词尾音是辅音、后一个单词的词首是元音时，便会产生辅音接元音的连音。

1. 短句

Stop it. 不要这样。

Prove it. 证明给我看。

Come on. 别这样。

Watch out! 小心！

I'll ask. 我问问看。

Have a look. 看一下。

2. 长句

Can I help you? 需要帮忙吗？

Did we lose anything? 我们掉了什么东西吗？

Switch off the light. 关灯。

You can always change your mind. 你总是可以改变主意的。

Do you want to share a taxi? 你想要共乘一辆出租车吗？

It didn't work out. 这件事没成功。

3. t + 元音的连音：t 弹舌音（见 **Chapter 3**, 第 **58** 页）

What a mess. 真是一团糟。

Put it on. 穿上。

Not at all. 一点也不会。

He's a lot of fun. 他很有趣。

That is what I mean. 我就是那个意思。

It's been quite a long time. 已经有好长一段时间了。

4. h 消音后的连音（见 **Chapter 3**, 第 **58** 页）

Is this his book? 这是他的书吗？

I think he is the one. 我觉得就是他。

We need him now. 我们现在需要他。

Did you tell him about Michael? 你跟他说了迈克尔的事吗？

Why don't you take her to that new restaurant?
你为什么不带她去那家新餐厅？

Did you ask her about that? 你问过她那件事吗？

■ **Rule 2：Vowel-to-Vowel 元音接元音的连音**

　　当前一个单词尾音是元音，后一个单词的词首也是元音时，便会产生元音接元音的连音。要注意的是，元音和元音连音的时候，听起来常常会像是中间多了一个辅音。

1. 当第一个单词词尾元音发 [o]、[aʊ]、[u]、[ʊ]、[ju] 时，与下一个单词的词首元音间以 [w] 连接

你读的是这样……	你听到的是这样……
do it	do wit
do I	do wI
how often	how woften
no other	no wother
you ought	you wought
due in	due win
know if	know wif
so I'll	so wI'll

2. 当第一个单词词尾元音发 [i]、[ɪ]、[aɪ]、[eɪ] 时，与下一个单词的词首元音间以 [j] 连接

你读的是这样……	你听到的是这样……
see it	see yit
may I	may yI
she is	she yiz
we ought	we yought
high up	hi yup
the end	the yend
be in	be yin
I am	I yam

3. 例句

Do I know this guy? 我认识这个人吗？

How often do you think this happens?
你觉得这种事多久会发生一次？

I don't know how to do it. 我不知道该怎么做。

Don't you see it? 你还不明白吗？（你还看不清吗？）

We've finally come to the end of the tunnel.
我们终于来到黑暗的尽头了。（辛苦的日子终于快过去了。）

She is the one I told you about. 她就是我以前和你说的那个人。

■ **Rule 3：Consonant-to-consonant** 辅音接辅音的连音

当前一个单词的词尾是辅音，后一个单词的词首也是辅音时，便可能产生辅音接辅音的连音。辅音与辅音的连音包括下面几种情形：

Unit 2 连音规则

1. 前一个辅音与后一个辅音发音相同时，两个辅音当一个声音发

Do you want to? 你想这么做吗？

Open the red door. 打开那道红色的门。

I wish she'd come. 我真希望她能来。

That's a bad dog. 那是一只坏狗。

Our luck could change. 我们的运气可能会改变。

Leave it to me. 把它交给我。

2. t + y 的连音

I'll meet you there. 我跟你在那里见面。

He's gonna beat you. 他会揍你。

Don't you like it? 你不喜欢吗？

I hate you. 我恨你。

I went there last year. 我去年去过那里。

I don't care what you say. 我不在乎你说什么。

3. d + y 的连音

Would you come? 你会来吗？

Could you say that again? 你可以再说一次吗？

Did you hear that? 你听到了吗？

Where did you get that from? 你那是哪来的？

How would you like your steak? 你的牛排要几分熟？

How could you do that? 你怎么可以那样做？

4. k + c / k 的连音

Mark can run fast. 马克跑得很快。

Mike keeps a diary. 迈克有写日记的习惯。

Nick couldn't say a word. 尼克一个字也说不出来。

Your neck can get badly injured. 你的脖子可能会严重受伤。

You should thank Kim for her help. 你应该感谢金的帮忙。

I see moms pick kids up at school every day.
我每天都看见妈妈们在学校接小孩放学。

5. s + s 的连音

Sue's stupid. 苏很笨。

James studies science. 詹姆士是学理科的。

The cake is sweet. 这个蛋糕很甜。

My baby brother loves stickers. 我年幼的弟弟喜爱贴纸。

My mom has seven sisters. 我妈妈有七个姐妹。

It rains so much in London. 伦敦经常下雨。

6. d + d 的连音

It's a mad dog. 它是一条疯狗。

Have you had dinner yet? 你吃晚餐了吗？

It's a made decision. 这是已经做好的决定。

What's the planned delivery date? 东西计划何时寄到？

Flights are delayed due to heavy rain. 航班因大雨延误。

The university had to send down a few students.
这所大学必须开除几个学生。

现在，请各位同学开口练习连音。记住，只有多练习才是学好的唯一途径！

Unit 2 连音规则

收尾练习 Exercise 上完课是不是头昏脑涨了？来做做收尾练习吧！

再听听看下面的短文，注意连音，并跟着说说看。

I'm studying this Pronunciation and Listening book. There's a lot to learn, but I find it very enjoyable. I think I will find it easier and easier to listen to native speakers speak in English, but the only way to really improve, is to practice all of the time.

Now I can distinguish different vowels and consonants that sound similar, and I also pay more attention to stresses when I listen than I used to. I have been talking to a lot of native speakers of English lately and they tell me I'm easier to understand. Anyway, I could go on and on, but the important thing is to listen well and sound good. And I hope I'm getting better and better!

提醒便条纸 Reminder 舒葳老师的小叮咛，提枪上阵也不怕。

熟悉连音的规则，可以帮助我们在说英语时说得既顺又快！不过同学要记得，学会了规则后还得要常常练习，让连音成为你平时说话时自然的习惯。同学不妨多听广播或有录音的英语文章或对话，一边听一边画下连音记号，多听几次并跟着念。平时自己阅读文章时，也可以尝试着自然地把单词与单词连在一起！

Unit 3

再听听看

热身运动 Warm Up 学习英语前，先来做个热身操吧！

请听 MP3，写出你听到的句子。

题目 Questions

1. _____
2. _____
3. _____
4. _____
5. _____
6. _____
7. _____
8. _____
9. _____
10. _____

解答 Answers

1. Can you tell me your office hours?
2. That wasn't a fair answer.
3. I'm in a rush I'm afraid.
4. When did he go there?
5. He is practicing as much as he can.
6. What you see is what you get.
7. Have you heard of this singer?
8. It's due in two weeks.
9. I'll be in in a minute.
10. It'll be over in an hour.

实际演练 Explanation

通过认真的解题练习打下扎实的基础。

题目 Question

① Can you tell me your office hours?
你可以告诉我你们的办公时间吗？

解析 Resolution

office hours 会说成 officehours，其中 h 消音，因此 ce [s] 会直接连到 ours [auəz]；用连音记号表示就是：Can you tell me your‿office h̶ours? 句子中的 office hours 就是"办公时间、营业时间"，也可以说成 business hours。请念念下面的句子，听 MP3，练习跟着说说看。

■ 你也可以这么说

What are your business hours?
你们的营业时间是几点到几点？

What time do you get off work?
你几点下班？

■ 可活用的补充例句

Our business hours are from nine a.m. to five p.m. Monday through Friday.
我们的营业时间是周一到周五，早上九点到下午五点。

U.S. Postal Service reduces office hours to offset reduced volume.
美国的邮政服务通过缩短营业时间以减少需求量降低的影响。

How long does it take to get there during rush hour?
在高峰期到那里需要多久？

The traffic is very bad during rush hours.
高峰时期交通非常差。

Off-peak public parking is paid for with cash or credit card at a ticket machine.
在非高峰时段停车须使用现金或信用卡通过缴费机付费。

题目 ❷ **That wasn't a fair answer.**
Question 那么说不公平。

解析
Resolution

wasn't a 会说成 wasn'ta，fair answer 会说成 fairanswer；用连音记号表示就是：That wasn't‿a fair‿answer. 请念念下面的句子，再听 MP3，练习跟着说说看。

■ 可活用的补充例句

He isn't‿a good cook. 他不是个好厨师。

It isn't‿a bad‿idea. 那不是个坏主意。

题目 ❸ **I'm in a rush I'm afraid.**
Question 很抱歉我在赶时间。

解析
Resolution

这句话说得快时，除了 a 和 rush 不连音外，每个单词都会跟前一个单词连音，因此这句话可以说成 Imina rushimafraid. 用连音记号表示就是：I'm‿in a rush‿I'm‿afraid. in a rush 就是"赶时间"；I'm afraid 是"恐怕"的意思，用在告诉对方坏消息、表达歉意时。请念念下面的句子，再听 MP3，练习跟着说说看。

■ 可活用的补充例句

I won't be available‿I'm‿afraid. 恐怕我没空。

We're‿in a hurry. 我们在赶时间。

I'm‿in‿a very difficult position. 我处在一个很难的位置。

Unit 3 再听听看

题目 **4** When did he go there?
Question
他什么时候去那里的？

解析
Resolution

did he 可以说成 didhe，其中因为 h 消音，did 的尾音 d [d] 会直接连到 he 的 e [i]；用连音记号表示就是：When did he go there? 请念念下面的句子，再听 MP3，练习跟着说说看。

■ 可活用的补充例句

How did he do it?
他是怎么办到的？

When is he going to get married?
他何时才要结婚？

题目 **5** He is practicing as much as he can.
Question
他现在一有空就练习。

解析
Resolution

he is 中 he 的 e [i] 和 is 的 i [i] 连音，元音与元音的连音中间可加上 [j]，帮助连音连得更顺，说成 Heyis，as much as he 说成 as muchashe，h 消音，因此 as 的 s [s] 会直接连到 he 的 e [i]。用连音记号表示就是：He is practicing as much as he can. 句子中的 as much as 就是"尽可能、尽量多"的意思；as much as he can 就是"他只要有机会就会做"的意思。请念念下面的句子，再听 MP3，练习跟着说说看。

■ 可活用的补充例句

She can have as much as she wants.
她要有多少就可以有多少。

We should communicate as much as possible.
我们应该尽可能多沟通。

题目 **❻ What you see is what you get.**
你看到的就是你会得到的。

解析

what you 的 t 和 y 连音会发 [tʃ]，see is 连音则可以说成 see‿is。这句话用连音记号表示就是：What‿you see‿is what‿you get. 这句话的意思就是"你现在看到的就是你能得到的"，表示你眼前的一切都是真实的，不会改变，不会有假；这句话也可以用来表示"我就是这样的一个人，你不要想改变我"。

请念念下面的句子，再听 MP3，练习跟着说说看。

■ 可活用的补充例句

I mean what‿I say. 我说的话是认真的。

You asked for‿it; you got‿it. 这是你要的，现在你得到了。

To see‿is to believe. 眼见为实。

题目 **❼ Have you heard of this singer?**
你听说过这个歌手吗？

解析

have you 中 have 的 v（e 消音）和 you 的 y 连音，说成 havyou；heard of 的 d 和 o 连音，说成 heardof；this singer 中 this 的尾音 s 和 singer 的字首 s 连音，说成 thisinger。这句话用连音记号表示就是：Hav‿e you heard‿of this‿singer? 请念念下面的句子，画上连音记号，再听 MP3，练习跟着说说看。

■ 可活用的补充例句

We both think‿it's good. 我们俩都觉得挺好。

Pleas‿e say you love me. 请说你爱我。

Unit 3 再听听看

题目 **❽** It's due in two weeks.
Question
两周后到期。

解析 due in 的 ue [ju] 和 in 的 i [ɪ] 连音，元音与元音的连音中间可加
Resolution 上 [w] 的声音，帮助连音连得更顺，发成 duewin。这句话用连
音记号表示就是：It's due‿in two weeks. 句子中，due 的意思是
"到期"，in two weeks 是"两周后"，所以这句话的意思就是
"两周后到期"，通常用来指两周后要完成某项工作。请念念下
面的句子，再听 MP3，练习跟着说说看。

■ 可活用的补充例句

The bank loan‿is due‿in a month.
银行贷款一个月后就要到期了。

Her train‿is due‿at 8 a.m.
她的火车预计早上八点到。

题目 **❾** I'll be in in a minute.
Question
我马上回家。

解析 be 的 e [i] 和 in 的 i [ɪ] 连音，元音与元音的连音中间可加上 [j] 的
Resolution 声音，帮助连音连得更顺，发成 beyin。in 和 in 连音，in 和 a
又连音，因此这句话会说成：I'll beyinina minute. 用连音记号表
示就是：I'll be‿in‿in a minute. 在这里，I'll be in 的意思就是"我
会进去"，可以用来表示"进办公室"；in a minute 就是"一
分钟后"，其实就是"很快"的意思。请念念下面的句子，再听
MP3，练习跟着说说看。

■ 可活用的补充例句

Will you be‿in? 你会在家吗？

I'll be‿out. 我会出去。

题目 Question ⑩ It'll be over in an hour.
一个小时之内就会结束。

解析 Resolution

be 的 e [i] 和 over 的 o [o] 连音，元音与元音的连音中间可加上 [j] 的声音，帮助连音连得更顺，发成 be‿yover。此外，over 和 in 连音，in 和 an 连音，an 和 hour 又连音，因此这句话会说成：It'll be‿yoverinan‿hour。用连音记号表示就是：It'll be‿over‿in an‿hour。请念念下面的句子，再听 MP3，练习跟着说说看。

■ 可活用的补充例句

It's not‿over yet. 事情还没结束。

It's all‿over now. 全完了；都结束了。

Start‿it all‿over‿again. 再从头开始一次。

提醒便条纸 Reminder

舒葳老师的小叮咛，提枪上阵也不怕。

- 老外说话时，会自然地把单词连在一起说。熟悉了连音的发音，才不会反应不过来老外在说什么。

- 多听英语的 MP3，一边看文本，一边听。体会老外说的连音，并跟着模仿，让耳朵和嘴巴都能习惯各种组合的连音。一旦听过了，也熟悉了，再听到时就不会听不懂了。

- 平时在阅读英语时，也可以根据连音的规则，自己练习用连音读出英语句子。长期下来可以让自己说英语时自然地使用连音。如此一来，你的英语听说能力就都能有长足的进步了！

Chapter 8

语调与弦外之音
What would you like?

听力 Listening
口语 Speaking

Unit 1 听听看,说说看
Unit 2 语调变化
Unit 3 再听听看

学习重点
Main Point

我们先看看这章的标题:"What would you like?"这句话的重音应该放在哪里呢?试着说说看。

你知道吗?当重音放在不同地方的时候,也会改变这句话的意思!如果你能掌握重音位置所传达的意义,就会帮助你听得更容易、理解得更轻松!

现在,我们就来看看英语中音调的各种改变所代表的意义。了解了英语音调的变化规则,不但听力会进步,而且你也能说出更地道的英语!

Unit 1

听听看，说说看

热身活动 Warm Up 学习英语前，先来做个热身吧！

请听 MP3，想想看 A、B、C 与 D 各组中，每个句子各表达什么意思。

题目 Questions

① A. **I** didn't hire Jane.
B. I **didn't** hire Jane.
C. I didn't **hire** Jane.
D. I didn't hire **Jane**.

② A. **What** would you like?
B. What **would** you like?
C. What would **you** like?
D. What would you **like**?

③ A. **Where** can we go?
B. Where **can** we go?
C. Where can **we** go?
D. Where can we **go**?

④ A. **Who** did you see?
B. Who **did** you see?
C. Who did **you** see?
D. Who did you **see**?

Unit 1 听听看，说说看

实际演练 Explanation

通过认真的解题练习打下扎实的基础。

题目 Question

① **I didn't hire Jane.**
我没有雇用简。

解析 Resolution

上面的这句话，重音放在不同的位置，强调的意思也不同！

A. 重音放在 I，I didn't hire Jane. "我没有雇用简"，强调雇用她的人不是我，是别人。

B. 重音放在 didn't，I didn't hire Jane. "我没有雇用简"，表示简可能从头到尾都没有被雇用，这件事情根本没有发生。

C. 重音放在 hire，I didn't hire Jane. "我没有雇用简"，强调我也许是面试了她、跟她谈过或甚至讨论是否雇用她的这个可能性，但我从未做"雇用"她的这个决定或举动。

D. 重音放在 Jane，I didn't hire Jane. "我没有雇用简"，要表达的是"我雇用的不是简，而是别人，你们可能搞错了"。

■ 地道英语随便说

　　是不是很有趣呢？懂得听老外的音调和重音，才能正确掌握对方要表达的意思！下面我们再听一次 MP3，练习说说看吧！

A. I didn't hire Jane.
└ 是别人雇用的简，不是我。

B. I didn't hire Jane.
└ 完全不是事实，我根本没雇用简（简可能根本没被雇用）。

C. I didn't hire Jane.
└ 简也许是我面试的，但我没有做雇用简的决定或动作。

D. I didn't hire Jane.
└ 我雇用的人不是简，而是另有其人。

题目 ❷ **What would you like?**

你想来点什么？

解析

What would you like? 这句话一般而言，句子的最重音会放在 like，也就类似上面的 D. What would you like? 意思是说："你想来点什么？"用在替人点餐的时候。不过，这句话重音放在不同的位置，想强调的意思也不同。

A. 重音放在 What，What would you like? 强调"你想来点什么？"可能是他在说这句话时对方听错了而回答了"他想要某个人之类的"，因此问问题的人再次强调他问的是他想要"什么"。

B. 重音放在 would，What would you like? 强调"你想来点什么？"翻译成中文就有"你到底想要什么"的意思，表示对方已经说了他不要这个，也不要那个，似乎给他什么他都不能满意。因此问话的人这么说，意思是"那你到底要什么"。这样的语气，有抱怨的意思。

C. 重音放在 you，What would you like? 强调"你想来点什么？"表示别人已经点过餐了，该你点了。那"你"要什么呢？

■ 地道英语随便说

是不是很有趣呢？懂得听老外的音调和重音，才能正确掌握对方要表达的意思！下面我们再听一次 MP3，练习说说看吧！

A. What would you like?
└ 我不是问"谁"，我问的是"什么"。

B. What would you like?
└ 你已经说了你不要什么了，那到底什么你才想要呢？

C. What would you like?
└ 其他人已经点餐了或已经表达他们的喜好了，现在该你点餐或表达你的喜好了。

D. What would you like?
└ 一般性问题：你想要来点什么？

题目
Question

③ Where can we go?
我们可以去哪里？

解析
Resolution

"Where can we go?"这句话一般而言，句子的最重音会放在go，也就是上面的 D. Where can we go? 意思是说："我们可以去哪里？"不过，这句话如果重音放在不同的位置，想强调的意思也不同！

A. 重音放在 Where，"Where can we go?"强调"我们可以去哪里？"我问的是哪里，而不是其他事情。

B. 重音放在 can，"Where can we go?""我们可以去哪里？"表示我们好像哪儿都不许去。重点是问到底有什么地方是我们"可以"去的。

C. 重音放在 we，"Where can we go?""我们可以去哪里？"他们，或你们，已经知道可以去哪里了。那我们呢？这句的重点在于：轮到告诉我们可以去哪儿了吧？

D. 重音放在 go，"Where can we go?""我们可以去哪里？"是一般性问题。没有特别要强调什么意义，只是单纯地问"我们可以去哪里"的时候，重音就会放在最后一个内容词：go。

■ 地道英语随便说

是不是很有趣呢？懂得听老外的音调和重音，才能正确掌握对方要表达的意思。下面我们再听一次 MP3，练习说说看吧！

A. Where can we go?
└ 我想知道的是"哪里"，不是"什么时间"或"怎么去"，等等。

B. Where can we go?
└ 我们好像哪里都去不得。到底有什么地方是我们可以去的吗？

C. Where can we go?
└ 他们可以去那些地方，那我们呢？我们可以去哪里？

D. Where can we go?
└ 一般性问题：我们可以去哪里？

题目 ❹ Who did you see?

你看到谁了？

解析

"Who did you see?" 这句话一般而言，句子的最重音会放在 see，也就类似上面的 D，意思是说："你看到谁了？"不过，这句话如果重音放在不同的位置，想强调的意思也不同。

A. 重音放在 who，"Who did you see?" 强调"你看到谁？"可能是说话者很惊讶听到对方表示他看到某人，因此问问题的人再次确认，你看到的是"谁"啊？

B. 重音放在 did，"Who did you see?" 强调"你看到谁了？"翻译成中文就有"你到底看到了谁"的意思，表示对方已经对于他似乎谁都没看到有所不满意。因此问话的人这么说，意思是："那么你究竟有没有看到任何人呢？"这样的语气，有抱怨的意思！

C. 重音放在 you，"Who did you see?" 强调"你看到了谁呢？"表示别人看到其他人了，那"你"看到谁了呢？

■ 地道英语随便说

是不是很有趣呢？懂得听老外的音调和重音，才能正确掌握对方要表达的意思喔！下面我们再听一次 MP3，练习说说看吧！

A. Who did you see?
└ 我想知道的是"谁"。

B. Who did you see?
└ 似乎对于谁都没看到而不满意，有抱怨的意思。你到底看到谁？

C. Who did you see?
└ 别人看到其他人了，那你呢？你看到了谁呢？

D. Who did you see?
└ 一般性问题：你看到谁了？

提醒便条纸 Reminder

舒葳老师的小叮咛，提枪上阵也不怕。

　　英语重音及语调的变化会影响所要表达的语意。如果同学不知道语调对语意的影响，永远都只照字面上去听、去理解，可能还是没办法正确抓住对方想表达的意思！也难怪有的时候，我们即便是每个字都听清楚了，却还是觉得前后逻辑不通或语意合不起来，原来就是因为我们不了解"语调"所传达的"弦外之音"！下面，我们就来进一步了解英语重音和语调的变化和其所要表达的意思吧！

Unit 2

语调变化

学前准备 Preparation 准备充足的话，必能事半功倍。

老外会自然地经由强调句子中不同的单词，来表达不同的意思。中文其实也有一样的现象！以 Unit 1 举的例子"我没有雇用简"这句话为例，如果你试试看把重音放在不同的位置说说看，是否也会有不同的效果呢？如下：

我没有雇用简。

我**没有**雇用简。

我没有**雇用**简。

我没有雇用**简**。

这是英语语调变化的最基本出发点——加重你最需要强调的单词。这节课我们就来认识英语不同类别的重音及语调的变化，并练习听听看、说说看。

■ 句子的重音规则

每一个句子都会有很多的"内容词"，也因此会有很多的重音。但每一个句子都会有最重音，也就是句子的重点。句子重音的变化便造成了音调的改变，也改变了所要传达的意义。句子重音与音调的变化有以下几种类别：

■ Rule 1：句子的最重音通常在最后一个内容词

What's the matter? 有什么问题？

Unit 2 语调变化

What are you doing**?** 你在做什么？

That rat is bigger than the cat**.** 那只老鼠比这只猫还大。

I find learning a new language is difficult**.**
我觉得学习一个新的语言蛮难的。

I have something **for you.** 我有东西要给你。

Put the coffee **in it.** 把咖啡倒进去。

  注意，在后两句中，因为句子的最后一词 you 和 it 都是"架构词"。"架构词"因不带重要字义，我们不会特别强调。something 和 coffee 分别是两个句子的最后一个内容词，因此为句子的重音。（"架构词"和"内容词"的分辨，请见 Chapter 5 Unit 2，第 93 页。）

■ Rule 2：句子的最重音有时不止一个

I lost **my** purse**.** 我弄丢了我的钱包。

The scooter **ran the** red light**.** 那辆摩托车闯了红灯。

I lost the battle**, not the** war**.**
我输了这场战役，但还没输了这场战争。

■ 语调的变化
 Rule 1：新信息要加重音

  虽然一般而言，句子的重音都在最后一个"内容词"，但当我们说出新信息，也就是对方还不知道的信息时，我们一定也希望对方能听见、听清楚。因此，当这个新信息不在最后一个内容词时，我们便会把重音放在这个新的信息，以免对方没听见！

1. **W: I have lost my** coat**.** 我掉了我的外套。

  └ coat 是最后一个关键词。

 M: What kind **of coat?** 什么样的外套？

  └ 我们已经知道是 coat 了，这里 kind 是新的重点。

 W: It was a rain**coat.** 是雨衣。

  └ raincoat 是最后一个关键词，也是新信息。

M: **What color was your raincoat?** 你的雨衣是什么颜色？
  └ 颜色是这个问题的新重点。

W: **It was gray. Gray with floral patterns.**
  灰色。灰色有花的图案。

  └ 前半句中 gray 是最后一个关键词，也是重点。后半句中，我们已经知道是灰色了，因此 floral patterns 变成新的重点。

2. W: **I could use a drink.** 我想喝点酒。

   M: **What kind of drink?** 你想喝哪种酒？

   W: **I'd love some wine.** 我想来点葡萄酒。

   M: **What type of wine do you prefer?** 你喜欢哪种酒？

   W: **Any white wine will do. Any white, but not a very dry white.** 任何白酒都好。白酒，但不要太涩的白酒。

   M: **Let's have some white wine in the pub.**
   我们去酒吧喝点白酒吧。

■ Rule 2：更正错误信息时，正确信息加重音

当对方说错了什么，我们要加以纠正时，自然也是希望对方听得清清楚楚。因此，当我们说出正确的信息以纠正对方时，也会把这个正确的信息加重。

1. W: **Did you go on Thursday?** 你周四去的吗？

   M: **No, I went on Thursday and Friday.** 不，我周四和周五都去了。
     └ 不但是周四，还有周五！

2. W: **You should've worked harder.** 你应该更努力点的。

   M: **I did work hard.** 我有努力啊。
     └ 这里用助动词 did 强调"我的确有"。

3. W: **It seems expensive.** 好像有点贵。

   M: **It doesn't seem expensive to him.** 他可不觉得贵。
     └ 你觉得贵，但他可不这么觉得。

4. **W: I heard you have lived in Beijing for 10 years.**
   我听说你在北京住十年了。

   M: Actually, I have lived here for 15 years.
   事实上，我已经在这里住了十五年了。

   不止十年，已经十五年了。

5. **W: We all forgot about Mom's birthday.** 我们都忘了妈妈的生日。

   M: I didn't. 我可没忘。

   那是你们忘了，我可没忘。

6. **W: Where's your bike? Did someone borrow it?**
   你的自行车呢？借给谁了吗？

   M: No. Someone stole it. 不是，自行车被偷了。

   不是借给别人了，是让人偷了。

■ **Rule 3**：确认对方信息时，所要确认的信息加重音

　　当不确定自己是否已听清楚对方所说信息而欲确认时，也会将想确认的部分加重音。

1. **W: You did want two Cokes, didn't you?**
   你说要两杯可乐，没错吧？

   确定是要两杯吗？

   M: No, I didn't. Just one. 不是。一杯就好。

2. **W: Did you say you will speak to them about the new project?** 你是说你会跟他们谈新案子，对吗？

   你会去谈，不用我或别人再去谈了吧？

   M: Yes, that's right. Leave it to me. 是的，没错。交给我处理吧。

3. **W: It cost me six thousand to buy this dress.**
   这件连衣裙花了我六千。

   M: Six thousand? 六千？

   是六千吗？不是六"百"？除了确认外，还有不以为然或不可置信之意。

4. **W: Tina's already quit.** 蒂娜已经辞职了。

   M: She has? 她已经这么做了吗？

   └ 原本就知道她可能会辞职。但已经辞了吗？有表示惊讶之意。

5. **W: Alan has done some beautiful drawings of his dream house.** 艾伦画了几幅他梦想中的房子。

   M: So he has finished them! 所以他已经完成了啊！

   └ 原本就知道他在画，但已经完成了。

6. **W: You'll have to visit National Park sometime. It really is amazing!**
   你有空一定得去国家公园看看。真的很令人惊艳！

   M: Oh, so you did go there for your holiday!
   哦，所以你们真的去那里度假了！

   └ 事前可能就知道对方要去那里度假，所以真的去了，有表示确认之意。

■ Rule 4：重音改变时，意思也跟着改变

当不确定自己是否已听清楚对方所说信息而欲确认时，也会将想确认的部分加重音。

1. **I have two. / I have, too. / I have to.**

   请说说以下问答重音在哪儿。

   (1) **W: How many kids do you have?** 你有几个小孩？

   M: I have two. 我有两个。

   (2) **W: I have tried my best.** 我已经尽力了。

   M: I have, too. 我也尽力了。

   (3) **W: Why do you work so hard?** 你为什么工作那么努力？

   M: I have to. 我必须这么做。

Unit 2 语调变化

你知道"I have two""I have, too"和"I have to"听起来有什么不一样吗？现在听 MP3 跟着说说看。

(1) W: How many kids do you have? 你有几个小孩？

　　M: I have two. 我有两个。
　　└ 重点在 two，因此重音在 two。

(2) W: I have tried my best. 我已经尽力了。

　　M: I have, too. 我也是。
　　└ 强调你尽力，我也是。因此重音在 I 和 too。

(3) W: Why do you work so hard? 你为什么工作那么努力？

　　M: I have to. 我必须这么做。
　　└ have 在这个句子中是强调的动词"必须"，也是最后一个内容词。

2. thought

请说说下面句子重音在哪儿。

(1) M: I thought you'd enjoy it.
　　我以为你会喜欢。

　　W: So did I. It was too cold though.
　　我也是啊。但是真的是太冷了。

(2) M: I thought you'd enjoy it.
　　我早知道你会喜欢。

　　W: Yeah, the beach resort is the bomb.
　　是啊，那个海滩度假胜地真是太棒了。

(3) M: I thought it was going to rain.
　　我以为会下雨。

　　W: So did I. I'm glad it didn't though.
　　我也是。不过我很高兴没下。

(4) M: I thought it was going to rain.
　　我就知道会下雨。

　　W: I know. The weather is terrible.
　　是啊。天气真的太糟了。

是不是很有趣？强调的重音不同，表达的意思完全不一样。现在听 MP3 跟着说说看。

(1) M: I thought you'd enjoy it. 我以为你会喜欢。
└ 结果对方并不喜欢。

W: So did I. It was too cold though.
我也是。但是真的是太冷了。

(2) M: I thought you'd enjoy it. 我早知道你会喜欢。
└ 对方也真的喜欢。

W: Yeah, the beach resort is the bomb.
是啊，那个海滩度假胜地真是太棒了。

(3) M: I thought it was going to rain. 我以为会下雨。
└ 结果并未下雨。

W: So did I. I'm glad it didn't though.
我也是。不过我很高兴没下。

(4) M: I thought it was going to rain. 我就知道会下雨。
└ 真的下雨了。

W: I know. The weather is terrible. 是啊，天气真的太糟了。

thought 是一个有趣的词，它是 think 的过去式。think 用作 thought 时是"我本来/过去这么想"的意思，可以当"我原本以为（其实我想错了）"用，也可以当"我原本就想到（所以我是对的）"。

当我们以正常的语调说话，也就是把重音放在最后一个内容词时，这时 thought 仍然是重音，因为它原本就是"内容词"，thought 的意思当"以为"用；而当我们又更特别强调 thought 这个单词时，便是要表达"我早就想到了！"

再听一次，你是否能体会不同重音想传达的不同感觉呢？

Unit 2 语调变化

收尾练习
Exercise

上完课是不是头昏脑涨了？来做做收尾练习吧！

请练习说说看下面句子。重音在哪儿？

题目 Question

① I didn't say he stole the money. Someone else said it.
② I didn't say he stole the money. That's not true at all.
③ I didn't say he stole the money. I only suggested the possibility.
④ I didn't say he stole the money. I think someone else took it.
⑤ I didn't say he stole the money. Maybe he just borrowed it.
⑥ I didn't say he stole the money, but rather some other money.
⑦ I didn't say he stole the money. He may have taken some jewelry.

解答 Answers

① **I** didn't say he stole the money. Someone else said it.
我没有说他偷了钱。别人说的。
└ 强调"我"没有说，因此强调 I。

② I **didn't** say he stole the money. That's not true at all.
我没有说他偷了钱。这完全不是真的。
└ 强调我"没有"说，因此强调 didn't。

③ I didn't **say** he stole the money. I only suggested the possibility.
我没有说他偷了钱。我只是暗示了这个可能性。
└ 强调我没有"说"，因此强调 say。

④ I didn't say **he** stole the money. I think someone else took it.
我没有说他偷了钱。我想是别人拿的。
└ 强调我没有说是"他"，因此强调 he。

⑤ I didn't say he **stole** the money. Maybe he just borrowed it.
我没有说他偷了钱。也许他是借的。
└ 强调我没有说他"偷"，因此强调 stole。

⑥ I didn't say he stole **the** money, but rather some other money.
我没有说他偷了这些钱，而是其他的钱。
└ 强调我没有说他偷"这些"钱，因此强调 the。

⑦ I didn't say he stole the **money**. He may have taken some jewelry.
我没有说他偷了钱。也许他只是拿了些珠宝。
└ 强调我没有说他偷这些"钱"，因此强调 money。

提醒便条纸 Reminder 舒葳老师的小叮咛，提枪上阵也不怕。

英语中以重音加强所要强调重点的表达方式，其实和中文并没有什么不同。但是同学们却往往因为英语是"外国语"，一味地背诵语法、单词，反而忽略了语言沟通时最自然、最基本的元素。一旦习惯让听重音、听语调成为听英语的一部分，你会发现你更能以平常心面对说英语的老外。你会更轻易地抓住对方想表达的意思和感觉，不仅如此，你自己在说英语的时候也会更自然！

MEMO   **Listening & Speaking**

Unit 3

再听听看

 学习英语前，先来做个热身吧！

请听 MP3，并选择最适当的回应。

① A. Oh, I thought you wanted tea.
B. Oh, I thought you wanted one.

② A. No, I also bought a dress and a pair of shoes.
B. Come on. It's an expensive bag. I had to think carefully.

③ A. Oh, so who did?
B. Oh, so which song did you write?

④ A. Oh, sorry. I thought you were asking about the salmon. No, it's on the table.
B. No, it's on the table. It doesn't require refrigeration.

⑤ A. Yeah, I enjoyed some sports but not football.
B. Yeah, I can't get enough of televised sports.

⑥ A. No, this is my first time.
B. Yes, I love this place.

解答 Answers　① B　② B　③ A　④ A　⑤ A　⑥ B

实际演练 Explanation
通过认真的解题练习打下扎实的基础。

题目 Question

① **But we asked for two coffees!**
但我们要的是两杯咖啡！

解析 Resolution

这里强调的是 two，表示对方可能是弄错了数量，说话者才需要强调是两杯，而不是其他的数目，因此，可能的回应应该是：B. Oh, I thought you wanted one.（我以为你要的是一杯）

■ 地道英语随便说

下面我们听听看，强调不同的重点时语调会有什么样的变化。请跟着练习说说看。

W: But we asked for two coffees!
但是我们要的是两杯咖啡！

M: Oh, I thought you wanted one.
噢，我以为你要的是一杯。

W: But we asked for two coffees!
但是我们要的是两杯咖啡！

M: Oh, I thought you wanted tea.
噢，我以为你要的是茶。

■ 你也可以这么说

I said I wanted a black coffee.
我说我要黑咖啡。

I said I wanted a black coffee.
我说我要黑咖啡。

That woman in pink is my teacher.
那位穿粉红色衣服的女人是我的老师。

That woman in pink is my teacher.
那位穿粉红色衣服的女人是我的老师。

Unit 3 再听听看

题目 ❷ **You spent 4 hours just to buy this bag?**
Question   你花了四小时买这个袋子？

解析 这里强调的是 4 hours，表示对方觉得不可思议的是"四小时"
Resolution 这么长的时间。因此较适合的回应应是针对时间做解释，也就
是选项：B. Come on. It's an expensive bag. I needed to think
carefully.

■ 地道英语随便说

下面我们听听看，强调不同的重点时语调会有什么样的变化。请跟着练习说说看。

M: You spent 4 hours just to buy this bag?
你花了四小时就为了买这个袋子？

W: Come on. It's an expensive bag. I needed to think carefully. 不要这样。这个袋子很贵，我得考虑清楚。

M: You spent 4 hours just to buy this bag?
你花了四小时就为了买这个袋子？

W: No, I also bought a dress and a pair of shoes.
不是，我还买了一件连衣裙和一双鞋子。

■ 你也可以这么说

It takes me two hours to go home by taxi every day.
我每天要花两小时坐出租车回家。
└ 强调我每天要花"两小时"回家，不是更少时间。

It takes me two hours to go home by taxi every day.
我每天要花两小时坐出租车回家。
└ 强调我每天要搭"出租车"回家，不是搭公车。

My mom spends ten thousand US dollars on makeups every year. 我妈妈每年花一万美金在化妆品上。
└ 强调妈妈要花"一万"美金在化妆品上，不是更少钱。

My mom spends ten thousand US dollars on makeups every month. 我妈妈每个月花一万美金在化妆品上。
└ 强调妈妈要花一万"美金"在化妆品上，不是人民币。

161

题目 ❸ **I didn't write that song.**
Question 　　我没有写那首歌。

解析
Resolution

> 这里强调的是 I，表示对方可能以为是他，但事实上不是他，因此说话者才需要强调"我"没写。较适合这个情境的回应应该是：A. Oh, so who did?

■ 地道英语随便说

　　下面我们听听看，强调不同的重点时语调会有什么样的变化。请跟着练习说说看。

W: I didn't write that song.
　　我没有写那首歌。

M: Oh, so who did?
　　噢，那是谁写的？

W: I didn't write that song.
　　我没有写那首歌。

M: Oh, so which song did you write?
　　噢，那你写的是哪一首？

■ 你也可以这么说

You didn't win that game. 你没有赢那场比赛。
└ 强调你"没有"赢，不要再说你赢了。

You didn't win that game. 你没有赢那场比赛。
└ 强调你没有赢"那场"比赛，你赢的是别的比赛。

I can't sing. 我不会唱歌。
└ 强调"我"不会唱歌，别人会。

I can't sing. 我不会唱歌。
└ 强调我不会"唱歌"，我会做别的事。

Unit 3 再听听看

题目 **❹ Is the cured ham in the fridge?**
Question
火腿在冰箱吗？

解析
Resolution

> 这里说话者强调的是 cured ham，表示对方可能以为问的是别的食物，但事实上不是，因此说话者需要强调"火腿"。因此较适合这个情境的回应应该是：A. Oh, sorry. I thought you were asking about the salmon. No, it's on the table.

■ 地道英语随便说

下面我们听听看，强调不同的重点时语调会有什么样的变化。请跟着练习说说看。

W: Is the cured ham in the fridge?
火腿在冰箱吗？

M: Oh, sorry. I thought you were asking about the salmon. No, the ham is on the table.
噢，抱歉，我以为你问的是鲑鱼。不，火腿在桌上。

W: Is the cured ham in the fridge?
火腿在冰箱吗？

M: No, it's on the table. It doesn't require refrigeration.
不，火腿在桌上。它不需要冷藏。

■ 你也可以这么说

Does her parents live with you? 她的父母跟你住在一起吗？
└ 强调"她的父母"，不是你的父母。

Does her parents live with you? 她的父母跟你住在一起吗？
└ 强调"跟你住"，不是跟她住。

Didn't you come all the way here to see Sarah?
你不是大老远来这里看萨拉的吗？
└ 强调"你"大老远来，要看萨拉的不是你吗？

Didn't you come all the way here to see Sarah?
你不是大老远来这里看萨拉的吗？
└ 强调你要来看"萨拉"，你要看的不是萨拉吗？

163

题目 **5** **I thought you like sports.**
Question   我以为你喜欢运动。

解析
Resolution

> 这里他以正常的语调说这句话，也就是强调所有"内容词"，最重音在 sports。因此这里的 thought 指的是"以为"，表示对方似乎不喜欢运动比赛，因此 A 是恰当的回应。
>
> 注意第一句重音也可以放在 like，强调我以为你"喜欢"，但你似乎不太喜欢？

■ 地道英语随便说

　　下面我们听听看，强调不同的重点时语调会有什么样的变化。请跟着练习说说看。

W: **I thought you liked sports.**
　　我以为你喜欢运动。

M: **Yeah, I enjoy some sports but not football.**
　　我是喜欢某些运动，但我不喜欢足球。

W: **I thought you like sports.**
　　我就知道你喜欢运动。

M: **Yeah, I can't get enough of televised sports.**
　　是啊，电视转播的运动我怎么看都看不够。

■ 超级实用句型

I thought I could do it. 我以为我做得到。

I knew I could do it. 我就知道我做得到。

Unit 3 再听听看

题目 **❻** I thought you'd been here before.
Question 我就知道你来过这里。

解析
Resolution

> thought 可以当"我原本以为（但其实我想错了）"，也可以当"我原本就有想到（所以我是对的）"用。这里强调的是 thought，当后者，也就是"我就知道"用，表示对方的确来过，因此 B 是恰当的回应。

■ 地道英语随便说

下面我们听听看，强调不同的重点时语调会有什么样的变化。请跟着练习说说看。

M: I **thought** you'd been here before.
我以为你来过这里。

W: No, this is my first time.
不，这是我第一次来。

M: I **thought** you'd been here before.
我就知道你来过这里。

W: Yes, I **love** this place.
是啊，我爱极了这地方。

■ 超级实用句型

I **thought** I **lost** you. 我以为我失去你了。

I **knew** I lost you. 我就知道我失去你了。

I **thought** you'd **never** pick me. 我以为你永远不会选我。

I **knew** you'd never pick me. 我就知道你永远不会选我。

165

提醒便条纸 Reminder 舒葳老师的小叮咛，提枪上阵也不怕。

- 老外在说话时，除了单词、句型外，语调也是重要的传达意义的工具。了解语调背后的意义，才能真正听懂英语。

- 英语的语调和中文一样，都是加重特别需要强调的单词，包括强调新信息、更正对方的误解或确认对方所说的信息。因此当一个句子的重音位置不同时，也代表对方想表达的重点也不同。

- 英语的重音就是声调提得较高的部分，在重音的部分说得也较慢、较清晰，以确保听话者听得清楚。

- 平时听英语的时候，多体会老外在说每一句话时的节奏，何时轻何时重，何时拉得长何时一带而过。相信你很快就能听懂老外要表达的真实意思。

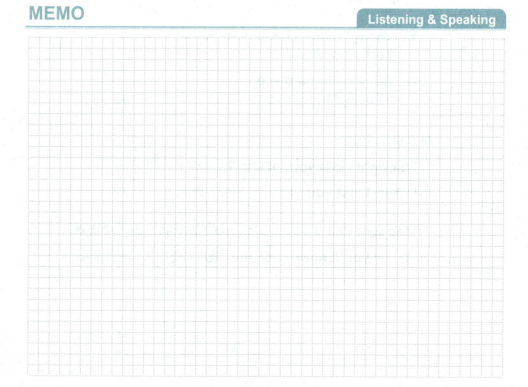

Chapter 9

语意单位及英语笔记
I don't think I know.
I don't think. I know.

听力 Listening
口语 Speaking

Unit 1 听听看，说说看

Unit 2 语意单位

Unit 3 再听听看

学习重点 Main Point

你知道吗？老外在说话时，不同的地方停顿、换气，也会产生不同的意思！看看本章的标题，"I don't think I know"和"I don't think. I know"意思是否不同呢？（请见本章 第177页）

理解老外语句的声调及停顿的位置所代表的意义，不但能够帮助你更能听懂老外在说什么，在听长篇听力的时候还能帮助你跟上老外的节奏，避免只听得懂前两句，然后就什么也听不懂了。

除了听懂外，同学也常会有用英语做笔记的机会，如听英语演讲、听英语报告、跟老外开会、甚至是在考试时，如托福、IELTS 及其他的英语考试都需要考生有做英语笔记的能力。但你可能不知道，听懂声调及停顿语句也是训练自己做英语笔记的重要方法之一。今天我们就来带同学一起学习如何利用语句段落听懂老外的话，如何听英语、做笔记吧！

Unit 1

听听看，说说看

热身活动 Warm Up　学习英语前，先来做个热身吧！

请听听看，试着做笔记、写下你听到的句子。快速写下重点即可，不需要写出完整的句子。

题目 Questions

1. _____.
2. _____.
3. _____.
4. _____.
5. _____.
6. _____.
7. _____.
8. _____.

解答 Answers

1. It's J-O-S-E-P-H-I-N-E.
2. 886-2-2393-4939
3. suwei.wang@msa.hinet.net
4. 5F, No.7, Alley 8, Lane 111, Moon Lake Road Section 3, Taipei, Taiwan.
5. We need sugar, flour, milk, butter and a dozen eggs.
6. I have been to Germany, France, Belgium, England, Spain and Greece.
7. Seattle or Portland — which is better, and why?
8. Which name would you opt for a baby girl? Natasha, Miranda, Sylvia, Andrea or Olivia?

实际演练 Explanation 通过认真的解题练习打下扎实的根基。

题目 Question

① It's J-O-S-E-P-H-I-N-E.
是约瑟芬。

解析 Resolution

在这道题目中，说话者拼出一个名字：Josephine. 你是否发现，她在拼单词的时候，说完每一个字母后音调都提高，一直到最后才落下呢？

当你听到老外声调上扬时，便知道他还没拼完，需要继续注意听；反之，当你听到他的声调落下时，便知道他已经说完了。

在听英语时，最怕就是一闪神，声音就过了，听不见也来不及。如果能事先知道对方是否会继续说下去，也会提升你听的能力！

再听一次试试看，是不是这样呢？

题目 Question

② 886-2-2393-4939
八八六——二——二三九三——四九三九

解析 Resolution

在这道题目中，说话者说出一个电话号码。数字说起来简单，但是听老外说一整串的数字还得写下来时，同学们就常常反应不及了。因此，平时常练习听数字并写下来是很重要的练习！

除了确实熟悉数字并能迅速反应外，声调和"语意单位"也能帮助你在听老外说话时有好的临场反应！老外在说电话号码时，和我们在说中文的时候一样，会自动替数字分组，以免说得上气不接下气。这一小组的数字就是所谓的"语意单位"。"语意单位"不仅能帮助说话者说得较轻松，也能帮助听话者听得较清楚！你是否也注意到，说话者在说完每一个数字后音调都提高，一直到一小组数字说完时，声调才会落下呢？

再听一次试试看，是不是这样呢？

题目 ③ *suwei.wang@msa.hinet.net*
（电子邮件信箱）

解析

在这道题目中，说话者说出一个电子邮件信箱。在现代生活里，拼姓名、说电话号码和电子邮件信箱都已经是生活中常有的事。我们在听老外说这些基本资料时，也都往往需要能把听到的正确迅速地记下来，在这里，语调和停顿同样也能帮助你。

如同上一题替数字分组，在说其他信息时我们也同样会替文字或信息分组，说话者不至说得上气不接下气，听话者也能听得较轻松、较清楚。因此说话者在说完每一个字时音调也会提高，直到说完一个"语意单位"时才落下。

以本题为例，他语气的停顿如下（斜线表示停顿）：

suwei/.wang@/msa/./hinet/.net

在听英语时，最怕就是一闪神，声音就过了，听不见也来不及。如果能事先知道对方的节奏，也会提升你听的能力！再听一次试试看，是不是这样呢？

题目 ④ **5F, No.7, Alley 8, Lane 111, Moon Lake Road Section 3, Taipei, Taiwan.**
台湾台北市月河路三段——一巷八弄七号五楼。

解析

听地址并能够正确记录也是我们常要做的事。

同样的，你也会发现老外在每说完一个部分时，音调都会提高，并做短暂停顿，直到说完一个"语意单位"时才落下。

以这题为例，他语气的停顿如下（斜线表示停顿）：

5F,/ No.7,/ Alley 8,/ Lane 111,/ Moon Lake Road/ Section 3,/ Taipei,/ Taiwan.

再听一次，练习跟着说话者一起说，模仿他的呼吸与节奏。

Unit 1 听听看，说说看

题目 **❺** **We need sugar, flour, milk, butter and a dozen eggs.**
Question
我们需要糖、面粉、牛奶、奶油，以及一打鸡蛋。

解析
Resolution

这里，说话者告诉你他需要哪些东西，而你必须记下来。这时，你必须养成挑"重点"，也就是挑"关键词"写。以这题为例，你只要写下需要的东西即可，即便如此，你都可能反应不及。因此，你可以利用语气停顿的空格，每个字都只先拼一半，看得懂即可，等对方说完了，你再回去把词拼完整、写好。

甚至你也可以写中文或拼音！毕竟重要的是听懂了、记下来。什么方法对你管用，就是最好的方法。

当然，同上面的几道题一样，你也应该用声调来预知他后面是否还有更多的东西要说，帮助你专心去听并掌握对方节奏。一旦声调落下了，你便可以回头把刚才的笔记重新写好、写清楚。

上面这句话，他语气的停顿如下：

We need sugar,/ flour,/ milk,/ butter/ and a dozen eggs.

再听一次，练习跟着说话者一起说，模仿他的呼吸与节奏。

题目 **❻** **I have been to Germany, France, Belgium, England, Spain and Greece.**
Question
我去过德国、法国、比利时、英国、西班牙，以及希腊。

解析
Resolution

这里，说话者告诉你他去过哪些国家，而你必须记下来。这时，你同样只需挑"重点"，也就是挑"关键词"。以这道题目为例，你只要写下去过的国家即可。你可以利用语气停顿的空档，每个词都只先拼一半，看得懂即可，等对方说完了，你再回去把词拼完整、写好。你也可以写中文或拼音。

同上面的几道题一样，你也应该用声调的上扬来预知他后面是否还有更多的东西要说，帮助你专心去听并掌握对方节奏。一旦声调落下了，你便可以回头把刚才的笔记重新写好、写清楚。

上面这句话他语气的停顿如下：

I have been to Germany,/ France,/ Belgium,/ England,/ Spain/ and Greece.

再听一次，练习跟着说话者一起说，模仿他的呼吸与节奏。

题目 **7** **Seattle or Portland — which is better, and why?**
Question

西雅图和波特兰，哪一个城市比较好？为什么？

解析 这里，说话者给你两个选项让你选择。注意他语气的停顿如下：
Resolution
Seattle/ or Portland//— which is better/, and why?

再听一次，练习跟着说话者一起说，模仿他的呼吸与节奏。

题目 **8** **Which name would you opt for a baby girl? Natasha, Miranda, Sylvia, Andrea or Olivia?**
Question

你会为刚出生的女宝宝选哪一个名字？娜塔莎、米兰达、西尔维娅、安德莉亚，还是奥莉维亚？

解析 这里，说话者问你女宝宝名字的意见，而你必须记下来。如同上面的几题，你也可以用声调来预知他后面是否还有更多的东西要说，帮助你掌握对方节奏。一旦声调落下了，你便可以回头把刚才的笔记重新写好、写清楚了。opt for 是选择的意思。
Resolution

上面这句话，他语气的停顿如下：

Which name would you opt for a baby girl?// Natasha,/ Miranda,/ Sylvia, /Andrea/ or Olivia?

再听一次，练习跟着说话者一起说，模仿他的呼吸与节奏。

Unit 1 听听看，说说看

提醒便条纸
Reminder

舒葳老师的小叮咛，提枪上阵也不怕。

老外说话时，即便速度很快，也会呼吸、停顿的。这些停顿对英语学习者有两层意义：第一，这些停顿配合声调，能帮助我们知道对方说到哪里了，是说到一半，还是已经说完并准备开始说下一个重点了，掌握及预测对方的节奏能帮助我们的听力。第二，句中停顿的位置不同，有时会改变语意。因此，下一课我们就一起来看看英语"语意单位"能如何帮助我们提升听力，以及它如何影响了说话者的语意吧！

MEMO   **Listening & Speaking**

Unit 2

语意单位

学前准备 Preparation 准备充足的话，必能事半功倍。

　　"语意单位"能帮助同学们提高听力水平，是听长篇听力的好工具及重要的技巧。

　　"语意单位"的意义，是让我们通过声调及停顿的位置判断说话者的语句是否已经完成。如果语调上扬并停顿，表示针对这个部分，后面还有重要信息要补充，这时我们要继续专心听，不能松懈；反之，如果对方语调落下，则表示这个语句已经完成。

　　我们一直强调听力最难的地方，便在它"稍纵即逝"。一个闪神，对方已经说完了，没听见也来不及了。掌握"语意单位"，便能帮助我们跟上对方的节奏，一个不小心没听懂前一句话时，也能追上下一个句子。下面我们便来看看我们究竟应该怎么听吧。

■ **Rule 1**：数字和名字：上扬、上扬、落下

　　当前一个词尾音是辅音、后一个单词的词首是元音时，便会产生辅音接元音的连音。

数字	名字
106	LA
94768	IBM
May 11, 1974	MRT
September 21, 2016	ASAP
0933 909 226	X, Y, Z
886 2 2394 1666	Nicole
	Sophia
	Hoffman

Unit 2 语意单位

一连串的数字或字母，老外会将它们分为几段来说。如果是名字，则通常会以音节作为分段的标准。而在段落结束或整串数字或字母结束前，语调皆会上扬，此我们就知道对方尚未说完，就要继续专心听下去。当对方语调下降时，便表示对方已经说完了。

■ **Rule 2**：一连串的人、事、物：上扬、上扬、落下

当前一个单词尾音是辅音、后一个单词的词首是元音时，便会产生辅音接元音的连音。

They sell Fords, Buicks, and Toyotas.
他们卖福特、别克和丰田汽车。

There are only three primary colors: red, yellow and blue.
只有三个原色：红、黄和蓝。

I'd like two hamburgers, soup and salad, and a drink.
我要两份汉堡、汤、沙拉和一杯饮料。

I bought a tie, two shirts, underwear, and a pair of pants.
我买了一条领带、两件衬衫、内衣裤和一条裤子。

I watched TV, played on-line games, did some work, and slept a bit. 我看了电视、玩了线上游戏、做了点工作、还睡了一小会儿。

We grow basil, lemon grass, lavender, and rosemary.
我们种罗勒、柠檬草、薰衣草和迷迭香。

当老外在说一连串的事物时，说到前面几个事物时语调皆会上扬，据此我们就知道对方尚未说完，要继续专心听下去。当对方说 and 并且语调下降时，表示对方已经说完了。

■ **Rule 3**：语意未完，语调上扬；语意结束，语调落下

当前一个单词尾音是辅音、后一个单词的词首是元音时，便会产生辅音接元音的连音。

She works for I'm Publishing. 她在"我识"出版社工作。
└ 上面这句话语气完结了，因此语调落下。

There's no easy answer to this. 这个问题不容易回答。

现在请比较下面这组句子。每组都有两个相似的句子,只是第二句的后面较第一句多了段补充说明。请注意两句话语调的不同。

I enjoy playing card games. 我喜欢玩牌。
  └ 语句结束,语调直接落下。

I enjoy playing card games with my family. 我喜欢跟家人玩牌。
  └ 因为后半句进一步加注了更多的信息,说完后,语调变成先上扬,最后补充完后语调才落下。

下面是更多例子。注意第一句和第二句语调的变化:

I remembered to bring the notebook.
我记得带笔记本。

I remembered to bring the notebook, but I forgot my pen.
我记得带笔记本,但我忘了带我的笔。

She's going to come back. 她会再上门的。

She's going to come back with her friends.
她会带她朋友一起再上门的。

I'm planning to get a Master degree. 我计划读硕士。

I'm planning to get a Master degree in the United Kingdom.
我计划去英国读硕士。

Babies like to play with sounds. 婴儿喜欢玩声音。

Babies like to play with the sounds that they are making.
婴儿喜欢玩他们自己发出来的声音。

I don't like strawberries. 我不喜欢草莓。

I don't like strawberries, but I love strawberry ice cream.
我不喜欢草莓,但我爱极了草莓冰淇淋。

Unit 2 语意单位

■ **Rule 4**：一段语意的开始，语调会提高；一段语意的完成，口气会稍加停顿

以下斜线" / "代表短暂停顿，" // "代表较长停顿，也就是一段语意的完成。

I really want to learn to play the guitar.// It has a great sound/ and there are a lot of great songs/ I want to learn.// The best thing about the guitar/ is that it's easy to carry!// I play the piano and I like it,/ but I can only play at home.// I would love to be able to play anywhere.// With a guitar,/ I could take it to my friends' house/ or to the park.// It would give me more time/ to practice/ and to improve my singing.//

在同一个句子中会因"语意单位"的结束而做短暂的停顿" / "，这可以帮助我们依照意思分割对方说的句子，增进理解。而在每一句话结束时，说话者的语气都会稍稍停顿，帮助读者准备听下一个重点。并且，在新的一句话开始时，句子中的第一个内容词声调也会较高，以吸引我们的注意。因此，当你听到语气停顿、声调提高的时候，你就知道一个新的主题或重点又要开始了。

这个技巧在你错过了前一句的重点并且已经不知道老外在说什么的时候最能派上用场。只要你能掌握下一个重点开始的地方，并专心听，你还是有机会能再次掌握到重点，抓到大部分的信息！

请再听一次。这次不要看书，用心体会语气停顿和声调的变化。

■ **Rule 5**：语意单位与意义改变

I don't think I know.

I don't think. I know.

上面两句话的意思有何不同呢？第一句话是一个完整的"语意单位"，说话者一气呵成，意思是："我不认为我知道。"也就是："我不知道"的意思。

第二句则是两个"语意单位"：I don't think. 和 I know. 因此说话者会在 I don't think. 后面先停顿，再接着说 I know. 那么这又是什么意思呢？I don't think. I know. 的意思就变成了："我不用思考。我就是知道。"

所以听老外说话时，听清楚停顿的地方也很重要！

收尾练习 Exercise

上完课是不是头昏脑涨了？来做做收尾练习吧！

请不要看书，听听看下面的短文。注意音调，什么时候后面还有未完的语句？什么时候已经说完了？什么时候又是一个新的重点？

I'm studying this Pronunciation and Listening book.// There's a lot to learn,/ but/ I find it very enjoyable.// I think I will find it easier/ and easier to listen to native speakers speak in English,/ but the only way to really improve, is to practice all of the time.//

Now I can distinguish different vowels/ and consonants/ that sound similar,// and I also pay more attention to stresses when I listen/ than I used to.// I have been talking to a lot of native speakers of English lately/ and they tell me I'm easier to understand.// Anyway,/ I could go on and on,/ but the important thing is to listen well and sound good.// And I hope I'm getting better and better!//

提醒便条纸 Reminder

舒葳老师的小叮咛，提枪上阵也不怕。

英语听力困难的主要原因之一，是因为声音一下就过去了，若是没听到也没办法了。这节课的重点之一，是帮助同学通过注意"语意单位"正确听懂对方的意思，避免误解。另一个重点，即是练习听出说话者何时会说完，何时要开始新的重点。这样的技巧能帮助我们在听的时候知道在什么时候要格外专心，什么时候可以松懈一下。下面我们来实际练习看看。

Unit 3

再听听看

热身活动 Warm Up 学习英语前，先来做个热身吧！

请听 MP3，并依指示选择正确的答案。

题目 Questions

① "Dave," said the boss, "is stupid!" 谁笨？
  A. Dave.
  B. The boss.

② He sold his houseboat and farm. 他卖什么？
  A. Houseboat and farm.
  B. House, boat, and farm.

③ I had pie and apples. 他吃了什么？
  A. Pineapples.
  B. Pie and apples.

请听听看，写下你听到的句子。一边听一边快速写下重点，不需要写出完整的句子。

④ _____.

⑤ _____.

⑥ _____.

解答 Answers

① A ② A ③ B

④ I bought tissues, two toothbrushes, toothpaste, slippers, mineral water, and batteries.

⑤ The teachers are from Japan, Taiwan, Spain, Brazil, Greece, and France.

⑥ I knew I was going to be late for work, so I drove too fast and got a speeding ticket.

> **实际演练**
> **Explanation** 通过认真的解题练习打下扎实的基础。

题目 Question

① "Dave," said the boss, "is stupid!"
"大卫，"老板说，"是笨的。"

- ☑ **(A) Dave.** ································· 大卫。
- ☐ **(B) The boss.** ······························ 老板。

解析 Resolution

请注意，在这句话中，说话者在什么地方有稍微停顿换气呢？换气表示一段"语意单位"已经结束了。在这里，他说的是（/ 表示停顿换气）：

Dave/ said the boss/ is stupid.

这表示 said the boss 是一个独立的单位，也就是"老板说"，是插入语。说什么呢？"Dave is stupid."。反之，下面的第二句中，The boss is stupid. 就是一完整的语句，中间并无停顿或换气。因此这里的正确答案应是 A。

■ 超级实用句型

"...," said sb.（某人）说："……。"

■ 地道英语随便说

请比较下面两句并练习跟着说说看。

"Dave," said the boss, "is stupid!"
"大卫，"老板说，"是笨的！"

Dave said, "The boss is stupid!"
大卫说："老板是笨的！"

"Mary," replied Grandma, "likes to shop."
"玛丽，"祖母回答，"爱购物。"

Mary replied, "Grandma likes to shop."
玛丽回答，"祖母爱购物。"

题目 ❷ He sold his houseboat and farm.
Question 他卖了他的游艇和农场。

☑ (A) Houseboat and farm. ················ 游艇和农场。

☐ (B) House, boat, and farm. ············· 房子、船和农场。

解析
Resolution

请注意，在这句话中，说话者在什么地方有稍微停顿换气呢？在这里，他的 houseboat 是连在一起说的。表示 houseboat 是一个独立的单位，也就是"游艇"。下面的第二句"He sold his house, boat, and farm"中，house 语调上扬，house 和 boat 中有停顿，因此这里的 house 和 boat 是两个独立的东西，正确答案应是 A。

■ 超级实用句型

sb. sold + N（某人）卖了（名词）。

■ 你也可以这么说

请比较下面两句并练习跟着说说看。

He sold his houseboat and farm.
他卖了他的游艇和农场。

He sold his house, boat, and farm.
他卖了他的房子、船和农场。

■ 地道英语随便说

I bought some ice, cream and bananas.
我买了一些冰、奶油和香蕉。

I bought some ice cream and bananas.
我买了一些冰激凌和香蕉。

Do you have any milk tea or coffee?
你有奶茶或咖啡吗？

Do you have any milk, tea, or coffee?
你有牛奶、茶或咖啡吗？

| 题目 Question | ❸ I had pie and apples.
我吃了派和苹果。

☐ (A) Pineapples. ·· 凤梨。

☑ (B) Pie and apples. ·· 派和苹果。

解析 Resolution

> 在这句话中，重音在哪儿？说话者在什么地方有稍微停顿换气呢？在这里，他的重音在 pie 和 apple，表示 pie 和 apple 是两个独立的单位，也就是"派"和"苹果"。下面的第一句"I had pineapples"中，重音在 pine，pineapple 中也未停顿，因此 pineapples 是一个独立的东西。正确答案应是 B。

■ 你也可以这么说

I had pineapples. 我吃了凤梨。

I had pie and apples. 我吃了派和苹果。

■ 地道英语随便说

That's a cupboard. 那是个橱柜。

That's a cup on the board. 那是个杯子在黑板上。

Read the newspaper. 读报纸。

Read the news in the paper. 读报纸里的新闻。

There's snow and storm. 有雪和暴风雨。

There's a snowstorm. 有暴风雪。

题目 Question

④ I bought tissues, two toothbrushes, toothpaste, slippers, mineral water, and batteries.

我买了卫生纸、两把牙刷、牙膏、拖鞋、矿泉水和电池。

解析 Resolution

在这里,他说的是("/"表示停顿):

I bought tissues,/ two toothbrushes,/ toothpaste,/ slippers,/ mineral water,/ and batteries.

边听边写下一两个英语字母或中文翻译以代表各个单词,听语调上升了解对方尚未说完,继续专心听接下来要说的信息。一连串的事物后接 and 再加上语调下降,表示语句完成,可回头整理笔记。

■ 地道英语随便说

The 7 colors of the rainbow in order are: red, orange, yellow, green, blue, indigo and violet.
彩虹的颜色包含了七个颜色:红、橙、黄、绿、蓝、靛、紫。

We are interested in buying all kinds of jewelry, diamonds, watches, vintage antique and estate jewelry.
我们有兴趣收购各式各样珠宝、钻石、手表、古董和传家珠宝。

We sell all kinds of goods online — cell phones, cameras, notebooks, TV, books, fragrances, cosmetics, and electrical appliances.
我们在网上出售各种商品——手机、相机、笔记本电脑、电视机、书籍、香水、化妆品,以及其他电子设备。

题目 Question **❺** **The teachers are from Japan, Spain, Brazil, Greece, and France.**
这些老师来自日本、西班牙、巴西、希腊和法国。

解析 Resolution

> 在这里，他说的是（"/"表示停顿）：
>
> The teachers are from Japan,/ Spain,/ Brazil,/ Greece,/ and France.
>
> 边听边写下一两个英语字母或中文翻译以代表各个单词，并通过听语调上升了解对方尚未说完，继续专心听接下来要说的信息。一连串的事物后接 and 再加上语调下降，表示语句完成，可回头整理笔记。

■ 地道英语随便说

Our students are from all over the world — Japan, China, Korea, Spain, Mexico, Germany, Russia, and many other countries.
我们的学生来自世界各地：日本、中国、韩国、西班牙、墨西哥、德国、俄罗斯以及许多其他的国家。

Rome, Paris, London — these are among the typical stops for every traveler coming to visit Europe.
罗马、巴黎、伦敦——这些是所有来欧洲旅行的人必去的地方。

Here is a list of destinations that are my personal favorite to travel alone — Chiang Mai, Melbourne, Milan, Amsterdam and Madrid.
这里是一些我个人最喜欢去独自旅行的地方：清迈、墨尔本、米兰、阿姆斯特丹和马德里。

Chiang Mai is a scenically beautiful place where I felt safe, made friends easily, and found a lot of fulfilling activities to do.
清迈有很美丽的风景，在这里，我感到安全，容易交到朋友，还发现了很多令人感到充实的活动。

Unit 3 再听听看

题目 **❻ I knew I was going to be late for work, so I drove too fast and got a speeding ticket.**
Question

我知道我要迟到了，所以车开得太快，结果被开罚单。

解析
Resolution

在这里，也可以说（"/"表示停顿）：

I knew I was going to be late for work,/ so I drove too fast/ and got a speeding ticket.

每次语气的停顿，都代表了一个"语意单位"。边听边利用一两个英语单词写下每一个"语意单位"的重点，并通过听语调上升了解对方尚未说完，继续专心听接下来要说的信息。语调下降，表示语句完成，可回头整理笔记。

■ 你也可以这样说

My little girl was getting shouted at by my husband because she was supposed to be in bed, not playing in the bathroom.
我女儿被我先生训，因为她应该上床睡觉，而不是在浴室玩耍。

■ 地道英语随便说

Jo, the second eldest sister, was very honest and brave, but she often got into trouble because too impetuous.
二姐，乔，为人非常诚实、勇敢，但她常常因为太冲动鲁莽而惹上麻烦。

From 1st to 7th grade at school, I was really bright and always did my homework and everything, but then I completely lost all my focus towards school in 8th grade.
从一年级到七年级，我很聪明做功课也认真，但八年级的时候我对学校完全失去了兴趣。

At the start, it wasn't so bad, but starting towards the end of year 9, I started to get into a lot of trouble.
刚开始还好，但九年级快结束的时候我开始陷入了很多麻烦里。

提醒便条纸 Reminder

舒葳老师的小叮咛,提枪上阵也不怕。

- 一个英语的句子中可能有数个"语意单位",老外在说话时会以短暂换气或停顿来代表一个"语意单位"的结束。
- "语意单位"使说话者可以在正确的地方换气,也能帮助听话者通过"语意单位"正确地了解对方所传达的信息。我们在听老外说话时,要注意对方的声调和"语意单位",这样可以帮助我们跟上老外的节奏,知道现在说到了哪里。
- 每一个新句子的开头,声调都会特别提高。这也是我们需要特别专心听的地方。
- 当说完一个"语意单位",语调却上扬时,表示句子还没说完。
- 当语调下降,表示本句完成,可准备听新句子。

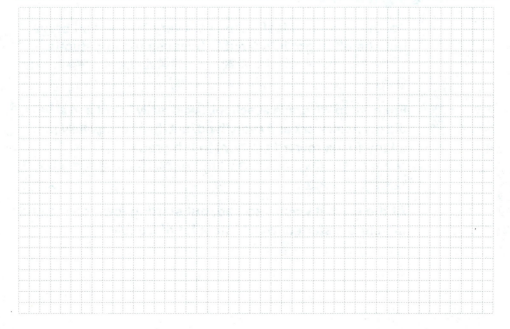

Chapter 10

成语、惯用语及短语

听力
Listening
口语
Speaking

Unit 1 听听看，说说看

Unit 2 成语、惯用语及短语

Unit 3 再听听看

学习重点
Main Point

前面从 Chapter 1 到 Chapter 9，我们帮同学整理了英语中困扰同学听力的"声音"问题。同学听力不好，往往是因为一直在用眼睛学英语，并用中文的声音系统去理解英语的声音，所以一直无法突破。在前面，我们一起了解了英语声音的运作并多加练习后，同学的听力水平必定可以大大提升！

在掌握了"声音"的因素后，我们还得学习英语中的成语、惯用语和短语，才能更进一步！这是因为老外在说话时使用的字句和写文章时是不同的。有许多口语中常用的成语、惯用语及短语都是我们在阅读英语时不会看到的，也正因为如此，当我们突然听老外满口"英语口语"时，就会听不懂了！

现在我们就一起来看看常用的成语、惯用语及短语，熟悉口语英语，提升英语听力！

Unit 1

听听看，说说看

热身活动 Warm Up 学习英语前，先来做个热身吧！

听听看MP3中的对话，并选择第二个人回应所表达的意思。

题目 Questions

1 _____ A. It'll just take a minute.

2 _____ B. It's easy.

3 _____ C. It's a regular part of her job.

4 _____ D. It's best to get it over with now.

5 _____ E. It's a good idea to work together.

6 _____ F. It's good that you went at all.

7 _____ G. To be honest, ice-skating's not really my cup of tea.

8 _____ H. The grass is always greener.

解答 Answers   ❶ B ❷ C ❸ E ❹ D ❺ A ❻ F ❼ H ❽ G

实际演练 Explanation

通过认真的解题练习打下扎实的根基。

题目 Question

① M: **Man, I have to do all the homework for chapter 6 tonight!**
我今晚要做完第六章全部的功课！

W: **Don't worry about it. It's a piece of cake.**
别担心，小意思而已。

解析 Resolution

正确答案：B. It's easy. 很容易。

It's a piece of cake. 就是"小意思、很容易，难不倒人"的意思。另一个类型用法的成语是"as easy as pie"，是"易如反掌"的意思。或是你也可以说"it was a breeze"同样都是"易如反掌"的意思。

■ 你也可以这么说

The test was as easy as pie.
考试真是太简单了。

The test was a breeze.
考试真是太简单了。

■ 地道英语随便说

M: **How was the test?**
考试考得如何？

W: **A piece of cake!**
太简单了。

M: **Thank you so much for your help. You saved my life.**
真是太感谢你的协助了。你帮了我一个大忙。

W: **No problem. When you know what you're doing, it's a piece of cake.**
没问题。这是我的专长，没花什么力气。

题目 Question

❷ M: Thanks for the coffee. That was really great service.
谢谢你的咖啡。你的服务真好。

W: It's all in a day's work.
这是我工作分内的事。

解析 Resolution

> 正确答案：C. It's a regular part of her job.
> 这是她平时工作的一部分。
>
> "It's all in a day's work"，就是"这是我工作分内的事"，用来形容某些事虽然困难或听起来很奇特，但其实是这个人日常工作的一部分。

■ 你也可以这么说

Drinking champagne with Hollywood stars is all in a day's work for top celebrity reporters.
对于专门访问名人的记者而言，和好莱坞明星们喝香槟只是日常工作的一部分。

We worked till twelve last night on the presentation. It's all in a day's work for an executive at my company.
我们昨晚准备报告工作到十二点。对我们公司的管理人员来说这只是日常工作的一部分。

A fancy dinner with a Hollywood celebrity is all in a day's work for this reporter.
对于这个记者而言，和好莱坞明星一起享用昂贵晚餐只是日常工作的一部分而已。

■ 地道英语随便说

M: You're such a good cook!
你真是厨艺高超！

W: Actually, I don't particularly like to cook, but it's all in a day's work.
事实上，我不是很别喜欢做菜，但是这是我日常工作的一部分。

Unit 1 听听看，说说看

题目 ❸ **M: Maybe we should work on this project together.**
也许我们应该联手做这个项目。

W: Yes, two heads are better than one.
是啊，三个臭皮匠胜过一个诸葛亮。

解析

正确答案：E. It's a good idea to work together.
合作是个好主意。

Two heads are better than one. 两个头好过一个头，其实就是俗语说的"三个臭皮匠胜过一个诸葛亮"的意思，用来表示两个人的合作会比一个人努力或苦思好。这句话也可以用在形容"寡不敌众"！

■ 你也可以这么说

Two heads are better than one when it comes to solving complex political issues.
当解决复杂的政治争端时，双方合作胜过单兵作战。

Come over here and help me balance my checkbook. Two heads are better than one.
过来帮我算一下账。两个人比一个人强。

■ 地道英语随便说

W: Can you figure out what this legal document means?
你知道这个法律文件是什么意思吗？

M: Why ask me? It's not like I know anything about the law.
为什么问我呢？我又不懂法律。

W: But two heads are better than one.
两个人一起想总比一个人想破头好吧。

题目 **④** **M:** I've got to get started on the report or I'll never finish it today.
我得赶紧开始写报告,不然的话我今天绝对写不完的。

W: There's no time like the present.
此时不做更待何时?

解析

正确答案:D. It's best to get it over with now.
现在就把它完成是最好的方式。

There's no time like the present. 就是"不现在做还等待何时",表示说话者认为应该立即行动。present 是"礼物",也是"现在",所以我们会说"现在"就是任何人给你最好的礼物。因为只要能把握现在,live in the present,也可以说 live in the present moment,你就能够创造无限可能!

■ 你也可以这么说

Live in the present. Do not look back and grieve over the past.
活在当下。不要回头看,不要为过去懊恼悲伤。

Go ahead and call him — there's no time like the present.
你就赶紧给他打电话吧,现在不做更待何时?

Why don't you start preparing for your presentation now instead of waiting till the night before? There's no time like the present.
你为什么不现在就开始准备你的报告?不要等到前一天晚上,要把握当下每一个时刻。

■ 地道英语随便说

M: When do you think I should phone Mr. Davison about that job?
你觉得我应该什么时候打电话给戴维森先生,询问关于那份工作的事?

W: Well, there's no time like the present.
这个嘛,不如现在就行动吧。

题目 Question

⑤ M: Could you be a dear and give me a hand with these boxes?
你可以好心帮我搬这些箱子吗？

W: No sooner said than done.
马上就做。

解析 Resolution

正确答案：A. I'll just take a minute. 马上就做。

No sooner said than done. 就是"马上就做"，意思是对方在提出请求的同时，这件事就可以完成了。这句话是用来表示马上就会去做，或这件事已经要完成了。类似表达热忱与效率的说法还有："Consider it done." 或直接说："Done."

■ 你也可以这么说

The service at the hotel was really remarkable. Everything we asked for was no sooner said than done.
这间饭店的服务真是令人赞叹。我们提出的所有要求，他们都非常高效率地完成了。

Just ask and consider it done.
只要你开口，我们就能帮你办好。

■ 地道英语随便说

M: Would you mind closing the window?
你介意把窗户关上吗？

W: No sooner said than done.
马上关。

W: Could you give me a copy of this page, please?
可以请你帮我复印这页吗？

M: Consider it done.
马上办。

题目 **6** **M:** I was late for class on Friday. I had a doctor's appointment.
我星期五上课迟到。我去看医生了。

W: Better late than never.
迟到总比缺勤好。

解析

> 正确答案：F. It's good that you went at all.
> 你去了就已经很好了。
>
> "Better late than never"，意为"迟到总比没发生好"，就是"虽然晚了，但至少你做了，总比什么都没做来得好"。

■ 你也可以这么说

I'm sorry I'm late to the party. Better late than never, right?
很抱歉迟到，但至少我来了，对吧？

The achievement is long overdue, but better late than never.
这项成就姗姗来迟，但总算实现目标了。

■ 地道英语随便说

M: Cathy's card arrived 10 days after my birthday.
凯茜的卡片在我生日过了十天后才到。

W: Oh well, better late than never.
这个嘛，迟来的卡片总比没有卡片好。

W: Going to college? Now? But I'm already 40!
上大学？现在？但我已经四十岁了！

M: Well, better late than never.
总比永远不做好吧？

题目 **❼ M:** I hate my job! I'd love a job like Mary's. She seems really happy.
Question
我讨厌我的工作！我想要一份玛丽的那种工作。她看起来很快乐。

W: The grass is always greener.
别人的看起来总是比自己的好。

解析
Resolution

> 正确答案：H. The grass is always greener.
> 别人的看起来总是比自己的好。
>
> "The grass is always greener"是"别人的草地看起来总是比较绿"的意思。我们也可以说完整的句子"The grass is always greener on the other side of the fence"或是"The grass is always greener on the other side"，意思是说，我们总是容易羡慕别人的东西，如工作、房子、生活等，但别人的东西其实只是"看起来"很好而已，我们总是太容易羡慕别人好的地方，看见别人不好的地方。

■ 地道英语随便说

M: You're so lucky. You went to a great college, have money, and you're so smart. You will probably accomplish more by the time you're 30 than I will ever achieve in my entire life.
你真幸运。你上了好的大学，有钱，又这么聪明。你大概三十岁就会有我一辈子都无法达到的成就。

W: Are you serious? I've always envied you. People expect so much out of me. I wish I could just be a regular guy with normal expectations and a normal life.
你是认真的吗？我一直都很羡慕你。大家对我的期望太高。我真希望我是普通人，别人对我有一般的期待，自己过一般的生活就好。

M: Wow, I honestly never looked at it that way. I guess it's true that the grass is always greener on the other side of the fence.
哇，老实说我从来没有这样想过。我猜人总是觉得别人的生活比自己的好。

题目 Question	**8** M: **Would you like to go bowling tomorrow evening with me?** 你明天傍晚可以跟我一起去打保龄球吗？
	W: **To be honest, bowling's not really my cup of tea.** 事实上，我不喜欢保龄球。

解析 Resolution	正确答案：G. To be honest, bowling's not really my cup of tea. 事实上，我不喜欢保龄球。
	"It's not my cup of tea" 是 "我对……没兴趣" 的意思。在句中加上 really 这个字，可以听起来比较缓和、客气：
	It's not my cup of tea. = I don't like it. 我不喜欢。
	It's not really my cup of tea. = I don't like it very much. 我不是太喜欢。
	你也可以说 It's my cup of tea. 表示"这是我有兴趣的事"。

■ 你也可以这么说

"Going to the KTVs," Mary said, "is not really my cup of tea."
"去唱歌这件事，"玛丽说，"我不是很有兴趣。"

I realize a fantasy computer game is not everyone's cup of tea, but this one is amazing.
我知道酷炫的电脑游戏不是每个人都会有兴趣的，但这个游戏真的很赞。

I like suspense in movies. It's my cup of tea.
我喜欢电影中的悬疑情节。那很吸引我。

■ 地道英语随便说

M: **Let's go to the British Museum today. There's a lot to see there.**
我们今天去大英博物馆吧。那里有很多可以看的东西。

W: **You three visit the museum without me. Looking at ancient collections is not my cup of tea.**
你们三个自己去吧。我没兴趣看古老的收藏。

Unit 1 听听看，说说看

| 提醒便条纸 Reminder | 舒葳老师的小叮咛，提枪上阵也不怕。

有的时候我们听老外讲话时，明明听懂了每个单词，却还是搞不懂对方的意思，不明白这些单词为什么在这个情境下被组合在一起。这时，很可能是因为老外用了英语的成语。和中文一样，成语所表达的意思不一定和字面的意思相同，它有弦外之音。这时候，如果我们对这些用语不熟悉，就有可能摸不清对方的所指。除了成语之外，要听得懂老外说话，我们还得多多学习英语的惯用语及短语。英语中的成语、惯用语及短语数量众多，下面我们先介绍一些比较常听到的吧。

MEMO　　　　　　　　　　　　　　　　　　　Listening & Speaking

Unit 2

成语、惯用语及短语

> **学前准备 Preparation**　准备充足的话，必能事半功倍。

英语的短语及惯用语很多，我们不可能一一说明。在这里，我们只能先介绍一些常用的，让同学先体会一下老外在英语口语中时常挂在嘴边的惯用语，帮助我们加强听力！

■ 与钱有关

1. tighten your belt 勒紧裤带

如果你需要 tighten your belt，表示你必须开始小心你的开销了。是不是听起来很熟悉呢？其实中文里也有这个说法，形容经济拮据，手头不宽裕，需要节衣缩食度日。

W: Do you think you can pay this bill sometime this week?
你想你这周可以缴这个账单的钱吗？

M: Another bill? I'll have to tighten my belt this month!
又有账单了吗？我这个月得勒紧裤带了！

2. get money to burn 钱太多了

如果有人可以把钱拿来烧，表示这个人钱多到可以花在休闲娱乐上了，跟我们说"烧钱"的意思可是差了十万八千里！

M: How would you like to go to Paris with me?
要不要跟我一起去巴黎啊？

W: Where did you get money to burn?
你哪里来的闲钱啊？

3. cost an arm and a leg 花了我非常多的钱

如果我们形容某事 costs an arm and a leg，意思就是说这个东西非常昂贵。说 cost me a fortune 也是一样的意思。

This house cost us an arm and a leg, but we have no regrets.
这栋房子花了我们很多钱，但是我们并不后悔。

Katie cost me a fortune! 凯蒂花了我很多钱。
└ 可能是他的女友或老婆很爱花他的钱买昂贵的东西。

■ 与人有关

1. the apple of your eye 最珍贵的人

如果你说某人是 the apple of your eye，表示这个人是你最关心、喜欢的人。有一首歌就是这么唱的："You're the apple of my eye. That's why I'll always be with you."

My granddaughter is the apple of my eye.
我孙女是我最珍爱的人。

2. be not cut out for something 不是那个料

如果你是 not cut out for something，表示你不是那样的人或你不适合做那样的事。你也可以说：not cut out to be…。

I started studying finance but I quickly realized I wasn't cut out for it.
我开始读财经，但我马上就意识到我不是那块料。

He is not cut out to be President.
他不是当总统的料。

3. to each his own 人各有所好

To each his own. 指的是每个人的品位、喜好不同。

W: This place is great. I love the noise and activity in here. You don't like it?
这地方太棒了。我爱死了这里的热闹和这里的活动。你不喜欢吗？

M: Not really. To each his own though.
不太喜欢，不过个人喜好不同。

199

■ 与工作有关

1. burning the candle at both ends 一根蜡烛两头烧

说某人 burning the candle at both ends 表示这个人太忙了，简直里外煎熬。

W: John stays out all night at bars and then goes to work at 6 a.m.
约翰整夜都待在酒吧，到早上六点就直接去上班。

M: He's really burning the candle at both ends.
他真是一根蜡烛两头烧。

2. a blank check 空白支票；充分授权

如果你给某人 a blank check，就是说你给他一张空白支票，他想写多少金额，就写多少金额，意思就是你充分授权他以他认为最好、最恰当的方式处理问题。

2008 年 9 月奥巴马在竞选美国总统时恰巧遇到美国金融风暴和金融业 7000 亿援助案的争议，他就说了："No 'blank check' for Wall Street." 意思是说 7000 亿援助案不该是让华尔街用在任何他们想用的地方，而应该保障一般美国人也能得到帮助。

We are not giving the redevelopment project a blank check. The organizers will be working within a strictly limited budget.
我们并不是给这个改造计划一张空白支票。这些组织机关都会在严格把关的预算下进行这个计划。

3. a done deal 定案了

"A done deal" 是用来表示已经达成一项协议或一个决定。我们通常会说 "It's a done deal" 或 "It's not a done deal"。

We've already hired someone for the position, so this is a done deal.
这个职位我们已经雇用了一个人，所以尘埃落定了。

We told them we needed more time to think about it, so it's not a done deal.
我们告诉他们我们还需要点时间考虑，所以这件事尚未定案。

Unit 2 成语、惯用语及短语

■ 有问题的时候

1. get the runaround 被对方迂回地拒绝

"You get the runaround"意思就是对方间接迂回地拒绝你,也可以说"Someone gives you the runaround"。

M: I got the runaround when I asked my mother for a new car.
我问我妈妈能不能买一辆新车时,她跟我打迷糊仗。

W: I know what you mean. That's happened to me.
我懂你的意思。我也有过一样的体验。

2. We're in the same boat. 我们同在一条船上。

we're in the same boat 指我们处境相同,也就是都必须做类似的事情。

W: I have to go to school, and then go to work every day this week.
这个星期我每天必须上学,放学后再去上班。

M: We're in the same boat.
我们处境相同。

3. take a crack at it 试试看

take a crack at it 就是指尝试看看做某件事情。注意听,在说话的时候,这几个字都会连音。

W: I just can't uncork the bottle.
我打不开这个瓶子。

M: Can I take a crack at it?
我可以试试看吗?

■ 与天气/气氛有关

1. once in a blue moon 非常少见

once in a blue moon 这个跟天气有关的成语可以用来形容某事非常少见。说 blue moon 是因为老外觉得有时候因天气的状况,月亮看起来有可能感觉蓝蓝的呢!

We only see our daughter once in a blue moon.
我们很少见到我们的女儿。

2. in the dark 一无所知、被蒙在鼓里

如果某人在某件事情上 be kept in the dark，表示他没有被告知跟此事相关的发展，因为 in the dark 就是黑漆漆、什么都看不见的意思。相同的意思，你也可以说 be left in the dark。

The personnel were kept in the dark about the merger until the last minute.
关于这个公司的合并案，人事部门一直到最后一刻都还被蒙在鼓里。

3. It never rains but it pours 福无双至，祸不单行

这个表达法是用来形容当坏事发生的时候，其他的坏事也会接踵而来。就是中文说的："福无双至，祸不单行。"

First of all, it was the car breaking down, then the fire in the kitchen and now Mike's accident. It never rains but it pours!
刚开始是车子抛锚，然后厨房着火，现在麦克又发生这个意外。真是祸不单行！

英语常用的动词短语同样也是不胜枚举，这里我们只是列举几类常听见的，帮助同学学习！

■ 与计划有关

1. call off 取消

call off 就是 cancel，是取消的意思。仔细听，call off 会连音。跟着说说看。

W: What's going on? Why are you leaving already?
发生什么事？你为什么已经要走了？

M: The bride called off the wedding, so I'll be going home, I guess.
新娘取消婚礼了，所以我想我该回家了。

2. carry out 执行、实行

carry out 就是执行一项计划或命令。去做一个测试或实验也可以说 carry out。

The plan was carried out to perfection.
这个计划执行得很完美。

The government is carrying out tests on growing genetically modified crops.
政府正在测试经基因改造农作物。

3. fall through 失败、未发生

我们说一个计划、案子等 fall through，表示最后并没有实现。

The project fell through at the last minute because of a lack of funding.
因为缺乏资金，计划在最后一刻告吹了。

4. get on / Get along 继续／使有进展

get on with something，就是继续做某事，让某事有进展的意思。也可以说 get long。

Stop all the fuss and get on with your work!
别再小题大做地抱怨了，赶快回去工作吧！

How are you getting on with your new job?
你的新工作进展得如何啊？

How is he getting along with his studies?
他书读得如何？（他的研究进行得怎么样？）

5. go ahead 照常进行

我们说某事会 go ahead 就是说某事会发生、会照计划进行。

The conference will go ahead as scheduled.
会议会按照原定计划举行。

6. put off 延期、拖延

put off 就是 delay，是延期、拖延的意思。我们会说 put off 某事，如果某事用代名词 it 代替时，就会说 put it off。注意，在说话时，put off 和 put it off 都会连音！

W: Why are you going to the dentist today? I thought we were going to SOGO.
你今天为什么要去看牙医？我还以为我们今天要去崇光百货呢。

M: Well, I just can't put it off any longer.
我实在是不能再拖了。

■ 开始与结束

1. back down 让步、放弃

在某事上 back down 就是因为别人对立的立场或其他阻碍而放弃、打退堂鼓了。

He has backed down from the position he took last week.
他已经放弃了上星期的立场。

Local authorities backed down on their plans to demolish the building.
当地的政府已放弃他们拆除这栋建筑的计划。

2. break out 爆发

break out 就是很突然地开始,通常用于疾病、战争、暴乱等。

He was twelve when the war broke out.
战争爆发时,他十二岁。

Recently, a fatal disease broke out in China infecting thousands of children and causing the death of some of them.
最近有一种致命的疾病在中国扩散开来,数以千计的孩童受到感染,其中一些孩子因此死亡。

3. die down 逐渐减弱

die down 就是平静下来,或逐渐减弱的意思。

The humidity has gone and the wind has died down. It's actually a pretty nice day today.
潮湿已经远离,风也渐渐减弱。今天天气其实蛮不错的。

When the applause died down, she started to sing.
当掌声渐落,她便开始唱歌。

4. drop out 辍学

drop out 指的是念书念到一半就离开学校,没有完成学业。

Dropping out of school has become more and more common at school.
学生辍学越来越常见了。

Some students drop out of school because they suffer setbacks at school.
有些学生辍学是因为在学校经历了挫折。

5. move in / move out 搬进去 / 搬出去

　　move in 是搬进去，move out 就是搬出去。如果是搬进去跟某人住就是 move in with someone。

We have just moved in.
我们刚搬进来。

Tom decided to move in with his girlfriend.
汤姆决定搬去跟他女朋友同住。

Moving out is a great way to become independent.
搬出去独居是训练独立的好方法。

6. opt out 选择退出

　　opt out 是选择结束或退出某项已经在进行的服务或计划等，常用于在市场行销或组织的政策等。

You may click the "opt-out" button to notify the sender that you wish to receive no further e-mails.
你可以点"选择退出"键来告知寄件者你以后不希望再收到邮件。

Are patients given the chance to opt out of having medical information stored on the database?
病人有选择不将医疗资料存在资料库的机会吗？

■ 人的关系

1. break up 分手

　　break up 就是和男女朋友分手。当动词用是 break up，两个音节皆重；当名词用是 breakup，重音变成在第一音节。

My brother has just broken up with his girlfriend.
我哥哥才刚跟他女友分手。

Is it harder for the person who gets broken up with to get over the breakup?
被甩的人是否不容易从分手的低潮中走出来呢？

He's still not over the breakup, but he's finally ready to move on.
他还没完全走出分手的低潮，但总算是准备好要继续过他的生活了。

2. count on 依靠

count on 是依靠、信赖的意思，可以 count on 人、也可以 count on 某件事会发生。我们也常说 Don't count on it. 表示不要相信这件事、不要对这件事太有信心。

You can count on me.
你可以信赖我。

Don't count on lower fuel prices lasting very long.
不要期待低油价会持续多久。

M: Are you coming to our party this weekend?
你周末会来我们的派对吗？

W: You can count on it.
一定去！

3. get on / get along 相处

我们上面有学过，get on with something 是继续进行某事的意思。如果我们说 get on with someone 就是和某人的相处情形了。get on well 就是相处融洽，你也可以说 get along well。

I've always got on well with Henry.
我和亨利一向相处融洽。

The two boys get on well most of the time.
这两个男孩通常都相处融洽。

My sister and I don't get along.
我跟我姐姐处不来。

4. get together 聚在一起

When can we get together again?
我们何时才能再相聚？

We get together once in a while.
我们隔一阵子就聚一次。

5. hang out 和朋友一起消磨时光

hang out 就是和朋友一起度过休闲的时间，如聊天、吃喝、逛街、玩乐，等等。你可以说 hang out at / in...，表示没事常在那里度过休闲时光。你也可以说 hang out with someone，表示你常和谁在一起。

He hangs out in the pub down the street. He's there most nights.
他没事都会去那间酒馆，几乎每晚都在那里。

That new café in the city centre is a nice place to hang out with friends.
市中心的那间新咖啡店是和朋友一块儿出来玩的好地方。

I work long hours and don't want to hang out with people from work.
我工作时间很长，所以不想下班还和同事一起打发时间。

6. look down on 鄙视、看轻

look down on someone 就是看不起、鄙视某人的意思。

He looks down on his colleagues because he thinks he's better than them.
他瞧不起他的同事，因为他自觉高人一等。

A lot of people look down on her because of her family background.
很多人因为她的家庭背景而鄙视她。

提醒便条纸 Reminder 舒葳老师的小叮咛，提枪上阵也不怕。

英语中的成语、惯用语和短语是阻碍同学理解的一大因素。不熟悉这些成语、惯用语和短语，就算背再多的单词，往往也是听不懂。那是因为英语口语和英语书面语有一定的差别，最大的差别便是英语口语中有自己独特的表达方法。我们在这里介绍的只是部分的成语、惯用语和短语，同学一旦有了概念，以后便要多学习这些口语常用的表达方法，才能听得轻松顺畅！下面我们就来做更多的练习吧！

Unit 3

再听听看

热身活动 Warm Up　学习英语前，先来做个热身吧！

请听 MP3，并填写空格中的成语、惯用语及短语。并想想这些成语、惯用语各代表什么意思。

题目 Questions

① W: Wow, you ate that ice cream fast.
　M: Yeah, _____. It was so good.

② M: Well, I am sorry for what I did. Thank you for telling me about it.
　W: It is OK. I just had to _____.

③ W: It's _____ out there!
　M: I know. We won't be going shopping today!

④ W: So, how does the story end?
　M: Well, _____, the titanic sinks and the girl lives.

⑤ M: I don't think our classmates should confront Professor Simms with these issues.
　W: I know. I'm going to try to _____.

⑥ She may not like the coffee cake, but _____.

⑦ James _____ while we painted the entire house.

⑧ Allen was _____ thinking about how to please his parents with good grades.

Unit 3 再听听看

请听 MP3，并填写空格中的短语。并想想这些短语各代表什么意思。

题目 Questions

⑨ He's impossible! How do you _____ him?

⑩ I will have to _____ on the workers to make this deadline.

⑪ Please _____ and let me out of the car. I need to get out of here.

⑫ Wow, you really _____. Why were you so _____ him?

⑬ Could you _____ for Chris while he is _____?

⑭ M: I don't go to the bars like I did as a young man.
   W: Actually, I've noticed that you've really _____ your drinking altogether.

⑮ W: Why do you get so upset when Ralph tells his stories?
   M: I think he feels the need to _____ his life stories in an attempt to make his life feel more grand and fulfilling. I wish he would simply tell the truth.

⑯ W: I don't understand what you are _____. What are you trying to say about my dress? Do you or don't you like it?
   M: Well, to be completely honest, I was trying to _____, but I really don't like it.

解答 Answers

❶ I couldn't help it
❷ get it off my chest.
❸ raining cats and dogs
❹ in a nutshell
❺ talk them out of it
❻ I'll cross that bridge when I come to it
❼ didn't lift a finger
❽ beside himself
❾ put up with
❿ crack down
⓫ pull over
⓬ told him off / mad at
⓭ fill in / on vacation
⓮ cut down on
⓯ play up
⓰ getting at / spare your feelings

209

实际演练 Explanation

通过认真的解题练习打下扎实的基础。

题目 Question

① **W:** Wow, you ate that ice cream fast.
哇，你冰激凌吃得真快。

M: Yeah, I couldn't help it. It was so good.
是啊，我无法自制。实在是太好吃了。

解析 Resolution

"I couldn't help it"就是"我没办法控制自己；没办法改变"，常用在找借口，或合理化自己的行动的时候。

■ 你也可以这么说

I've tried to stop smoking, but I can't. I must smoke! I can't help it!
我尝试戒烟，但失败了。我得抽烟，我没办法不抽！

I should control my temper better, but I can't help getting angry.
我应该要控制自己的脾气，但我就是不由自主地生气。

I couldn't help but wonder what I'd done to deserve this.
我想不通，我究竟是做了什么，得到这样的报应。

I couldn't help but wonder, "What does he look like?"
我不禁猜想："他究竟长什么样子？"

■ 地道英语随便说

M: Why do you spend so much time on the Internet?
你为什么花这么多时间上网？

W: I can't help it. Maybe I'm addicted.
我也没办法。也许我有网瘾了。

Unit 3 再听听看

题目 ❷ M: Well, I am sorry for what I did. Thank you for telling me about it.
Question
嗯，我为我的行为感到抱歉。谢谢你告诉我。

W: It is OK. I just had to get it out of my chest.
没关系，我只是需要一吐为快。

解析 get it out of my chest 从字面上理解就是"从胸中丢出来"，也
Resolution 就是"一吐为快"的意思，表示"说出来就没事了"。

■ 你也可以这么说

Thanks for the chat. I really just needed to get it out.
谢谢你陪我聊天，我真的很需要倾诉。

We helped him get it out about his ex-girlfriend.
我们让他尽情地倾诉他前女友的事。

题目 ❸ W: It's raining cats and dogs out there!
Question
外面正倾盆大雨！

M: I know. We won't be going shopping today!
是啊。我们今天不会去购物了！

解析 raining cats and dogs，雨大得猫和狗都从屋顶上被冲下来了，
Resolution 就是"倾盆大雨"的意思。我们也可以用下面的说法来表示"倾盆大雨"。

■ 你也可以这么说

It's pouring. 雨下得很大。/ 正在下倾盆大雨。

It's pouring down rain. 雨下得很大。/ 正在下倾盆大雨。

I was caught in a downpour. 我被困在一场倾盆大雨中。

题目 Question ❹ W: So, how does the story end?
所以，故事最后怎么了？

M: Well, in a nutshell, the Titanic sinks and the girl lives.
这个嘛，长话短说，泰坦尼克号沉了，女孩活下来了。

解析 Resolution

in a nut shell，照字面上理解是"在坚果壳里"。坚果的壳很小，不能装很多东西，因此"在坚果壳里"就是"简单地说""一言以蔽之"的意思。你也可以说：to put it in a nutshell 或 putting it in a nutshell。相同的意思，你也可以说 long story short。

■ 你也可以这么说

Just give me the facts in a nutshell.
长话短说。

I've got bills to pay, I've got to have my car repaired and I've just lost my job — putting it in a nutshell I'm fed up!
我有账单要付，我有车要修，而且我刚失业——总之，我真是受够了！

■ 地道英语随便说

W: **What took you so long? I've been waiting here for ages!**
你为什么这么久？我等好久了！

M: **Well, to put it in a nutshell, we got lost.**
这个吗，长话短说，我们迷路了。

W: **Hey, why the long face? Did you have a bad day?**
嗨，你怎么脸这么臭？你今天不顺利吗？

M: **Long story short, I got fired.**
长话短说，我被炒鱿鱼了。

Unit 3 再听听看

题目 Question ❺ **M:** I don't think our classmates should confront Professor Simms with these issues.
我认为我们的同学不应该在这些问题上和西姆斯教授正面起冲突。

W: I know. I'm going to try to talk them out of it.
我知道，我会试着说服他们不要这么去做。

解析 Resolution

talk someone out of something 就是"说服某人不要做某事"。如果是要"说服某人要去做某事"就要说 talk someone into something。另外，get out of it 则是"想办法摆脱、逃避"的意思。

■ 你也可以这么说

You've got to talk him into exercising.
你得说服他开始运动。

I don't know why I let you talk me into going.
我不知道我为什么会让你说服我去。
└ 说话者去了，但后悔这么做。

Please talk me out of buying this bag!
拜托你说服我不要买这个包！

I reckon her backache was just a way of getting out of the housework.
我想，她说背痛只不过是为了逃避做家务的借口罢了。

If I can get out of going to the meeting tonight, I will.
如果有可能的话，我不想参加今晚的会议。

题目 Question ❻ She may not like the coffee cake, but I'll cross that bridge when I come to it.

她有可能不喜欢这个咖啡蛋糕，但到时再说吧。

解析 Resolution

"I'll cross that bridge when I come to it"照字面上理解是"等到我看到桥再过吧"。看到了桥再过桥，都还没看到桥当然也就不需要想过桥的事，其实就是中文说的"船到桥头自然直"，碰到问题再解决吧。

■ 地道英语随便说

M: **What if Mom says no?**
如果妈妈不答应怎么办？

W: **I'll cross that bridge when I come to it.**
到时候再说。

题目 Question ❼ James didn't lift a finger while we painted the entire house.

我们在给这整间房子刷油漆时，詹姆斯一点忙都没帮。

解析 Resolution

"didn't lift a finger"照字面上理解是"一根手指头都没举起来"。如果别人在做事，他却一根手指头都没举起来，就表示"他一点忙都没帮"。通常用来形容懒惰不帮忙的人。"didn't lift a finger"也可以说"didn't raise a finger"。

■ 你也可以这么说

He spends all day stretched out on the sofa and never lifts a finger to help.
他整天躺在沙发上，从来不帮一点忙。

He never raises a finger to help with the housework.
他从不做家事。

Unit 3 再听听看

题目 8 Allen was beside himself thinking about how to please his parents with good grades.
艾伦为想出如何能以好成绩取悦他的父母感到很焦虑。

解析 beside oneself 照字面上理解是"在他自己旁边"。这是什么意思呢？这个意思是说某人的情绪已经到了很极端、不像自己的程度，很像灵魂已经出窍，在旁边看着自己一样。

■ 你也可以这么说

He was beside himself with anger.
他快气疯了。

She is beside herself with excitement because her holiday is approaching.
她因为假期的即将到来而欣喜若狂。

题目 9 He's impossible! How do you put up with him?
他简直是不可理喻！你是如何能忍受他的？

解析 put up with 就是"忍受"的意思。

■ 你也可以这么说

I can't put up with this weather for much longer.
我没办法再忍受这种天气了。

I can't put up with this shit any more.
我再也无法忍受这些垃圾事了。

题目 ⑩ I will have to crack down on the workers to make this deadline.
我得好好地逼一下这些工人，才有办法在限期内赶工完成。

解析 Resolution
crack down 就是"严厉地要求"的意思，在这里表示强加要求及催赶员工的工作。

■ 你也可以这么说

The presidential candidate promised to crack down on corruption.
总统候选人承诺要严惩贪污。

The library is cracking down on people who lose their books.
图书馆打算严厉处罚丢书的人。

题目 ⑪ Please pull over and let me out of the car. I need to get out of here.
请靠边停车让我下车。我需要离开这里。

解析 Resolution
pull over 就是"靠边停车"的意思，也可以用在"警察叫车子靠边停"。

■ 你也可以这么说

James pulled the car over to the side of the road and stopped.
詹姆斯把车子靠边停了。

The police pulled the car over and tested the driver for alcohol.
警察让车子靠边停，然后测了驾驶员的酒精浓度。

The police pulled the speeding motorist over.
警察让超速的驾驶员靠边停车。

Unit 3 再听听看

题目 Question ⑫ **Wow, you really told him off. Why were you so mad at him?**
哇，你真的狠狠地骂了他一顿。你为什么对他这么生气？

解析 Resolution | tell off 就是"责怪、责骂"的意思。mad at someone 就是"对某人非常生气"的意思。

■ 你也可以这么说

His girlfriend told him off for arriving nearly half an hour late.
他的女朋友因为他迟到了将近半小时而责骂他。

My boss gave me a good telling-off for forgetting the meeting.
由于忘了会议，我被老板狠狠地训了一顿。

题目 Question ⑬ **Could you fill in for Chris while he is on vacation?**
克里斯放假的时候，你可以替他代班吗？

解析 Resolution | fill in 有两个意思，在这里是"替某人代班"的意思；另外也可以当"填表格"的意思。

■ 你也可以这么说

She has to take care of her mother in the hospital, so we have hired a temp to fill in for her.
她必须去医院照顾她妈妈，所以我们请了一个临时工来代她的班。

Could you please fill in the application form and send it back to us?
可以请你把申请表填完并寄回来吗？

题目 ⓴ **M:** I don't go to the bars like I did as a young man.
我现在不像年轻的时候那样常去酒吧了。

W: Actually, I've noticed that you've really cut down on your drinking altogether.
事实上，我注意到你连酒都不怎么喝了。

解析 cut down on something 就是"减少某物的量"。cut down on... 也可以说成 cut back on...，都是减少某物使用量的意思。

■ 你也可以这么说

The doctor told me to cut down on the fat in my diet.
医生叫我减少饮食中的油脂。

In order to cut down on mailing expenses, we have asked members to send us their e-mail addresses for future correspondence.
为了减少邮资开销，我们已请会员发送电子邮箱，为以后通信之便。

I'm trying to cut down on caffeine.
我在努力减少咖啡因的摄入量。

The government has announced plans to cut back on defence spending by 10% next year.
政府宣布了明年国防开支缩减百分之十的计划。

■ 地道英语随便说

W: Look at how much our cost has increased.
看看我们的成本增加了多少。

M: We simply must cut back on office expenses.
我们必须减少办公成本。

题目 **⑮ W: Why do you get so upset when Ralph tells his stories?**
拉尔夫在说他的故事时，你为什么那么不高兴呢？

M: I think he feels the need to play up his life stories in an attempt to make his life feel more grand and fulfilling. I wish he would simply tell the truth.
我觉得他需要借着夸大他的人生故事，来让他的人生显得比较伟大、充实。我真心希望他能实话实说。

解析 play up something 就是"夸大某事的重要性"的意思。相反就是 play down，表示"轻描淡写或贬低了某事的重要性"。

■ 你也可以这么说

The ad plays up the benefits of the product but doesn't say anything about the side effects.
那则广告夸大了产品的优点，但丝毫没提及其副作用。

He tried to play down my part in the work and play up his own.
他全力抹煞我在这个工作中的重要性，而夸大他自己的作用。

The newspapers have really played up the government's election results.
报纸实在是夸大了政府的选举结果。

■ 地道英语随便说

M: If you play down your part in the project, you won't get the credit you deserve.
你如果对自己在这个项目中的表现过分谦虚，就得不到应得的肯定了。

W: I don't mind it. I couldn't have done it without the others' support.
我不介意。如果没有其他人的协助，我也没办法完成。

题目 **⑯** W: I don't understand what you are getting at. What are you trying to say about my dress? Do you or don't you like it?

我不懂你是什么意思。你对我的连衣裙有什么意见？你到底是喜欢还是不喜欢？

M: Well, to be completely honest, I was trying to spare your feelings, but I really don't like it.

这个嘛，老实说，我刚才只是不想伤你的心，我实在不喜欢。

解析
Resolution

> get at something 就是"暗示"，是"意有所指"的意思，也可以当"批评"用。get at something 有很多意思，可以当"暗示""意有所指""批评"用，也可以用来表达"挖掘真相"的意思。

■ 你也可以这么说

What do you think she is getting at? I don't have a clue what she wants.
你觉得她到底是在暗示什么？我完全不知道她到底要什么。

Her boss is always getting at her for being late.
她老板老是批评她迟到的事情。

This was an attempt to stop journalists getting at the truth.
这是企图阻止记者挖掘出真相的。

■ 地道英语随便说

M: Why are you always getting at me?
你为什么老是在找我麻烦？

W: I have no idea what you are talking about.
我不懂你在说什么。

提醒便条纸 Reminder

舒葳老师的小叮咛，提枪上阵也不怕。

- 听力对大多数同学来说很难的原因之一，在于老外在说话时用的是"英语口语（spoken English）"，包含了大量的成语、惯用语及短语。

- 从小习惯学校所教的"英语书面语（written English）"的同学，一下子听英语口语，自然会听不懂。

- 大量学习英语中的成语、惯用语及短语必定能迅速提升英语听力的水平。

- 平时在听英语的时候，如果遇到听不懂的地方，先不要慌，听关键单词、靠前后文了解大意。等听完后，如果有录音稿可看，再把听不懂也看不懂的地方找出来。

- 通常每个单词都认识，却怎么也觉得文义不通的时候，都是因为你碰到了成语、惯用语及短语！强行用字面的意义解释，当然怎么说都说不通了！

- 查"成语惯用语字典"或问老师，学习你不懂的成语、惯用语及短语。

- 当你的成语、惯用语及短语使用能力增强时，不仅你的听力会变强，你的口语能力必定也会更上一层楼！

MEMO   Listening & Speaking

MEMO

Listening & Speaking

Practice 1

听力实战练习 1
Conversational Exchange
常见表达用语及对话模式

听力 Listening
口语 Speaking

Unit 1 必备日常用语

Unit 2 赞美与回应

Unit 3 同意与反对

Unit 4 告知坏消息

学习重点 Main Point

前面三十堂课,我们学习了十个听力诀窍,教你如何"有效率"地听。没有掌握"听的方法"时,得花上很长的一段时间才能有些许的进步;一旦掌握了"听的方法",就能在最短的时间掌握要领,提升听力水平。

学会了方法后,更要充分地练习,才能将这些"技巧"变成自己在听的时候的"本能"。接下来的 Practice 1 到 Practice 4,我们便要练习使用这些技巧。也就是说,同学在听的时候,务必记得运用之前学到的方法,把专注力放在听关键词,听不懂的地方,也要注意是否是连音、弱化,或是你自己发音的问题!

Unit 1

必备日常用语

热身活动 Warm Up 　学习英语前，先来做个热身吧！

请听 MP3，并写下你所听到的。你知道这些用语各是什么意思吗？

题目 Questions

1. _____
2. _____
3. _____
4. _____
5. _____
6. _____
7. _____
8. _____
9. _____
10. _____
11. _____
12. _____

解答 Answers

1. How's it going?
2. Wha's up?
3. Look out!
4. Watch out!
5. Hurry up!
6. Who's here?
7. Come on!
8. It's about time!
9. How about that!
10. It's great. Isn't it?
11. He won't go. Will he?
12. Shouldn't I tell him about that?

Unit 1 必备日常用语

实际演练 Explanation 通过认真的解题练习打下扎实的基础。

请注意连音与消音，听 MP3，并跟着说说看。

题目 Questions

① How's it going? 最近如何？

② What's up? 怎么样？

③ Look out! 注意！

④ Watch out! 小心！

⑤ Hurry up! 快点！

⑥ Who's here? 是谁啊？

⑦ Come on! 快点！

⑧ It's about time! 是时候了！

⑨ How about that! 这样如何！

⑩ It's great. Isn't it? 很棒，不是吗？

⑪ He won't go. Will he? 他不会去，对吧？

⑫ Shouldn't I tell him about that?
我难道不该告诉他那件事吗？

提醒便条纸 Reminder 舒葳老师的小叮咛，提枪上阵也不怕。

第一句到第九句都是日常生活中很常听到的打招呼的方式或普通用语，第 10、11、12 句则是"附加问句"的例子。这些句子常听到且用词简单，如果是阅读，我们一看就懂，但是要是听的话，可能就不知道对方说了什么。事实上，只要我们能抓住连音及消音的特性，多听几次，自己也学着说说看，下次听到老外这么说时，我们一定就都能听懂了！

Unit 2
赞美与回应

热身活动 Warm Up 学习英语前，先来做个热身吧！

想象老外对你说出下面的赞美，并写出你会有的回应。

题目 Questions

1. You're looking smart today!

2. I like your shirt. It really suits you.

3. This is really delicious. You're such a good cook.

4. Wow! You look absolutely stunning!

5. What lovely flowers!

解答 Answers

1. Oh! I've got an interview.
2. Oh thanks. I've had it for years actually.
3. Do you really think I am?
4. Don't I always?
5. Glad you like them.

实际演练 Explanation

通过认真的解题练习打下扎实的基础。

老外常赞美人，因此赞美的用语以及回应的方式我们都应该要熟悉。回应的方式有很多种，要视当时情境及你与对方的关系交情而定。可以是正经八百地道谢，如"Thank you. I'm flattered"；也可以是俏皮地开个玩笑，如"Don't I always?"

请再听一次并跟着说说看。

题目 Question

1
M: **You're looking smart today!**
你今天打扮得很好看！

W: **Oh! I've got an interview.**
噢！我要去参加一个面试。

解析 Resolution

smart 在用来形容穿着时，就是看起来"整洁、好看、吸引人"的意思。

■ 你也可以这么说

Guy looks very smart in his new suit, doesn't he?
盖伊穿上新西装显得精神十足，不是吗？

Sherry works in a very smart new office overlooking the River Cam.
雪莉在一间非常漂亮的新办公室里工作，从那里可以俯瞰康河。

We went to a very smart party on New Year's Eve.
我们参加了一个非常时尚的跨年派对。

■ 可活用的补充句型

Don't get smart with me.
请放尊重点。／请你礼貌点。

The boys were punished for being smart in class.
这几个男孩因为在课堂上不尊重老师、卖弄小聪明而受了责罚。

题目 ❷

M: I like your shirt. It really suits you.
我喜欢你的上衣,很适合你。

W: Oh thanks. I've had it for years actually.
噢,谢谢。这件衣服已经穿了很多年了。

解析 Resolution

"It really suits you"是常用的赞美人衣着的说法。注意 suits you 的连音,以及 I have had it for years 的连音。blouse 是女生的短上衣。

■ 你也可以这么说

The dress / color suits you.
这件连衣裙 / 这个颜色很适合你。

You look good in that dress / color.
你穿这件连衣裙 / 这个颜色很好看。

题目 ❸

M: This is really delicious. You're such a good cook.
真好吃。你的手艺真好。你真是个好厨师。

W: Do you really think I am?
你真的这么觉得吗?

解析 Resolution

这是很客气的回应。"Do you really think I am?"就是"Do you really think I am a good cook?"的简单说法。

■ 你也可以这么说

Oh, that's really sweet of you.
噢,你的嘴真甜。

Oh, thank you. I really appreciate the compliment.
噢,谢谢。感谢你的赞美。

题目 **④** **M:** Wow! You look absolutely stunning!
Question   哇，你真是光彩四射！

W: Don't I always?
我不是一向如此吗？

解析
Resolution

> 这是较俏皮的回应方法，适合用在比较熟的朋友之间。"Don't I always?"就是"Don't I always look stunning?"的简单说法。stunning 就是非常亮眼、光彩四射的意思。

■ 你也可以这么说

I always do, don't I? 我不是一向如此吗？

■ 地道英语随便说

学习疲乏了吗？现在，静下心来安静地想想看。

M: Your article is the best I've ever read on this topic.
你的文章是我看过的同主题里写得最好的。

W: Thank you. I'm flattered.
谢谢你。我感到受宠若惊。

小贴士
Tip

> "I'm flattered"是很受人夸奖时最好的回应方式，就是"你这么说/这么做，我感到很开心且受宠若惊"。
>
> 当别人对你夸奖或奉承、令你感到高兴的时候，除了说"I'm flattered"外，你还可以这样说：
>
> I appreciate that. 我很感谢你这么说。
> Thank you for the compliment. 谢谢你的赞赏。
> That's nice of you to say. 你这么说真好。
> You have made me blush. 你让我脸红了。

例 I'm flattered you like my design.
你喜欢我的设计让我受宠若惊。

I'm flattered you read my blog.
你会读我的博客真让我受宠若惊啊。

题目 **⑤** **M: What lovely flowers!**
Question 这些花真美！

W: Glad you like them.
很高兴你喜欢。

解析
Resolution

> What lovely...! 真是美丽的……！是常用赞美的句子。"Glad you like it / them" 也是好用的回应。

■ 地道英语随便说

M: What a lovely evening! 今天真是美好的一晚！

W: Glad you enjoyed it. 很高兴你玩得愉快。

M: What beautiful eyes you have! 你的眼睛真美！

W: Thank you. It's very sweet of you. 谢谢。你嘴巴真甜。

M: What lovely weather! 天气真好！

W: It is lovely, isn't it? 真的是很好，不是吗？

M: Look at that smile. How beautiful! 看看那笑容，真美！

W: I appreciate the compliment. 谢谢你的夸奖。

M: You gave a great presentation.
你的报告做得很好。

W: We all put in a lot of effort. Thank you for acknowledging our hard work.
我们很努力，谢谢你看到了团队的用心。

■ 可活用的补充句型

That was really well done. Thanks for your work.
你做得真好。谢谢你的努力。

Unit 3

同意与反对

热身活动 Warm Up 　学习英语前，先来做个热身吧！

老外会常用特定的一些说法表达同意或反对对方的说法，所以熟悉这些用语很重要！

请听下面的表达，如果是同意请写〇，部分同意请写△，完全不同意请写×。

题目 Questions

1. _____
2. _____
3. _____
4. _____
5. _____
6. _____
7. _____
8. _____
9. _____
10. _____
11. _____
12. _____
13. _____
14. _____
15. _____
16. _____

解答 Answers

1. I would agree with that. 〇
2. I disagree, I'm afraid. ×
3. I take your point but... △
4. Well, it depends. △
5. You're absolutely right. 〇
6. Come on! ×
7. That's right. 〇
8. I don't think that's true. ×
9. I see what you mean, but... △
10. That's true in a way, but... △
11. Absolutely. 〇
12. I don't know about that. ×
13. To a certain extent, but... △
14. That's rubbish! ×
15. Exactly. 〇
16. Well, I'm not sure about that. ×

实际演练 Explanation

通过认真的解题练习打下扎实的基础。

请看下面各类别的表达用语。当老外不完全赞同对方意见时，会先礼貌地表示肯定，再继续说他不同意的地方！

■ 完全赞同

That's right. 没错。

I would agree with that. 我同意。

You're absolutely right. 你说得一点都没错。

Absolutely. 完全正确。

Exactly. 一点都没错。

■ 部分同意，但有意见

I see what you mean, but... 我知道你的意思，但是……

I take your point but... 我知道你的意思，但是……

To a certain extent, but... 某种程度上是没错，但是……

That's true in a way, but... 某种程度上是没错，但是……

Well, it depends. 这个嘛，要看情形。

■ 持反对意见

Well, I'm not sure about that. 这个嘛，我对那件事还不确定。

I don't know about that. 我可不确定那么说对不对（客气地否定）。

I don't think that's true. 我想那么说是不正确的。

Come on! 拜托！

I disagree, I'm afraid. 恐怕我不能同意。

That's rubbish! 简直是胡说八道！

Unit 4

告知坏消息

热身活动 Warm Up 学习英语前，先来做个热身吧！

当老外要告诉对方坏消息时，通常会先"警告"对方："我有坏消息要告诉你……"。也就是说，当你听到老外说类似下面的句子时，你就知道，大事不妙了！想想看，你是否能猜到他接下来要说什么？

题目 Questions

❶ Could I ask you a big favor?
我可以请你帮个大忙吗？
└─ 一定是个"大"忙。

❷ You know I said I could lend you my car this weekend?
你知道我说我这个周末可以借你车吗？
└─ 现在应该是没办法借了。

❸ You know that book you lent me?
你不是借给了我一本书吗？
└─ 可能是丢了，或毁损了。

❹ I've got a bit of a problem.
我不是很高兴 / 我有点问题。
└─ 对方应该是对你有所抱怨。

❺ I don't quite know how to put this, but...
我不知道该怎么说，但是……。
└─ 要说些难以启齿的事了。

❻ There's something I've been meaning to tell you.
有件事我一直想告诉你。
└─ 应该是会让你震惊的事吧。

7 I've a confession to make.
   我得承认一件事。
   └ 对方可能有什么事是你可能不想知道的。

8 I'm afraid I've got an apology to make...
   恐怕我有件事得向你道歉……
   └ 对方一定是做了对不起你的事。

提醒便条纸 Reminder
舒葳老师的小叮咛，提枪上阵也不怕。

- 同学应熟悉日常生活常用句型以及生活中惯用的应对用语，在练习听这些短句及常用表达法的同时，复习前面学过听重音、消音及连音的技巧。

- 所有本课的句子，同学都应该反复听 MP3 并开口跟着说。让自己的耳朵及说出来的英语与老外的声音融为一体。

- 最后不要打开书，试试看自己是否也可以说出这些句子。

- 当你熟悉老外的说话模式时，听力也会变得轻松自然！

Practice 2

听力实战练习 2
Daily Conversations
生活会话

听力
Listening
口语
Speaking

Unit 1 短篇对话

Unit 2 长篇对话

学习重点
Main Point

听完了常见句型与惯用的对话模式后,我们这节课要练习的是短篇及长篇的对话。

对话是日常生活中及各类英语考试中最常见的听力之一,听力重点在于听关键词,抓到每个对话的重点即可。当然,熟悉短语及惯用语也是很重要的!让我们来小试身手吧!

Unit 1

短篇对话

热身活动 Warm Up 学习英语前,先来做个热身吧!

请听对话,并选出适当的答案。

题目 Questions

1 What does the man mean?
A. The boss called and said he isn't coming.
B. The project has been cancelled.

2 What does the man mean?
A. The audience was too quiet.
B. The audience was too noisy.

3 What does the man mean?
A. He loves the place.
B. He loves to work with tools.

4 What does the man imply?
A. She helped him some time ago.
B. He owes her money.

5 What does the woman mean?
A. She doesn't like either black or white.
B. There's no one correct answer.

6 What does the man mean?

   A. He can meet anytime she wants.

   B. He wants to meet at the convenience store.

7 How does the woman feel about the project length?

   A. She found it agreeable.

   B. She didn't do the project at all.

8 What does the woman say about the driver's license?

   A. Her license has expired.

   B. Her friend has her license on a date.

9 How do they both feel about the job?

   A. They work so hard that they feel ill.

   B. They are unhappy with the job.

10 What does the woman mean?

   A. The movie is almost over.

   B. Their dinner is ready.

解答 Answers

① B ② B ③ A ④ A ⑤ B
⑥ A ⑦ A ⑧ A ⑨ B ⑩ A

实际演练 Explanation

通过认真的解题练习打下扎实的根基。

题目 Question

W: Jim, I thought you had a big project due tomorrow. How can you be taking such a long lunch break?
吉米，我还以为你明天有项目方案要交呢。你怎么午休了这么久？

M: The project has been called off. I have plenty of time to get the rest of my work done now.
这个项目被取消了。我现在有充裕的时间完成我的工作了。

What does the man mean?

☐ (A) The boss called and said he isn't coming.
　　　　　　　　　　老板打电话来说他不来了。

☑ (B) The project has been cancelled.
　　　　　　　　　　这个项目被取消了。

解析 Resolution

女方说"I thought you had a big project due tomorrow"，重音在 due，因此这句的意思是"我以为是这样，但看起来却好像不是如此"，表示疑问和惊讶。call off 是短语，就是 cancel（取消）的意思。因此答案是 B。

■ 你也可以这么说

If we have much more rain, the game might be called off.
如果雨再继续下，比赛可能会被取消。

■ 可活用的补充句型

A new version of the software is due in the next couple of weeks.
最新版的软件在几周后将发布。

Her baby is due in May.
她的预产期是五月。

The rent is due on the first day of each month.
房租每月第一天交。

Unit 1 短篇对话

题目 ❷ **W: Did you enjoy the movie?**
Question
你喜欢这部电影吗？

M: Yes, but I wish the crowd would've been more quiet during the show.
喜欢，但如果观众能安静点就更好了。

What does the man mean?

☐ **(A) The audience was too quiet.** ……… 观众太安静了。

☑ **(B) The audience was too noisy.** ……… 观众太吵了。

解析 would've 是 would have 在口语中的"缩音"说法。男方说
Resolution "I wish... would've"就是他这么希望，但事实上却不是如此。

■ 你也可以这么说

I wish I'd have enjoyed the movie more.
我希望我能更喜欢这部电影。
└ 但我不是太喜欢。

I wish I could've been there.
我真希望我那时候可以在那里。
└ 但我那时候不在。

I wish I hadn't eaten so much.
我真希望我那时候没吃这么多。
└ 但我那时候已经吃了。

I wish I had known that when I was 21.
我真希望我在二十一岁的时候已经知道那件事。
└ 但我那时候不知道。

■ 可活用的补充句型

Do you wish your parents would've given you a different name?
你希不希望你父母当初给你取一个不一样的名字？

题目 **❸** W: **I thought** you'd enjoy dinner here.
我就知道你会喜欢这里的晚餐。

M: You hit the nail on the head. I wish I'd've found it sooner.
你说得一点都没错。我真希望我早点发现这个地方。

What does the man mean?

☑ **(A) He loves the place.** ……………… 他爱死这里了。

☐ **(B) He loves to work with tools.** ……… 他喜欢使用工具。

解析 Resolution

男方说"I thought you'd enjoy dinner here"重音在 thought，表示他早就料到，并且成真了。从重音的位置我们便可以判断男生想的没错，女方是喜欢这里的。

女方说"You hit the nail on the head"，"正打中钉子的头"，是常用成语，表示"一针见血""完全正确"。

"I wish I'd've found it sooner"就是"I wish I would have found it sooner"的口语说法。表示她希望能早点发现，但事实上她现在才发现。

■ 你也可以这么说

Her comment about the situation was so exact. It hit the nail on the head. 她对此情形的评论一针见血。

Your analysis really hit the nail on the head.
你的分析真是一针见血。

■ 可活用的补充句型

She hit the jackpot with her first novel, which sold over a million copies. 她的一本小说非常成功，卖了一百多万本。

The company has hit the jackpot with its new line of cell phones. 这家公司因新款手机大获成功。

■ 地道英语随便说

M: **I knew you would say that.** 我就知道你会这么说。

W: **How did you guess?** 你怎么猜到的？

Unit 1 短篇对话

题目 **④ W:** Wow, thank you so much. You fixed that leak fast. How much do I owe you?
Question

哇,真谢谢你。你一下子就把漏水修好了。我应该给你多少钱?

M: You're welcome, and don't worry about it. It's **free of charge**. I owed you a favor anyway, right?

不用客气。这是免费的。反正我也欠你一分人情,不是吗?

What does the man imply?

☑ **(A)** She helped him some time ago. .... 女方以前帮过他的忙。

☐ **(B)** He owes her money. .... 男方欠女方钱。

解析 free of charge 是"免费",注意重音在 free 和 charge。of 中的
Resolution "o" 弱化。owe 是"欠钱";I owed you a favor 是"我欠你一分人情"的意思。

■ 你也可以这么说

I owe you. 我欠你一次。
└ 在口语中就是"谢谢你帮忙"的意思。

I owe you one.
我欠你一次。

■ 可活用的补充句型

How much do I owe you?
我欠你多少钱?

I owe them an apology.
我欠他们一个道歉。

He owes his success to chance.
他将其成功归功于机遇。

241

题目 ❺ **W: The answers to many questions aren't always black and white.**
很多问题的答案不总是非黑即白的。

M: I know, that's what makes working in this industry so hard.
我知道，那也是在这行工作这么困难的原因。

What does the woman mean?

☐ **(A) She doesn't like either black or white.**
　　　　　　　　　　　　　　她不喜欢黑色，也不喜欢白色。

☑ **(B) There's no one correct answer.**
　　　　　　　　　　　　　　　　没有一个正确的答案。

解析 | black and white 是"黑白分明、善恶分明"。注意重音在 black 和 white。and 弱化了，并且 d 和 t 消音。

■ 你也可以这么说

It's not a simple black-and-white issue. This is often called a grey area in the decision making process.
这不是个黑白分明的问题。在决策过程中，这就叫作灰色地带。
└ grey area 就是灰色地带，指不容易回答或难以界定的部分。

Black and white thinking can be the cause of many problems in our lives.
非黑即白的思维可能是造成我们生活中出现许多问题的原因。

■ 可活用的补充句型

We should acknowledge that there are grey areas in life.
我们应该明白生命中有许多的灰色地带。

Life is a paradox and is full of unknowns.
生命本身就是一个悖论，并且充满未知。

题目 Question ❻ **W:** When can we meet to discuss the project and transfer the data?
我们什么时候可以见面讨论这个案子并转交资料？

M: At your convenience.
看你什么时候方便（都可以）。

What does the man mean?

☑ **(A)** He can meet anytime she wants.
.... 女方要什么时候见面他都可以配合。

☐ **(B)** He wants to meet at the convenience store.
.... 他要约在便利商店见面。

解析 Resolution
at your convenience 是"看你方便"。正式的场合会听到这样的说法，就是"你决定，我都可以"的意思。这里要注意的是 at your 中 t 和 y 的连音。

■ 你也可以这么说

Please call me back at your earliest convenience.
请尽快在方便的时候回电。

Please call me to set up an appointment at your convenience.
方便的时候请打电话给我约时间。

The hotel has a restaurant for the guests' convenience.
饭店为了房客的方便开设了一间餐厅。

■ 可活用的补充句型

We can come visit you whenever it suits you.
看你何时方便，我们可以来拜访你。

We can leave whenever you're ready.
你准备好了我们随时可以走。

题目 Question	**❼ M: Didn't you find that the project took forever to finish?**

你不觉得这个案子好像永远没有做完的一天吗？

W: Not at all. I was prepared for everything.

不会啊。我准备得很完备。

What does the woman feel about the project length?

☑ **(A) She found it agreeable.** ················· 她可以接受。

☐ **(B) She didn't do the project at all.** ······ 她完全没有做。

解析 Resolution

took forever 是"好像永远都不会结束"，是表示很久的夸大说法。Not at all 是"一点也不"。注意连音，并且 t 在这里都发 [D] 弹舌音。

■ 你也可以这么说

It took forever to download the files from the Internet.
从网络下载这些档案花了好长的时间。

For some reason, my iPhone is taking forever to back up.
不知道为什么，我的苹果手机要花很久的时间备份。

■ 可活用的补充句型

You'd better like my present. It took me ages to make it.
你可一定要喜欢我的礼物啊。我花了好长的时间制作的。

It is taking me ages to learn to play this piano piece.
学习弹这首钢琴曲花了我好久的时间。

■ 地道英语随便说

M: When was the first time you heard that song?
你第一次听到这首歌是什么时候的事？

W: Oh, that was ages ago. I can't remember.
噢，好久好久以前了。我不记得了。

题目 **❽ M:** Why aren't you driving any more?
你为什么都不开车了。

W: My license is out of date.
我的驾照过期了。

What does the woman say about the driver's license?

☑ **(A) Her license has expired.** ·············· 她的驾照过期了。

☐ **(B) Her friend has her license on a date.**
·············· 她的朋友借去约会了。

解析 男方说 "aren't... any more" 就是 "再也不……了"。be out of date 是短语,是 "过时了" 的意思。注意这里的连音及消音,同时 of 弱化。另外 out of 中的 t 发 [D] 弹舌音。

■ 你也可以这么说

Their technology is pretty out-of-date.
他们的技术已经相当过时了。

The information on this website is out of date.
这个网站的信息过时了。

The information on this website is updated once a week.
这个网站的信息每周会更新一次。

■ 可活用的补充句型

This is his best book to date.
这本是有史以来最棒的书。

Bring us up to date on the news.
跟我们说说最新的新闻吧。

This magazine is up-to-date.
这本杂志是新的。

题目 **❾** **W:** This place just feels so unwelcoming now. I'm sick of it. I think I'll start looking for a new job.
这个地方现在真令人觉得冷漠。我受够了。我想我会开始找新的工作。

M: I know what you mean. I'm sick of this place, too.
我懂你的意思。我也受够了。

How do they both feel about the job?

☐ **(A) They work so hard that they feel ill.**
他们工作得太辛苦以至于都生病了。

☑ **(B) They are unhappy with the job.**
他们对于这个公司感到不愉快。

解析 "I'm sick of it" 就是对这件事感到生气、不开心，注意这句的连音。句子中的 of 弱化，t 消音。另外，要注意的是，在 "I'm sick of it" 中，f 在两个元音字母 o 和 i 中间，听起来会像是发有声音 [v]。

■ 你也可以这么说

I am tired of listening to your complaints.
我受不了听你抱怨了。

The way he treats his wife just makes me sick.
他对待老婆的方式令我反胃。

You make me sick! You're so lucky!
你真让我忌妒！你真是太幸运了！
└ 口语中 you make me sick 也有 "你让我忌妒" 的意思。

■ 可活用的补充句型

I'm sick of long songs.
我对情歌感到厌倦。

I'm sick and tired of hearing the same old excuses!
我厌倦听到重复的借口。

| 题目 Question | ⑩ M: Boy, this movie is lasting forever and I'm starving.
天哪，这个电影真长。我饿死了。

W: It'll be over in an hour. We'll get something to eat, then.
再有一个小时就结束了。我们那时候再去吃饭。

What does the woman mean?

☑ (A) The movie is almost over. ……………… 电影快结束了。

☐ (B) Their dinner is ready. ………………… 他们的晚餐好了。

| 解析 Resolution | ... is lasting forever，意为"……永远持续着"，就是"真长，怎么没完没了"的意思。所以我们知道他在抱怨这部电影太长了。女方说"It'll be over in an hour"就是"再一小时就结束了"。注意 It'll 的发音及连音。

■ 你也可以这么说

Don't worry. The situation won't last.
别担心。这个状况不会持续太久。

She's a horrible boss, but not to worry; her reign of terror won't last long.
她是个很糟的老板，但不要担心，她的恐怖统治不会维持多久的。

This will only last a week or two. It won't be like this for long.
这是最后一个星期了。这个情形不会维持太久了。

■ 可活用的补充句型

It won't be long before we can see you again.
我们很快就能再见到你了。

She's actually a very good person. It won't take long for you to see that.
她其实是个很好的人，不久后你应该就会有同感了。

It only takes a minute for a girl to fall in love.
女孩子爱上一个人只需要一分钟的时间。

Unit 2

长篇对话

热身活动 Warm Up 学习英语前，先来做个热身吧！

请听 MP3，选出适当的答案。

题目
Questions

1 What does the man say about the game?
  A. It was an excellent game.
  B. The referees didn't do a fair job.
  C. It was a dull game.

2 What does the woman feel about all employees taking English classes?
  A. It's useful for everyone.
  B. It's a waste of time.
  C. It's costly.

3 What are they going to do next?
  A. Get some instant coffee at 7-11.
  B. Ask people at the 7-11 where the coffee shop is.
  C. Have a cup of coffee in the coffee shop.

4 Where is this conversation taking place?
  A. A baseball court.
  B. A furniture shop.
  C. A restaurant.

5 What are they going to do?

　　A. Eat in a pricey restaurant.

　　B. Share the bill between the two of them.

　　C. Find a less expensive restaurant.

6 How did the man break his thumb?

　　A. Playing basketball.

　　B. Working out in the gym.

　　C. Falling down the steps.

7 What are they doing?

　　A. Discussing their annual report.

　　B. Talking about the boss's bad temper.

　　C. Explaining why they are angry at the boss.

8 What is the woman going to buy?

　　A. Food and flowers.

　　B. Flowers and alcoholic drinks.

　　C. Flowers and juice.

解答　**❶** B　**❷** C　**❸** B　**❹** B
Answers　**❺** A　**❻** C　**❼** B　**❽** B

实际演练 Explanation

通过认真的解题练习打下扎实的基础。

题目 Question

M: What did you think of the game last night?
你觉得昨晚的比赛如何？

W: Wow, what a finish. I couldn't've asked to see a better game.
哇，结局太棒了。不能更精彩了。

M: It was good, but I thought the referees really made some big mistakes. It wouldn't've been that close had they called the game correctly.
是很精彩，但我觉得裁判犯了些很大的错误。如果裁判判得正确，比分不会那么接近。

What does the man say about the game?

☐ (A) It was an excellent game. ……… 是一场精彩的比赛。

☑ (B) The referees didn't do a fair job. …… 裁判判得不好。

☐ (C) It was a dull game. ……………………… 比赛不精彩。

解析 Resolution

What did you think of...? 问对方的意见。注意 did you 和 think of 的连音。I couldn't've 就是 I couldn't have 的缩音；It wouldn't've 就是 it wouldn't have 的缩音。

男方最后说 It was good, but... 重音强调的是 was，其实就很像我们中文说的："是很好，但是……" 暗示了我们事实上虽然他也同意比赛精彩，却也有他觉得不满的地方。在这里，如果说话者只是要单纯地同意比赛很精彩，没有其他信息想要强调，则重音会在 good: It was good.

另外，最后一句的 had they called the game correctly 是倒装句，也就是 "if they had called the game correctly" 的意思。男方在表达他有意见后，提到了裁判的判决不正确，表示正确答案就是 B 了。

请再听一次，并实际体会运用我们上面提到的技巧。

■ 超级实用句型

What did you think of...? 你觉得……如何？

I couldn't've... 我没办法……了。

It was good, but I thought... 是很精彩，但我觉得……

It would't've been... had they... 如果他们……就会……了。

■ 你也可以这么说

What did you think of my new boyfriend?
你觉得我的新男友如何？

What did you think was going to happen?
你那时候觉得接下来事情会如何发展？

What did you think was the reason?
你觉得原因是什么？

I couldn't have had a better time.
我实在太开心了。

I couldn't have enjoyed it more.
我实在太开心了。

I couldn't have said it better.
我实在说得太好了。

■ 可活用的补充句型

You wouldn't have lost the game had you listened to my advice.
如果你听我的劝告，就不会输掉这场比赛了。

You wouldn't have missed the show had you left home earlier.
如果你早点离开家，就不会错过这场表演了。

题目 ❷ **M:** I think we all should take these English courses. I can already tell that my job performance is improving and the boss seems to notice that I'm more confident with clients now.

我觉得我们都应该上英语课。我真的可以感觉得到我工作表现进步了，而且老板似乎也注意到我现在面对客户比较有信心。

W: Well, to be honest, I think they would be useful for everybody, but some of us don't really work closely with many foreigners. It's not that I think it's a waste of time, but it costs the company a lot of money to send you to the classes.

这个嘛，老实说，我觉得英语课对每个人都有用。但是有些人其实不需要跟老外一起工作。我不是觉得浪费时间，只是送大家去上英语课会花公司很多钱。

What does the woman feel about all employees taking English classes?

☐ (A) It's useful for everyone. ……… 对每个人都很有用。

☐ (B) It's a waste of time. ……… 浪费时间。

☑ (C) It's costly. ……… 花费太大。

解析 Resolution

在男生说"I think we all should take English course"并表达对英语课的肯定之后，女方说"Well, to be honest, ..."就表示她持相反的意见。听到 well 和 to be honest 都表示否定的态度！

不只如此，女方说"It would be useful, but..."重音在 would，也表示她虽然同意"是会有用，但是……"，但有其他的看法，表示她并不赞同每个人上英语课的这个想法。

It's not that... 就是"我不是觉得……"的意思，表示她并不是觉得浪费时间。既然她不赞同，又不觉得是浪费时间，那么答案就应该是 C. It's costly. 请再听一次，并实际体会运用我们上面提到的技巧。

■ 超级实用句型

I think they would be useful for everybody, but...
我觉得是会对每个人都有用，但是……

Unit 2 长篇对话

题目 Question ❸ **W:** That's funny. I'm sure there was a coffee shop around here.
真奇怪。我确定以前这里有一间咖啡厅的。

M: Hmmm, I don't know. Maybe the 7-11 manager will know if there is one close to here.
嗯，我不确定。也许 7-11 店长会知道这附近有没有咖啡厅。

W: Alright, let's go in. Maybe they'll know.
好吧，我们进去吧。也许他们会知道。

What are they going to do next?

☐ (A) Get some instant coffee at 7-11.
去 7-11 买即溶咖啡。

☑ (B) Ask people at the 7-11 where the coffee shop is.
问 7-11 的人咖啡厅在哪里。

☐ (C) Have a cup of coffee in the coffee shop.
去咖啡厅喝咖啡。

解析 Resolution

that's funny 有两个意思："很奇怪"或"真好笑"。女方说 That's funny. 我们从她的语气知道她的意思是"真奇怪"。接着我们听关键词，知道她说 "I'm sure... coffee shop around here" 表示她觉得奇怪是因为她找不到 coffee shop。其实到这里，我们就知道主题是要找咖啡店在哪里了。

接着男方指出 "maybe the 7-11 manager will know..."，女方又说 "let's go in"，并接着说 "Maybe they'll know"，表示她同意男方的建议，决定进去问。因此答案是 B。

请再听一次，并实际体会运用我们上面提到的技巧。

■ 超级实用句型

That's funny. 真奇怪 / 真好笑。

I'm sure... 我确定……

Let's go in. 我们进去吧。

🎧 253

题目 Question ❹ **W: Can I help you, Miss?**
有什么能帮到你的吗?

M: Yes, is this couch marked down? It has a scratch here.
是的,这个躺椅打折吗?这里有刮痕。

W: Yes, this is one of the clearance items. I believe it is ten percent off the original price marked. I'll check to make sure.
是的,这是我们清仓货品之一。我记得是原价的九折。我去确认一下。

M: Thank you.
谢谢。

Where is this conversation taking place?

☐ (A) A baseball court. ················· 棒球场。

☑ (B) A furniture shop. ················· 家具店。

☐ (C) A restaurant. ······················ 餐厅。

解析 Resolution

题目问这段对话发生的场合,如果能串联内容中的关键词,我们就不难听出说话者在哪里。男方开头说"Can I help you?",表示他一定是在服务客人。女方问"Is the couch marked down?",couch 是"长沙发、躺椅"的意思,mark down 就是"打折"。接着男方的回答中 clearance items 是"清仓货",又说是 ten percent off the original price marked。综合这些关键词,我们就可以听出他们是在家具店了。因此答案是 B。

请再听一次,并实际体会运用我们上面提到的技巧。

■ 超级实用句型

Can I help you? 我可以为你服务吗?

Is the... marked down? 这个……打折吗?

I believe... 我相信…… / 我想……

It is ten percent off the original price marked.
这是原价的九折。

└ marked price 就是 tagged price，也就是"标价""定价"。

I'll check to make sure.
我去确认一下。

■ 你也可以这么说

We are offering a 10% markdown on children's shoes.
所有童鞋九折。

There's a 10% off this week on all children's shoes.
这周所有童鞋九折。

All children's shoes are subject to a 10% discount.
所有童鞋九折。

All children's shoes are now reduced to $20 a pair.
现在所有童鞋减价至二十美元一双。

■ 可活用的补充句型

I would like to make a complaint.
我要投诉。

My credit card was charged without authorization. I request a refund / credit to my credit card.
我的信用卡在我没有被授权的情况下就发生了扣款。我要求退款到我的信用卡。

I made a purchase on your website. The product came poorly wrapped and damaged.
我在你们的网上下了单。商品寄到时候包装很差而且有破损。

I was informed that order was to arrive on June 29. I waited and it never arrived.
我被告知我订的商品六月二十九日会到货。我一直在等，但商品一直都没来。

| 题目 Question | **5** | **M: What do you think of Le Petite?**
你觉得小餐厅如何？ |
|---|---|---|

W: The food is fantastic, but it's kind of small and a bit overpriced.
食物很棒，但分量有点少，而且也有点贵。

M: That's OK. I really want a good meal tonight. Do you want to go? I'll get the bill.
没关系，我今晚真的想吃点好的。你要去吗？我请客。

W: Sure, I really do like the food.
好啊，我真的挺喜欢那里的食物。

What are they going to do?

☑ **(A) Eat in a pricey restaurant.** ……… 去昂贵的餐厅吃饭。

☐ **(B) Share the bill between the two of them.**
                                                        分摊晚餐的花费。

☐ **(C) Find a less expensive restaurant.**
                                                        找一间不那么贵的餐厅。

解析 Resolution

题目问说话者接下去要做什么，如果能串联内容中的关键词，我们应该不难听出答案了。男方先说"What do you think of..."是问女方的意见。然后我们注意听重音，便可以听到女方的回应，强调的信息在 food... fantastic... small... overpriced；而当女方提到 overpriced 表示这间餐厅有点贵，但男方说"That's OK."表示不介意，并强调 really... good meal... 又说 I'll get the bill，表示他要请客付账。女方最后说 sure... like... food. 串联重音单词，我们可知他们在讨论去昂贵的餐厅吃饭。因此答案就是 A 了。

在发音方面我们要注意的是 kind of 的连音和弱化：kind of small，重音在 small。a bit overpriced 中 t 消音，overpriced 是复合形容词。kind of 和 a bit 都是有一点的意思，在口语中常常听到。

请再听一次，并实际体会运用我们上面提到的技巧。

■ 超级实用句型

It's kind of small. 分量有点少。

It's a bit overpriced. 有点贵。

I'll get the bill. 我请客。

■ 你也可以这么说

It's on me. 我请客。

It's my treat. 我请客。

■ 可活用的补充句型

Whenever we go out, my father picks up the tab.
我们出去吃饭时，总是我父亲付账。

Order whatever you want. The company is picking up the check.
想吃什么就点什么。公司请客。

■ 地道英语随便说

M: **Thanks for lunch. It was delicious. Next time lunch is on me.** 谢谢你请的午餐，很好吃。下次午餐我请客。

W: **Don't be silly.** 不用这么客气。

M: **I'm serious.** 我是说真的。

W: **Alright. Next time you'll treat.** 好吧，下次你请。

M: **How about trying that new French restaurant next door?**
我们今晚去试试附近新开的法国餐厅如何？

W: **Sure, but I hear it's expensive so let's go Dutch, OK?**
好啊，不过我听说那间餐厅很贵，所以我们各付各的，好吗？

M: **Let me pick up the tab this time. You treated me many times before when I was looking for a job. Now I'm making good money, so it should be my turn.**
这次让我请。之前我在找工作的时候，你请我吃好多次饭，现在我挣得不少，所以该是我回请了。

题目 Question ❻ **W:** Don't tell me you broke your thumb playing basketball. You always get injured playing ball.
不要告诉我你打棒球弄断了大拇指。你老是因为玩球受伤。

M: Actually, I tripped on the steps just outside the gym and never got to play last night. (laughing)
事实上，我在健身房外的阶梯上绊倒了，昨晚根本没去打球。（笑）

W: Wow, you really need to stop going anywhere near the gym.
天哪，你真的应该离健身房远点。

How did the man break his thumb?

☐ (A) Playing basketball. ⋯⋯⋯⋯⋯⋯⋯⋯⋯⋯⋯⋯⋯ 打棒球。

☐ (B) Working out in the gym. ⋯⋯⋯⋯⋯⋯⋯⋯ 健身房。

☑ (C) Falling down the steps. ⋯⋯⋯⋯⋯⋯⋯⋯ 在阶梯上绊倒。

解析 Resolution

女方说"Don't tell me..."，意为"不要告诉我……"，就表示她并不知道对方受伤原因，只是猜测。而当男方说"Actually..."时，我们就知道女方的猜测：playing basketball 是错误的了。注意，听到 actually，就表示说话者有"否定对方意见"的意思。男方继续说"I tripped on the steps..."表示"他在阶梯上绊倒"，trip 为动词是"绊倒"的意思，当名词才是"旅行"。所以答案是 C。

请再听一次，并实际体会运用我们上面提到的技巧。

■ 超级实用句型

Don't tell me... 不要告诉我……

I never got to... 我根本没能……

■ 你也可以这么说

I never got to know her.
我从来没有机会认识她

I never got to tell you what I wanted to do.
我从来没有机会告诉你我要做什么。

题目 **❼ M1:** **The boss seems so mad these days. We really should've finished the annual reports on time.**
老板最近好像很生气。我们那时真的应该准时交年度报告的。

W: **Yeah, his attitude has changed so much lately. I can feel it. His mood has worsened to the point that I can't even talk to him without making him mad about something.**
是啊，他的态度最近变化好大。我感觉得出来。他的情绪很差，每次跟他说话都会激怒他。

M2: **Yep, he has become a crotchety old man these days. You guys are so right. I feel like I'm walking on eggshells around here.**
他最近已经变成了一个坏脾气的糟老头了。你们说得一点都没错，我感到如履薄冰。

What are they doing?

☐ **(A) Discussing their annual report.**
讨论他们的年度报告。

☑ **(B) Talking about the boss's bad temper.**
谈论老板的坏情绪。

☐ **(C) Explaining why they are angry at the boss.**
解释为何他们生老板的气。

解析 题目问说话者在做什么。当一群人在讨论某事时，第一句话就是开场白，会带入主题。因此听懂第一句，就可以先预测这段对话大概是什么主题了。这里的第一句话是 "The boss seems so mad these days"，因此我们知道主题是 "老板的坏情绪"。

后面我们继续听关键词、听重音。这段对话中特别强调的是：attitude... much... feel... mood... worsened... point... mad... crotchety old man. 从关键词我们也可以得知他们讨论的内容主题是什么。因此答案是 B。

请再听一次，并实际体会运用我们上面提到的技巧。

■ 超级实用句型

We should've... 我们那时应该……
└ 但事实上并没有

I can feel it. 我感觉得出来。

to the point that... 已经到……的程度

I can't even... without... 我每次……都会……

You guys are so right. 你们说得一点都没错。

walking on eggshells 走在蛋壳上，比喻很危险、战战兢兢

■ 你也可以这么说

We shouldn't have left the office so late.
我们不应该这么晚离开办公室。

Emma and Madison seem to get along so well to the point that it seems fake.
艾玛和麦迪森的相处好到不像是真的。

Have you ever been so attracted to someone to the point of addiction?
你有没有喜欢一个人到上瘾的程度？

My wife and I can't even talk without arguing.
我太太和我甚至没办法谈话不吵架。

I was walking on eggshells trying to explain the remark to her without offending her further.
我想办法在不更加得罪她的情况下向她解释我的意见，就像是走在蛋壳上一样战战兢兢。

Everyone at the company was walking on eggshells until we heard that no one would be fired.
办公室的每一个人都如履薄冰，直到我们听说没有人会被炒鱿鱼。

■ 可活用的补充句型

Louis shouldn't have acted so foolishly!
路易斯不应该那么愚蠢。

Do you talk too much without thinking?
你常会不加思索就讲太多话吗？

Unit 2 长篇对话

题目 **8** M: **If you think about it, could you bring home some flowers for the dinner table tonight?**

想想看，你可以买一些花回来吗？可以放在今晚晚餐的餐桌上。

W: **Sure, with the boss and his wife coming to dinner, it will be a nice touch.**

没问题，今晚老板夫妇来吃饭，放些花感觉会蛮好的。

M: **Yeah. Oh, now that I think about it, we could also use some fine brandy for after dinner drinks. Could you pick some up?**

是啊。噢，我现在想一想，我们餐后可以来点高级的白兰地。可以买回来吗？

W: **Yeah, good idea. The boss loves a good drink after dinner.**

可以，好主意。老板可喜欢餐后小酌了。

What is the woman going to buy?

☐ (A) Food and flowers. —————— 食物和花。

☑ (B) Flowers and alcoholic drinks. —————— 花和酒。

☐ (C) Flowers and juice. —————— 花和果汁。

解析 题目问女生要买什么，是细节，因此要仔细听男方的要求和女方的回应。男方问：Could you bring home some flowers for the dinner table tonight? 重音是 flowers 和 dinner table，可推测要买花装饰餐桌。

后来男方又说"Now that I think about it, ..."表示他有新点子，因此接着说的也可能是重点：We could also use some fine brandy... Could you pick some up? 这句话的重音在 brandy，pick up 是短语，是口语中"买"的意思，表示要买 brandy。We could use... 是"我们需要……"，也是口语中常用的表达法。因此答案应该是 B。

请再听一次，并实际体会运用我们上面提到的技巧。

■ 超级实用句型

If you think about it, ... 想想看，……

It will be a nice touch. 感觉会蛮好的。

Now that I think about it, ... 我现在想一想……

We could use... 我们需要……

Could you pick some up? 你可以去买吗？

■ 你也可以这么说

The logic seems weird, but if you think about it carefully, you will get it.
逻辑听起来好像有点奇怪，但是如果你仔细想一下，你就会懂了。

Adding some flowers to the table was a nice touch.
桌上加点花是个很好的尝试。

It would be a nice touch if we could get his favorite baseball player to sign on his birthday card.
我们如果能够找到他最喜欢的棒球球员在他的生日卡上签名感觉会非常好。

Now that I think about it, it's really a very good idea.
我现在想想，这真是个非常好的建议。

Now that I think about it carefully, I know why John was upset.
我现在仔细想了想，知道约翰为什么不高兴了。

We sure could use a little good news today.
我们今天真的很需要一些好消息。

We could use some rain.
我们需要雨。

Could you pick up some milk on your way home?
你回家的路上可以买点牛奶吗？

提醒便条纸 Reminder

舒葳老师的小叮咛，提枪上阵也不怕。

- 当我们需要听一段长篇的对话时，因为内容较多，很容易抓不住重点，导致听不懂。以下几个步骤可以帮助我们听得更有效率：

- 理清目的：在日常生活中听老外说话时，都会有一个特定目的，也就是说，虽然对方传达的信息可能很多，却只有一些信息是我们真正要听的，如：开会的时间、约会的地点。另外有些时候，我们却只需知道对方谈论的主题、大意即可，如朋友间闲聊。如果能把注意力集中在听到我们需要听的重点，而非企图听懂每个单词，就能既听得懂又听得轻松！

- 抓住重音：说话者永远会把重要的信息加强、变慢且咬字更清楚。因此，我们往往只要听到重音词，把它们串联起来，便可以猜到七八成的内容了。

- 了解语气词及转承语：英语的语气词或转承语往往传达了说话者的态度，如：well，actually，to be frank，to tell you the truth 等，都有反面的意思。抓到这些语句传达的态度，我们其实就掌握了主要的信息。同时，因为我们可以预期对方说话的方向，也更容易听得懂。

- 熟悉句型：英语的句型也能传达意义。我们听不懂，也常常是因为"没听过这种说法"。一旦熟悉了常用句型，再听到就不会慌，也就能比较容易体会对方要传达的意思了。

MEMO

Listening & Speaking

MEMO

Practice 3

听力实战练习 3

Announcement and TV / Radio Commercials
广播与广告

听力
Listening
口语
Speaking

Unit 1 公共场合的广播

Unit 2 电视及广播的广告

学习重点
Main Point

除了日常生活的对话外，另一个我们常会需要听的，就是公共场合的广播及电视和电台的广告了！因为长度较长，又通常是一个人从头说到尾，对于听的人来说没有"喘息"的空间，一般的英语学习者都会觉得这类的听力很具挑战性。因此，在听这种长篇"独白"的时候，运用我们之前教过的"语调"及"语意单位"等技巧就变得很重要！

现在让我们来试试看吧！不要忘记运用声调的提高降落及语句的停顿，来判断说话者想表达的意义是已经告一段落，还是正要开始新的语意单位。尝试跟上说话者的节奏，掌握对方要说的重点吧！

Unit 1

公共场合的广播

热身活动 Warm Up 学习英语前，先来做个热身吧！

请听 MP3，并选择适当的答案。每一段广播有两至三道题目。

题目 Questions

A

① What is the purpose of the talk?

A. To tell people what to see on the lake.

B. To warn people against the unsafe conditions.

C. To advise people to stay inside because of the the bad weather.

② What should people do?

A. Take a closer look at the west end of the lake.

B. Eat ice near the river.

C. Not go beyond the orange safety markers.

B

① What is the purpose of the talk?

A. To announce a fire in the building.

B. To explain the location of a department store.

C. To instruct how to use elevators.

② What should people do now?

A. Call the fire department.

B. Move out of the building.

C. Collect their own stuff.

③ What should people use when moving out?

A. The stairs.

B. The elevators.

C. The escalators.

Unit 1 公共场合的广播

C **1** Where is this announcement being made?

  A. A department store.

  B. An airport.

  C. At school.

  2 How should people be using the escalators?

  A. Stand to the right.

  B. Stand to the left.

  C. Move quickly.

D **1** What is the reason for the delay?

  A. Bad weather.

  B. Mechanical problems.

  C. Meal preparation.

  2 What time should passengers arrive at the gate by?

  A. 8:30.　B. 8:00.　C. 10:00.

E **1** Who is listening to the announcement?

  A. Hotel guests.

  B. Company staff.

  C. University students.

  2 What is the party for?

  A. To welcome new staff.

  B. To celebrate a national holiday.

  C. To welcome hotel guests.

  你也可能被问

  Must everyone go to the party?

  A. It's optional. People can choose whether they want to go or not.

  B. It's mandatory. Everyone must attend it.

  C. The invited quests must attend.

F **1** What can people get at the repair shop?

   A. Well-prepared skis.

   B. A free maintenance package.

   C. Spare room keys.

2 What must people do to get assistance?

   A. Pay a minimum charge.

   B. Present your room key to the staff.

   C. See the manager.

你也可能被问

What is the main purpose of the announcement?

A. To sell skiing equipment.

B. To ensure the safety of the skiers.

C. To announce the housekeeping time.

解答 Answers

A **1** B **2** C
B **1** A **2** B **3** A
C **1** B **2** A
D **1** A **2** B
E **1** A **2** C **3** A
F **1** B **2** B **3** B

Unit 1 公共场合的广播

实际演练 Explanation 通过认真的解题练习打下扎实的基础。

题目 Question

A Hello skaters. Please note that the west end of the lake is closed due to unsafe conditions. The ice is very thin near the River George's mouth, so please stay inside the orange safety markers you see on the lake. Have a great time on the lake.

各位溜冰者，你们好。请注意湖的西边因为安全原因而关闭。乔治河口的冰层非常薄，所以请待在橘红色的安全标示内。祝你们在湖上玩得愉快。

❶ What is the purpose of the talk?
此篇广播目的是什么？

☐ (A) To tell people what to see on the lake. ⋯⋯⋯⋯⋯⋯⋯ 告诉人们湖上有什么值得观赏。

☑ (B) To warn people against the unsafe conditions. ⋯⋯⋯⋯⋯⋯⋯ 警告人们小心不安全的状况。

☐ (C) To advise people to stay inside because of the the bad weather. ⋯⋯ 建议人们因恶劣天气而留在室内。

❷ What should people do?
人们应该怎么做？

☐ (A) Take a closer look at the west end of the lake. ⋯⋯⋯⋯⋯⋯⋯ 近距离观赏湖的西岸。

☐ (B) Eat ice near the river. ⋯⋯⋯⋯⋯⋯⋯ 在河附近吃冰。

☑ (C) Not go beyond the orange safety markers. ⋯⋯⋯⋯⋯⋯⋯ 不越过橘红色的安全标示。

解析 Resolution

利用"语意单位",也就是语气的停顿和声调,可以帮助我们理解并跟上说话者的节奏。声调提高表示是一个新概念的开始。以下"//"符号表示较长停顿,也就是语句结束;"/"则表示短暂停顿,表示同一个句子内一个较小的"语意单位"的完成。

Hello skaters.// Please note/ that the west end of the lake is closed/ due to unsafe conditions.// The ice is very thin near the River Gorge's mouth,/ so please stay inside the orange safety markers you see on the lake.// Have a great time on the lake.//

一开头的 Hello skaters 告诉我们广播的对象正在溜冰。而当我们听到 Please note that... 就知道这个广播在请溜冰的人注意某件事情,也就是这段广播的目的。继续由重音抓关键词:... west... closed... unsafe... conditions... ice... thin 亦可以帮助我们知道主题跟安全有关。因此第一题的答案是 B。

第二题问"What should people do?",因此当我们听到说话者说:Please... 我们就应该特别留意。Please... 就是请听者做或不做某事,不但正是题目想问的重点,我们一般在听广播时当对方讲到 Please... 或 Please don't 也应该特别留意。结果我们听到他说的是:Please stay inside the orange safety makers... 因此答案是 C。这里的重点是抓句型。

Unit 1 公共场合的广播

■ **超级实用句型**

Please note that... 请注意……

Please stay inside... 请不要踏出……的范围

■ **你也可以这么说**

Multiple roads are closed due to flooding.
许多道路因为淹水而关闭。

Schools are closed due to the snow.
学校因为大雪而关闭。

Her financial adviser warned her against such a risky investment.
她的财务顾问已警告她这是一个很冒险的投资。

The police have warned tourists against leaving the main tourist centers.
警察已经警告旅客不要离开这个主要的游客中心。

■ **超级实用词汇**

unsafe condition phr. 不安全的状况、条件

adviser n. 顾问

risky a. 危险的

investment n. 投资

tourist center phr. 游客中心

unsafe a. 不安全的

condition(s) n. 情况

marker n. 游标

beyond adv. 超过；prep. 在（或向）……较远的一边

题目 | **B** May I have your attention, please. A fire has been reported on the top floor of the building. Do not panic. The fire department is on the way. Please exit the building now. Move quickly and do not stop for personal belongings. Exit using the stairways. Do not use the elevators.

请注意。顶楼据报有火灾。不要惊慌，消防队已经在赶来的路上。现在请离开这栋大楼。动作迅速，不要停留下来拿私人物品。请使用楼梯，不要使用电梯。

❶ What is the purpose of the talk?
此篇广播目的为何？

☑ **(A) To announce a fire in the building.** ······ 宣布大楼里的火警。

☐ **(B) To explain the location of a department store.** ······ 解释一间百货公司的地点。

☐ **(C) To instruct how to use elevators.** ······ 说明如何使用电梯。

❷ What should people do now?
人们现在应该怎么做？

☐ **(A) Call the fire department.** ······ 打电话给消防队。

☑ **(B) Move out of the building.** ······ 往大楼外移动。

☐ **(C) Collect their own stuff.** ······ 拿自己的物品。

❸ What should people use when moving out?
人们离开时应使用什么？

☑ **(A) The stairs.** ······ 楼梯。

☐ **(B) The elevators.** ······ 电梯。

☐ **(C) The escalators.** ······ 手扶梯。

Unit 1 公共场合的广播

解析
Resolution

利用"语意单位",也就是语气的停顿和声调可以帮助我们理解并跟上说话者的节奏。声调提高表示是一个新概念的开始。以下"//"符号表示较长停顿,也就是语句结束;"/"则表示短暂停顿,表示同一个句子内一个较小的"语意单位"的完成。

May I have your attention,/ please.// A fire has been reported on the top floor of the building.// Do not panic.// The fire department is on the way./ Please exit the building now.// Move quickly/ and do not stop for personal belongings.// Exit using the stairways.// Do not use the elevators.//

广播的主题都会在前一到两句出现。我们听到"A fire has been reported..."即知这是火警的广播。答案是 A。

第二题问:What should people do now? 因此当说"Please..."时,就应该特别注意,因为此时正要告诉听者应该做什么。而且 Please 的后面出现的通常也都会是重点。这里重音有"exit... building... now"。因此我们知道现在要离开这栋大楼。答案是 B。

最后一题问:What should people use when moving out? 因此当我们听到 ... exit using... 时就要特别注意听,因为 exit 就是 move out 的意思。结果他说的是"Exit using the stairways. Do not use the elevators"。我们听到重音有"... exit... stairways... do not... elevators"。我们知道要"使用楼梯,不要使用电梯"。因此第三题答案是 A。

■ 超级实用句型

... has been reported... 已被报告,已被报道

... is on the way ……在路上

Don't panic. 不要惊慌。

personal belongings 私人物品

■ 你也可以这么说

My iPad has been reported stolen and is now locked.
我的苹果平板已报警被窃,现在被锁住了。

This Facebook post has been reported.
这条脸书信息被举报了。

Is he here yet or is he on the way?
他已经到了吗,还是还在路上?

Mary is better now and on the way to recovery.
玛莉已经比较好了,她正在康复中。

We're now on the way to London.
我们正在去伦敦的路上。

They have three kids and another on the way.
他们有三个小孩,还有一个快出生了。

Don't panic. We'll sort it out.
不要慌张,我们会解决的。

Please make sure to take all your personal belongings with you when you leave.
离开时请记得携带所有的随身行李。

■ 可活用的补充句型

The government made a public announcement about the progress of the talks. 政府公开宣布谈话的进展。

When was the news announced to the public?
这个消息什么时候被宣布的?

These boxes are crowding up the room. Please move them out.
这些箱子占据了整个房间。请把它们搬出去。

I'm moving out. 我要搬出去住了。

■ 超级实用词汇

panic *n.* 惊慌失措;*v.* 使恐慌

fire department *phr.* 救火队

personal belongings *phr.* 私人物品

stairway(s) *n.* 楼梯

题目 Question

C Please be courteous and stand to the right while on the escalator. The left side is reserved for those preferring to walk more quickly in order to make their flight. Please be courteous and everyone will make their gate in time for their departure.

当使用电扶梯时，请有礼貌地靠右侧站。左侧是留给需要快速通过赶飞机的人使用的。请各位注重礼仪，让每个人都能够在起飞前赶到登机门。

❶ Where is this announcement being made?
这个广播在哪里进行？

☐ (A) A department store. ……………………… 百货公司。

☑ (B) An airport. ……………………………………… 机场。

☐ (C) At school. ……………………………………… 学校。

❷ How should people be using the escalators?
人们应该如何使用电扶梯？

☑ (A) Stand to the right. ……………………………… 靠右侧。

☐ (B) Stand to the left. ………………………………… 靠左侧。

☐ (C) Move quickly. …………………………………… 快速移动。

解析 Resolution

利用"语意单位"，也就是语气的停顿和声调，可以帮助我们理解并跟上说话者的节奏。声调提高表示是一个新概念的开始。以下 "//" 符号表示较长停顿，也就是语句结束；"/" 则表示短暂停顿，表示同一个句子内一个较小的"语意单位"的完成。

Please be courteous/ and stand to the right/ while on the escalator.// The left side/ is reserved for those preferring to walk more quickly/ in order to make their flight.// Please be courteous/ and everyone will make their gate/ in time/ for their departure.//

> 我们串联关键词 make flight，gate，departure，便知道这是机场的广播。第一题的答案是 B。
>
> 广播的第一话即说明广播目的，也必定会是广播的重点：stand to the right while on the escalator，也就是"使用电扶梯时请靠右侧站"。因此第二题的答案是：A。

■ 超级实用句型

is reserved for... 为……而预约的

make sb.'s flight 赶上（某人）的飞机

■ 可活用的补充句型

The clerks were helpful and courteous.
这些工作人员服务好且十分有礼。

The front row is reserved for faculty.
前排的位子是为教职员工保留的。

Cindy is a very reserved young woman.
辛迪是个很保守的年轻女孩。

We'll make sure that we are there in time for the performance.
我们一定能赶上演出。

Always stand on the right of the London Underground escalators. 在伦敦地铁的手扶梯，请靠右边站。

Washingtonians stand to the right of the escalators and walk on the left. 华盛顿的人站在手扶梯的右边，左边留给人走路。

小贴士 Tip：在国外的地铁站或百货公司，人们都会靠右边站，左边则是留出通道，让行人可以快速通过。无论是在国内还是在国外，这都是我们应该留意的行人礼仪！

■ 超级实用词汇

courteous a. 谦恭有礼的

escalator n. 手扶电梯

departure n. 离开

faculty n. 大学的教职员工

题目 Question | D

This is to announce a new departure time for Flight 856 to Los Angeles. Severe thunderstorms delayed the connecting flight from Tokyo. The plane is now on the ground and is being serviced. The new departure time is scheduled for 8:30.

Due to the delay, meal vouchers will be available for passengers scheduled on this flight. Passengers are asked to please be ready for boarding at Gate 10 by 8 o'clock. Thank you for your understanding.

我现在要宣布前往洛杉矶 856 航班次新的起飞时间。来自东京的转机航班由于剧烈暴风雨而延迟抵达。飞机现在已落地并在检查中。新的起飞时间预计为八点半。

由于时间的耽误，我们将会提供餐券给预定要搭乘这班航班的旅客。旅客请于八点前到达十号登机口准备登机。谢谢各位的谅解。

1 What is the reason for the delay?
延迟的理由是什么？

☑ (A) Bad weather. ······················ 天气不佳。
☐ (B) Mechanical problems. ······················ 机械问题。
☐ (C) Meal preparation. ······················ 餐点准备。

2 What time should passengers arrive at the gate by?
旅客应在几点前到达登机门？

☐ (A) 8:30. ······················ 八点半。
☑ (B) 8:00. ······················ 八点。
☐ (C) 10:00. ······················ 十点。

解析 Resolution

利用"语意单位",也就是语气的停顿和声调,可以帮助我们理解并跟上说话者的节奏。声调提高表示是一个新的"语意单位"的开始。以下"//"符号表示较长停顿,也就是语句结束;"/"则表示短暂停顿,表示同一个句子内一个较小的"语意单位"的完成。

This is to announce a new departure time for Flight 856/ to Los Angeles.// Severe thunderstorms have delayed the connecting flight from Tokyo.// The plane is now on the ground/ and is being serviced.// The new departure time is scheduled for 8:30.// Due to the delay,/ meal vouchers will be available for passengers/ scheduled on this flight.// Passengers are asked/ to please be ready for boarding at Gate 10/ by 8 o'clock.// Thank you/ for your understanding.//

第一句话即听到主题"This is to announce a new departure time...",所以我们知道这是机场的广播,告知乘客起飞时间的改变。第一题问:What is the reason for the delay? 因此接下来应该就会说原因,果然他说,"Severe thunderstorms delayed...",现在我们知道是thunderstorms,也就是天气的影响。第一题的答案是A。

第二题问的是:What time should passengers arrive at the gate by? 所以我们知道接下来我们应该注意的是到达 gate 的时间。然后我们听到他说:The new departure time is 8:30,但还不是我们要的信息。后面他又说"Passengers are asked to please be ready for boarding at Gate 10 by 8 o'clock",在八点前就要到登机口。因此第二题的答案是B。

事实上,当说话者提高语调,并说"Passengers are asked to please..."时,我们就应该知道后面可能就是重点了!因为当语调提高表示新信息要出现,而"Passengers are asked to please..."表示下面是乘客必须注意的信息,一定是很重要的!

Unit 1 公共场合的广播

■ 超级实用句型

This is to announce... 我现在要宣布……

sth. is scheduled for... 某事预计为（时间）

sth. will be available for sb. 我们将会提供某物给某人

Due to... 由于……

■ 可活用的补充句型

The flight has been delayed one hour, due to weather conditions.
天气状况的缘故，飞机已经晚点一个小时。

The flight was delayed because of mechanical problems.
因为机械故障，飞机被延误了。

The fog delayed the plane's landing.
大雾延迟了飞机的降落。

The Russian foreign minister has cancelled his trip to Washington.
俄罗斯的外交部部长取消了去华盛顿的旅程。

Over 80 flights were cancelled because of bad weather.
因为天气不好，超过八十个航班被取消了。

Dutch Airlines is changing winter schedule from Almaty to earlier departure time.
荷兰航空把从阿木拉图冬季航班的出发时间提前了。

What is the arrival time of your flight back to Beijing?
你回到北京的航班什么时候抵达？

■ 超级实用词汇

severe a. 严厉的
thunderstorm n. 暴风雨
connecting flight n. 转机
service n. / v. 服务
voucher n. 抵用券
delay v. 延迟
departure time / time of departure phr. 离开时间
arrival time / time of arrival phr. 抵达时间

Practice **3**

🎧 279

题目 | **E**
Question

Thank you for choosing the Grand Hyatt for your holiday stay. We will be having a welcoming party this evening for those of you that wish to attend. The party commences at 8:00 pm. Please attend and greet your fellow guests this evening. Thank you for your patronage and we hope you have a wonderful stay.

谢谢您选择君悦大饭店度过您的假期。今晚我们将会为想要参加的人举办一个欢迎晚会。晚会将在晚上八点钟开始。敬请光临，你有机会结识其他在此住宿的朋友们。感谢各位对我们的支持，预祝您有一个美好的假期。

❶ **Who is listening to the announcement?**
广播的对象是谁？

☑ **(A) Hotel guests.** ……………………………… 饭店顾客。

☐ **(B) Company staff.** …………………………… 公司员工。

☐ **(C) University students.** ……………………… 大学学生。

❷ **What is the party for?**
晚会的目的为何？

☐ **(A) To welcome new staff.** …………………… 欢迎新员工。

☐ **(B) To celebrate a national holiday.** ………… 庆祝国定假日。

☑ **(C) To welcome hotel guests.** ……………… 欢迎饭店顾客。

你也可能被问

Must everyone go to the party?
所有人一定要去参加派对吗？

☑ **(A) It's optional. People can choose whether they want to go or not.** ………… 选择性的，可以参加也可以不要。

☐ **(B) It's mandatory. Everyone must attend it.**
……………………………………………… 义务性的，每个人都应该参加。

☐ **(C) The invited quests must attend.**
……………………………………………… 受邀客人必须参加。

解析 Resolution

利用"语意单位",也就是语气的停顿和声调,可以帮助我们理解并跟上说话者的节奏。声调提高表示是一个新"语意单位"的开始。以下"//"符号表示较长停顿,也就是语句结束;"/"则表示短暂停顿,表示同一个句子内一个较小的"语意单位"的完成。

Thank you for choosing the Grand Hyatt/ for your holiday stay.// We will be having a welcoming party/ this evening.// The party commences at 8:00 pm/ for those of you that wish to attend.// Please attend/ and greet your fellow guests this evening.// Thank you for your patronage/ and we hope you will have a wonderful stay.//

第一题问的是:Who is listening to the announcement? 广播的听众是谁,也就是说,如果我们知道这段广播的主题或目的,就会知道听众是谁了。而广播的第一句话即是主题"Thank you for choosing the Grand Hyatt...",表示这是在饭店内,对住宿顾客所做的广播。答案是:A。

第二题问:What is the party for? 表示接下应该会听到关于party的信息,我们要知道的是 party 是为谁举办的。下面的关键词我们听到"We... having... welcoming party... you... attend",表示 party 是为听者举办的,之后的"Please attend... greet... fellow guests..."更说明 party 对象便是听者,而目的为欢迎新顾客。因此答案是 C。

第三题问:Must everyone go to the party? 听到"The party... 8:00 pm... for those of..."就要注意听是为谁办的。"For those of you that / who..."就表示要说明这个 announcement 是针对谁说的。接着他说"for those of you... wish ... attend"就表示是自由意愿参加。wish 是想要、希望的意思。因此答案是 A。optional 是选择性的意思;mandatory 是义务性的;也可以说 compulsory。

■ 你也可以这么说

Jackets are required at the restaurant, but ties are optional.
西装外套是必需的，但是是否打领带则随个人意愿。

Registration is optional, not mandatory.
会员注册是选择性的，非强迫参加。

It is mandatory that all students take two years of English.
所有的学生都必须修两年英语。

Travel insurance for the students is compulsory.
学生的旅游保险是强制的。

■ 可活用的补充句型

The festivities will commence with a parade.
节庆活动将以游行揭开序幕。

Their contract commences in January.
他们的契约一月开始生效。

My parents and I will both attend the banquet.
我父母和我都会出席宴会。

How many people will be attending?
有多少人会参加？

I won't be attending the conference.
我不会去参加会议。

Thank you for your patronage.
感谢你的光顾。

The new library is expected to have heavy patronage.
这家新的图书馆预期将有很多人使用。

The college relied on the patronage of its wealthy graduates to expand its funds.
这所大学依赖其富有校友的捐款，来增加他们的经费。

A sale is being held to raise funds for the school.
他们将举办一场拍卖会来筹措经费。

The museum is so short of funds; it may have to sell the painting.
这间博物馆经费短缺，可能得卖那幅画了。

The program relies on state funding.
这个计划依赖政府的经费。

Our guest receive the finest quality service.
我们的客人可以享受到最高品质的服务。

Frequent guests receive a discount.
常客可享有折扣。

■ 超级实用词汇

attend v. 出席
commence v. 开始
greet v. 打招呼
rely on phr. 依赖
expand v. 扩充
fund n. 基金、经费
raise funds phr. 募款
stay n. / v. 住宿
patronage n. 光临、照顾（通常在旅馆业、餐厅会听到）
guest n. （餐厅、饭店的）客人

题目 Question | **F** Hello skiers. Please note that skiing with unprepared skis can be very dangerous. We offer a free maintenance package here at Sunnyvale in order to make your experience here as safe as possible. Please see the repair shop and show them your room key. They will be happy to help you. Thank you and have a wonderful time on our mountain.

各位滑雪者，大家好。请注意，未准备完善的滑雪板是非常危险的。我们阳光谷提供免费的滑雪道清理器具，让您在此的体验尽可能安全无忧。请到修理室，并出示您的房间钥匙，他们会热心地协助您。谢谢，并预祝您在我们的山上度过愉快的时光。

1 What can people get at the repair shop?
人们可以在修理室得到什么？

☐ (A) Well-prepared skis. ················· 准备好的滑雪板。

☑ (B) A free maintenance package. ······ 滑雪道清理器具。

☐ (C) Spare room keys. ················· 备用的房间钥匙。

2 What must people do to get assistance?
人们要怎么做才能得到协助？

☐ (A) Pay a minimum charge. ············ 付最低消费。

☑ (B) Present their room key to the staff. 出示房间钥匙。

☐ (C) See the manager. ················· 见经理。

你也可能被问

What is the main purpose of the announcement?
这个广播的主旨为何？

☐ (A) To sell skiing equipment. ·········· 贩卖滑雪器具。

☑ (B) To ensure the safety of the skiers.
················ 确保滑雪人士的安全。

☐ (C) To announce the housekeeping time.
················ 广播清理房间的时间。

Unit 1 公共场合的广播

解析
Resolution

利用"语意单位",也就是语气的停顿和声调,可以帮助我们理解并跟上说话者的节奏。声调提高表示是一个新"语意单位"的开始。以下"//"符号表示较长停顿,也就是语句结束;"/"则表示短暂停顿,表示同一个句子内一个较小的"语意单位"的完成。

Hello skiers.// Please be aware/ that skiing with unprepared skis/ can be very dangerous.// We offer a free maintenance package/ here at Sunnyvale/ in order to make your experience here/ as safe as possible.// Please see the repair shop/ and show them your room key.// They will be happy to help you.// Thank you/ and have a wonderful time on our mountain.//

第一句话即听到主题,知道这是对滑雪者发布的广播。并且听到"Please be aware... dangerous"就知道目的在请听者注意某件事情的安全。第一题问的是:What can people get at the repair shop? 表示我们在广播中会听到 repair shop,并且要注意的是在 repair shop 能拿到什么。所以当他说"We offer..."时就要特别注意,因为"We offer..."和"What can people get"是一样的意思。他可能会说"We offer... at the repair shop"。

果然他先说了"We offer... a free maintenance package... Please see the repair shop...",表示提供的是 maintenance package("滑雪道清理器具"),而需要的话就 see the repair shop("找 repair shop")。因此这题的答案是 B。

第二题问的是:What must people do to get assistance? 要怎么做,repair shop 的人才会帮你?他说的是"Please see the repair shop and show them your room key"。也就是要给他看你的房间钥匙。答案是:B。

第三题问 What is the main purpose of the announcement? 这个广播的主要目的为何?因此这个题目问的是广播的主旨,需综合整篇广播的关键词来判断:"note that... unprepared skis... dangerous... free... package... in order to... experience... safe... repair shop... room key...",表示广播目的是为提醒滑雪人士滑雪器具的安全并提供相关服务,因此答案是 B。

■ 超级实用句型

Please be aware... 请注意……

... can be very dangerous ……是非常危险的

... can be... 是可以……的／有时是……的

■ 你也可以这么说

Please see the repair shop.
请到修理室。

Please be aware that we will be closed at 5 p.m. today.
请注意，我们今天下午五点就会结束营业。

■ 可活用的补充句型

She is aware of the problem.
她很清楚这个问题。

I was not fully aware of the danger.
我不是很清楚有这个危险。

BeiJing can be quite cold in winter.
北京冬天有时候很冷。

Sandy can be very rude at times.
桑迪有时候十分无理。

We don't need any help, but thank you for offering.
我们不需要帮忙，但谢谢你提供帮助。

Sophie was well-prepared and did well on the presentation.
索菲准备充分，报告很成功。

Be prepared for a busy start.
要有心理准备，一开始会很忙碌。

■ 超级实用词汇

skis   n.   滑雪板

maintenance   n.   清理、保养

repair   v.   修理

offer   v.   提供（帮助、工作等）

prepared   a.   有准备的

Unit 2

电视及广播的广告

热身运动 Warm Up 学习英语前，先来做个热身吧！

请听 MP3，并选择适当的答案。每一则广告有两道题目。

题目 Questions

A Who would be interested in this ad?
   A. Couples who want to buy a new house.
   B. People who are going to get married.
   C. Students who have a big exam coming.

② What should one do if he / she is interested?
   A. Take part in a draw.
   B. Call the number.
   C. Visit the shops.

B ① Who would be most interested in the product advertised?
   A. People who play computer games at Internet Cafés.
   B. People who want their house to be neat and clean.
   C. People who make frequent international calls.

② How is the central wireless network connected to your computer, telephone, cable TV and etc.?
   A. By cable.
   B. By wire.
   C. By radio signals.

C ❶ Who would most likely to be interested in this advertisement?

A. People who are considering getting a pet.

B. People whose pets need a heath check or treatment.

C. People who are looking for a new home for their pets.

❷ What is TAPP?

A. A pet store.

B. A pet hotel.

C. A pet hospital.

D ❶ What's the prize of this week's competition?

A. Two concert tickets.

B. Classical CDs.

C. Music magazines.

❷ What does a listener need to do to win the prize?

A. Be the first to say what the piece is.

B. Be the first to say the name of the composer.

C. Be the first to say what period this piece was written.

E ❶ Who would be most interested in this advertisement?

A. Children.

B. Computer programmers.

C. Tourists.

❷ How can one get a free tickets to Bonnie's Fun Fair?

A. To spend a particular amount of money on some product.

B. To send personal information and take part in a draw.

C. To call and answer questions carefully.

Unit 2 电视及广播的广告

F **❶** Who is the most possible target group of the advertisement?

A. People who seek to look prettier.

B. People who seek to be healthier.

C. People who want to lose weight.

❷ How often should a person use this product?

A. Before each meal.

B. Twice a day.

C. Every other day.

解答 Answers		
A ❶ B ❷ B	D ❶ C ❷ A	
B ❶ B ❷ C	E ❶ A ❷ A	
C ❶ B ❷ C	F ❶ A ❷ B	

🎧 289

实际演练 Explanation 通过认真的解题练习打下扎实的根基。

题目 Questions

A When the time has come for you to pop the question, will you be nervous or will you be confident in your decision? A purchase at Shay Company Diamonds will allow you to rest assured of your diamond decision. When the big day comes, you can be confident that she will love your selection, because the Shay Company has the very best diamonds in Chicago. She will fall in love with you all over again. You know that special moment deserves a special diamond for that special someone, so buy the perfect diamond. You can only find it at the Shay Company. Call 1-800-DIAMOND today.

当求婚时刻的到来，你会紧张还是会充满信心？在雪亿公司购买钻石是你最安心的选择。当大喜的那一天到来时，你可以确信她会爱死了你的选择，因为雪亿公司有芝加哥最好的钻石。她会再度与你坠入情网。你知道，特别的一刻，值得一颗特别的钻石，给特别的那个人，所以，要买最完美的钻石。这只能在雪亿公司找到。今天就打电话到 1 — 800 — DIAMOND.

❶ Who would be interested in this ad?
谁会对这个广告有兴趣？

☐ (A) Couples who want to buy a new house.
想买新房子的夫妻。

☑ (B) People who are going to get married.
将要结婚的男女朋友。

☐ (C) Students who have a big exam coming.
迎接大考来临的学生。

Unit 2 电视及广播的广告

② What should one do if he / she is interested?
有兴趣的人应该怎么做？

☐ (A) Take part in a draw. ——————— 参加抽奖。

☑ (B) Call the number. ——————— 打电话到那个号码。

☐ (C) Visit the shops. ——————— 到店里去。

解析
Resolution

我们应该善用"语意单位"、语气停顿和语调来帮助理解。以下"//"符号表示较长停顿，也就是语句结束；"/"则表示短暂停顿，表示同一个句子内一个较小的"语意单位"的完成。

When the time has come/ for you to pop the question,/ will you be nervous/ or will you be confident/ in your decision?// A purchase at Shay Company Diamonds will allow you to rest assured/ of your diamond decision.// When the big day comes,/ you can be confident/ that she will love your selection,/ because the Shay Company/ has the very best diamonds/ in Chicago.// She will fall in love with you/ all over again.// You know/ that special moment/ deserves a special diamond/ for that special someone,/ so buy the perfect diamond.// You can only find it/ at the Shay Company.// Call 1-800-/ DIAMOND/ today.//

第一句话"When the time has come for you to pop the question, will you be nervous or will you be confident in your decision?"就点出了这段话的主题，因此我们知道广告产品跟结婚有关。在英语里，pop the question 就有求婚的意思。

> 果然，"A purchase at Shay Company Diamonds will allow you..."，这里做广告的是雪亿钻石公司。同时，广告中被广告的商品一定会不断出现。这里我们一直听到 Shay Company Diamonds, diamond, 所以我们更确定这个广告卖的是钻石。再加上其他的关键词：make the right decision，she will love your decision，she will fall in love with you again, special moment... 也确定广告的对象是要结婚买钻戒的人。
>
> 广告的尾端通常是要你付诸行动。这里他说 "Call..."，所以是打电话。在美国为了让大家好记，商家的电话号码常常变成英语单词。像手机一样，一个数字会和数个字母共用一个输入按键。

■ 超级实用句型

pop the question 求婚（问这个重要的问题）

■ 可活用的补充句型

I have worked very hard to save money for the purchase of a car. 我很努力工作存钱买车。

That apartment was a wise purchase. 那间公寓很值得买。

You can rest assured that the salesman won't bother you again. 请放心，我们的业务不会再打扰你了。

You can rest assured that your son will be safe here. 你可以放心你的儿子在这里很安全。

Are you ready for the big day? 你准备好要迎接这个大喜之日了吗？

When's the big day? Have you set a date for your wedding yet? 大喜之日是什么时候？你们决定婚礼的日期了吗？

■ 超级实用词汇

purchase v. 购买
rest assured phr. 放心
the big day phr. 大喜之日
deserve v. 应得；值得

题目 **B** Do you have cable and telephone cords cluttering up your house? We have all had the trouble of sorting out computer, cable TV and telephone cords. But now we, here at Clean House, are pleased to present the solution to this unsightly mess. With our new universal wireless network, you can plug your cable TV, your DSL lines and your telephone lines into one central wireless network. Store it in your closet, in the attic, wherever, just get that unsightly mess out of the living room. Each set comes with a central hub and five satellite receivers capable of handling a 200,000 ping area. We are offering this today for the low, low price of only $79.95. Get it today.

你家有缠成一堆的电线和电话线吗？我们都有过试着把家中的电脑、数据机、有线电视和电话的电线整理出头绪的惨痛经历。但是现在，清洁屋推出了能够对付这脏乱有碍观瞻状况的解决方案。有了我们新出品的世界无线系统，你可以把有线电视电线、有线数据机电线或拨接数据机电线和电话线都插到一个中央无线系统。把它放置在你的衣柜、阁楼或任何地方，随你高兴，就能使客厅摆脱这种有碍观瞻的脏乱状况。每一组都附有一个中央分享器以及五个卫星接收器，可用于 200 000 平方米的面积。79.95 美元的低价就可以买到，今天就买吧。

❶ Who would be most interested in the product advertised?
谁会对此广告产品最有兴趣？

☐ (A) People who play computer games at Internet Cafés. ⋯⋯⋯⋯⋯⋯⋯⋯ 在网络咖啡店玩电脑游戏的人。

☑ (B) People who want their house to be neat and clean. ⋯⋯⋯⋯⋯⋯⋯⋯⋯⋯ 希望家里整齐干净的人。

☐ (C) People who make frequent international calls. ⋯⋯⋯⋯⋯⋯⋯⋯⋯⋯⋯⋯⋯⋯ 常常打国际电话的人。

❷ **How is the central wireless network connected to your computer, telephone, cable TV and etc.?**
电脑、电话等如何连接到这个中央无线系统？

☐ **(A) By cable.** ··· 电缆。

☐ **(B) By wire.** ··· 电线。

☑ **(C) By radio signals.** ··· 电波信号。

解析
Resolution

我们应该善用"语意单位"、语气停顿和语调来帮助理解。以下"//"符号表示较长停顿，也就是语句结束；"/"则表示短暂停顿，表示同一个句子内一个较小的"语意单位"的完成。

Do you have cable/ and telephone cords cluttering up/ your house?// We have all had the trouble of sorting out computer,/ cable TV/ and telephone cords.// But now/ we,/ here at Clean House,/ are pleased to present the solution to this unsightly mess.// With our new universal wireless network,/ you can plug your cable TV,/ your DSL line/ and your telephone lines/ into one central wireless network.// Store it in your closet,/ in the attic,/ wherever,/ just get that unsightly mess/ out of the living room.// Each set comes with a central hub/ and five satellite receivers/ capable of handling a 200,000 ping area.// We are offering this today for the low/ low/ price of only/ $79.95.// Get it today.//

Unit 2 电视及广播的广告

第一句话"Do you have cable and telephone cords cluttering up your house?"便会点出主题，因此我们知道这个广告产品希望解决的是家里 cable 和 telephone cords cluttering up 的问题。接下去叙述处理电线的痛苦后，果然，"We, at Clean House, are pleased to present the solution to this unsightly mess"，要提供你解决方案。

当我们听到"With our new universal wireless network..."就知道他会说明新产品的好处。每一个稍长的停顿都表示一个好处可能已经讲完。停顿后语调上扬，表示要开始说另一个好处。我们听重音，三个好处如下：

(1) plug... cable TV... DSL lines... telephone lines... one central wireless network...
也就是"通通插入一个中央无线系统"

(2) Store... closet... attic... get... mess out... living room.
也就是"把……放置某处，把脏乱赶出客厅"

(3) Each... central hub... five satellite receivers... 200,000 ping...
也就是"每一组都附有一个中央分享器以及五个卫星接收器，可用于 200 000 平的面积"。既然是无线的，就靠卫星接收器接收电波信号即可。

广告的最后自然会强调价钱有多么划算。

■ 超级实用句型

capable of... 有能力……的

■ 超级实用词汇

cable n. 电线

cord n. 电线

clutter up phr. 挤成一堆；缠成一堆

misfortune n. 不幸

sort out phr. 整理出头绪

unsightly mess phr. 有碍观瞻的脏乱

wireless a. 无线的

hub n. 活动中心；中枢

satellite receiver phr. 卫星信号接收器

题目 Question C Your pet deserves the best and only the good health and grooming experts at Advanced Pet Professionals can make sure your pet gets the best. Whether your dog has fleas, your cat has hairballs or a urinary tract infection, the professionals at Advanced Pet Professionals can help. We can and do take care of the minor problems as well as the serious injuries. We, at TAPP, can be trusted to help your pets heal from a broken leg or a cancerous lesion. You can trust us. You can trust Advanced Pet Professionals. At TAPP, we provide the most caring environments, the most up to date medical techniques, and the best veterinary service around. Let TAPP care for your pets like they deserve. They deserve the best, and TAPP provides it.

你的宠物值得你给它最好的，而只有在拥有健康和清洁专家的"卓越宠物专家"才能确保你的宠物得到最好的照顾。无论是你的狗可能有跳蚤，你的猫的毛起了毛球或是尿道感染，"卓越宠物专家"都能提供协助。我们能处理轻微问题，也能解决严重的受伤问题。在泰普，我们能帮助你治愈宠物的伤痛，小到骨折大到癌症。你可以信任我们，你可以信任"卓越宠物专家"。在泰普，我们提供最温暖的环境、最新的医疗技术和最优质的兽医服务。让泰普给你的宠物它们应得的照顾。让"卓越宠物专家"给你的宠物值得的照顾。它们值得最好的，泰普提供最好的。

1 Who would most likely to be interested in this advertisement?
谁最可能对这个广告有兴趣？

☐ (A) People who are considering getting a pet.
正考虑要养宠物的人。

☑ (B) People whose pets need a heath check or treatment. 有宠物需要健康检查或医疗的人。

☐ (C) People who are looking for a new home for their pets. 在寻找宠物新居的人。

❷ What is TAPP?

泰普是什么？

☐ (A) A pet store. ……………………………… 宠物店。

☐ (B) A pet hotel. ……………………………… 宠物旅馆。

☑ (C) A pet hospital. …………………………… 宠物医院。

解析
Resolution

我们应该善用"语意单位"、语气停顿和语调来帮助理解。以下"//"符号表示较长停顿，也就是语句结束；"/"则表示短暂停顿，表示同一个句子内一个较小的"语意单位"的完成。

Your pet deserves the best/ and only the good health and grooming experts/ at Taiwan Advanced Pet Professionals/ can make sure/ your pet gets the best.// Whether your dog has fleas,/ your cat has hairballs or a urinary tract infection,/ the professionals at TAPP can help.// We can/ and do/ take care of the minor problems/ as well as serious injuries.// We,/ at TAPP,/ can be trusted to help your pets heal/ from a broken leg/ or a cancerous lesion.// You can trust us.// You can trust/ Taiwan Advanced Pet Professionals.// At TAPP,/ we provide the most caring environments,/ the most up to date medical techniques,/ and the best veterinary service around.// Let TAPP care for your pets/ like they deserve.// They deserve the best,/ and TAPP provides it.//

第一句话"Your pet deserves the best"带入主题，我们就知道这个广告产品跟宠物有关，果然他说"... and only the good... experts at... make sure... pet gets... best"。

既然是广告，接下去必定是说明这家厂商的几点优势，听重音：

(1) ... dog... fleas... cat...hairballs... infection... professionals... TAPP... help

(2) We... can... minor problems... serious injuries

(3) We... TAPP... trusted... help... pets... heal... broken leg... cancerous lesion.

把所有关键词串联起来，我们知道这是一个宠物服务机构，负责照顾宠物清洁和医疗的问题。

较长的停顿后，听到"You can trust us"就知道服务项目已经说完了，接着是另一个主题，强调为什么可以信任他们。听重音："... most caring environments... most up to date medical techniques... best veterinary service... Let TAPP... pets... deserve"，这些是他们的优势。

■ 超级实用词汇

deserve v. 值得、应得
grooming n. 清理
advanced a. 高级的
professional n. 专家
fleas n. 跳蚤
urinary tract phr. 尿道
infection n. 感染
minor a. 小的；次要的；轻微的
injury n. 受伤
heal v. 治愈
caring a. 仁慈的；提供情感支柱的
up to date phr. 最新的
medical technique(s) phr. 医疗技术
veterinary a. 兽医的

Unit 2 电视及广播的广告

题目 Question **D**

Now, finally it's time for the highlight of the week — our weekly competition! Last week's prize of two National Theater tickets was won by Barry Jones. Congratulations, Barry. I hope you and your friend enjoyed the concert! This week we're offering a year's subscription to The World of Classical CDs to the first listener who can name this famous piece of music. I'm going to play the piece in a minute, but before I do, I'll give you some help, which should make your job a little easier. Are you ready? Right, now, listen carefully...

现在，终于到了一星期的高潮了——我们一周一次的竞赛。上星期的奖品是两张国家戏剧院的入场票，由贝利·琼斯赢得。贝利，恭喜了！希望你和你的朋友喜欢那场音乐会！这个星期，我们提供的奖项是一年期的《古典音乐世界》杂志。要得到这个大奖，你必须能够说出我放的这首曲子的名称。我马上就会开始放这首曲子，但是在开始之前，我会先给各位一点协助，好让各位能更轻松地说出答案。准备好了吗？好，现在，注意听……

❶ What's the prize of this week's competition?
本周比赛的奖品为何？

☐ (A) Two concert tickets. ················· 两张音乐会门票。
☐ (B) Classical CDs. ····················· 古典音乐 CD。
☑ (C) Music magazines. ··················· 音乐杂志。

❷ What does a listener need to do to win the prize?
想赢得奖品听众需要怎么做？

☑ (A) Be the first to say what the piece is.
 ················· 第一位说出这首曲子为何的人。
☐ (B) Be the first to say the name of the composer.
 ··················· 第一位说出作曲家的名字的人。
☐ (C) Be the first to say what period this piece was written. ········ 第一位说出这首曲子写于哪一个时期的人。

299

解析 Resolution

我们应该善用"语意单位"、语气停顿和语调来帮助理解。以下"//"符号表示较长停顿,也就是语句结束;"/"则表示短暂停顿,表示同一个句子内一个较小的"语意单位"的完成。

Now,// finally/ it's time/ for the highlight of the week//— our weekly competition.// Last week's prize of two National Theater tickets/ was won by Barry Jones.// Congratulations,/ Barry.// I hope you/ and your friend/ enjoyed the concert.// This week/ we're offering a year's subscription to/ The World of Classical CDs/ to the first listener/ who can name this famous piece of music.// I'm going to play the piece in a minute,/ but before I do,/ I'll give you some help,/ which should make your job a little easier.// Are you ready?// Right,// now,/ listen carefully... //

第一句话"Now, finally it's time for the highlight of the week..."带入主题,我们就知道这是一个节目的一部分,是什么节目呢?our weekly competition,一周一次的竞赛。

我们听到"Last week's prize..."就知道主持人先谈谈上周的状况:"two National Theater tickets was won by Bryan Jones..."。停顿后,我们听到"This week..."就知道今天的主题要开始了,他说"we're offering a year's subscription to The World of Classical CDs",给谁呢?听重音:"... first listener... name... famous music",第一个说出名曲名称的人。

接着比赛就要开始了:"I'm going to play... but before I do..."听到 but,表示还没有真正要开始,不开始要做什么呢?"I'll give you some help",也就是说主持人会先提供一些帮助!

■ 超级实用句型

the highlight of the week 一星期的高潮

I'll... but before I do... 我要……但是在那之前……

■ 可活用的补充句型

Both girls have entered the competition.
两个女孩都报名参加了比赛。

Competition from cheaper imports is making life tough for manufacturers.
低价进口货的竞争让制造商苦不堪言。

Name a price.
出个价吧。

I have named you for the position.
我提名你坐这个位子了。

Can you name the capital of India?
你说得出来印度的首都是哪里吗?

We must protect our company's good name.
我们必须保护我们公司的好名声。

■ 超级实用词汇

competition n. 比赛

offer v. 提供

subscription n. 订阅

name v. 说出……的名称

piece n. 曲子的单位

题目 **E** Tired of the daily grind? Ready for a day of excitement at Bonnie's Fun Fair? You can receive a free ticket to Bonnie's Fun Fair, by simply purchasing $ 1,000 worth of any Robinson Brothers games and puzzles. Send in the original dated receipt with the prices of the items circled and a completed redemption form to Galaxy Toy Offer, P.O. BOX 5112, Taipei, Taiwan. The redemption form must include your name, address, daytime phone and age and be postmarked no later than June 20th 2010. For detailed information, call 0-2-2345-7222.

你厌倦了日常生活中的琐事了吗？准备好要参加小白兔游乐园一日游了吗？只要你购买价值 1000 元的罗宾森兄弟游戏和拼图，就可以得到一张小白兔游乐园的免费入场券。把写有日期的收据上的价格圈起来，并填写申请表格，一起寄到台北邮政 5112 信箱，银河玩具公司。表格上必须填上你的姓名、地址、白天的联络电话和你的年龄，邮戳日期必须在 2010 年 6 月 20 日前！详细活动办法请自联系：0 — 2 — 2345 — 7222。

❶ Who would be most interested in this advertisement?
谁最可能对此广告有兴趣？

☑ **(A) Children.** .... 儿童。

☐ **(B) Computer programmers.** .... 软体工程师。

☐ **(C) Tourists.** .... 观光客。

❷ How can one get a free ticket to Bonnie's Fun Fair?
要如何才能得到小白兔游乐园的免费入场券？

☑ **(A) To spend a particular amount of money on some product.** .... 花一定的金额买游戏和拼图。

☐ **(B) To send personal information and take part in a draw.** .... 邮寄个人资料参加抽奖。

☐ **(C) To call and answer questions carefully.**
.... 打电话参加益智问答并小心回答。

解析
Resolution

我们应该善用"语意单位"、语气停顿和语调来帮助理解。以下"//"符号表示较长停顿，也就是语句结束；"/"则表示短暂停顿，表示同一个句子内一个较小的"语意单位"的完成。

Tired of the daily grind?// Ready for a day of excitement at Bonnie's Fun Fair?// You can receive a free ticket to Bonnie's Fun Fair,/ by simply purchasing NT$ 1000 worth of any Robinson Brothers games and puzzles.// Send in the original dated receipt/ with the prices of the items circled/ and a completed redemption form to Galaxy Toy Offer/ P.O. BOX 5112,/ Taipei,/ Taiwan.// The redemption form must include your name,/ address,/ daytime phone/ and age/ and be postmarked/ no later than June 20th/ 2010.// For detailed information,/ call 0-2-2345-7222.

第一句话"Tired of the daily grind? Ready for a day of excitement at Bonnie's Fun Fair?"告诉我们广告主题是 a day at Bonnie's Fun Fair。接下来一听到"You can receive a free ticket..."我们就可以预期他会说经由什么样的方法。果然他说"... by simply purchasing $ 1,000 worth of..."，购买价值一千元的东西即可。

接着，我们应可预期广告会详细叙述活动办法。听重音：

(1) Send... receipt... prices... circled... and... completed... form... Galaxy Toy Offer, P.O. BOX 5112, Taipei, Taiwan.
听到 and，知道是两个步骤。

(2) ... form must include... name, address, daytime phone... age...

(3) It must be postmarked no later than June 20th 2010.

听到 must 通常都是重点。

■ 超级实用句型

send A along with B 把 A 和 B 一起寄

■ 可活用的补充句型

The Natural History Museum in London is well worth a visit.
伦敦的自然历史博物馆很值得一去。

It was hard work, but it was worth it in the end.
过程很辛苦,但是最终的结果是值得的。

Keep your receipt in case you need to return anything.
保留收据,以免你需要退货。

The form should be completed and returned within 30 days of receipt.
请在收到表格三十天内填好并寄回。

Copying all the notes was a grind.
抄写这些笔记非常烦琐无聊。

How much do you think the house is worth?
你觉得这间房子值多少钱?

This ring must be worth a fortune.
这只戒指一定贵得不得了。

■ 超级实用词汇

grind n. 繁复;困难但无聊的活动

day tour phr. 一日游

fun fair phr. 游乐场

purchase v. 购买

worth n. 价值

receipt n. 收据

redemption form phr. 申请表格

personal information phr. 个人资料

postmark n. 邮戳

Unit 2 电视及广播的广告

题目 Question **F** Sylvia Internal Skin Care is a vital part of the way to take care of your skin. You'll see improvement not only on your face, but all over your body. Your skin would become smoother, softer, and more radiant. It's an all-over body approach, not the same old facial skin cream. Sylvia Internal Skin Care has been scientifically tested for efficacy. It has the clinically proven ability to improve the skin's density and appearance. Simply take two tablets of Sylvia Internal Skin Care each day – one in the morning and one at night, and you may notice a firmer, smoother, more radiant look in less than three months. And of course, a good moisturizer is still recommended for additional protection. Find Sylvia Care products at your local pharmacy. Your best skin is yet to come.

使用西微雅内服护肤产品，是你呵护自己皮肤的重要步骤。这样产生改变的不只脸部，而是全身。你的肌肤会变得更滑、更柔软、更有光泽。这是一种全身性的护肤方式，而非一般老式的面霜或乳液可比。西微雅内服护肤产品的效果经过科学测试，并经过临床证明能改变皮肤的紧实度和外观。每天只要服用两颗西微雅内服护肤产品——早上一颗、晚上一颗，你就可以在三个月内拥有更紧实、更柔滑、更有光泽的皮肤。当然，我们建议你仍需使用保湿乳液来护肤，以达到更多的保护。西微雅护肤产品在你家附近的药房有售。你最佳的肌肤状况即将来临了。

❶ Who is the most possible target group of the advertisement?
谁对这个广告的产品会最有兴趣？

☑ **(A) People who seek to look prettier.** 想看起来更美的人。

☐ **(B) People who seek to be healthier.** 想更健康的人。

☐ **(C) People who want to lose weight.** 想减重的人。

2 How often should a person use this product?
此产品如何使用？

☐ (A) Before each meal. —— 三餐前。

☑ (B) Twice a day. —— 每天两次。

☐ (C) Every other day. —— 每两天一次。

解析
Resolution

我们应该善用"语意单位"、语气停顿和语调来帮助理解。以下"//"符号表示较长停顿，也就是语句结束；"/"则表示短暂停顿，表示同一个句子内一个较小的"语意单位"的完成。

Sylvia Internal Skin Care/ is a vital part of the way/ you take care of your skin.// You'll see the improvement/ not only on your face,/ but all over your body.// Your skin becomes smoother,/ softer,/ and more radiant.// It's an all-over body approach,/ not the same/ old facial and skin cream.// Sylvia Internal Skin Care/ has been scientifically tested for efficacy.// It has the clinically proven ability/ to improve the skin's density/ and appearance.// Simply take two tablets/ of Sylvia Internal Skin Care/ each day// – one in the morning/ and one at night,/ and you may notice/ a firmer,/ smoother,/ more radiant look/ in less than three months.// And of course,/ a good moisturizer/ is still recommended/ for additional protection.// Find Sylvia Care products/ at your local pharmacy.// Your best skin/ is yet to come.//

> 第一句话 "...Skin Care... vital part... take care of your skin" 即带入主题，我们知道这个广告产品是跟护肤有关。
>
> 接着叙述产品的功效。听重音：
>
> (1) ... improvement not only... face... all over your body.
>
> (2) ... skin becomes smoother, softer, ... more radiant.
>
> (3) ... all-over body approach, not ... same old...
>
> 接着是不同层面的优势：... Skin Care... scientifically tested... efficacy... clinically proven... improve... density... appearance.
>
> 当我们听到 "Simply..."（"只要……"），就知道接下去是要告诉你怎么做。果然他说 "take two tablets... each day — one... morning and one... night"。听到 "And of course..." 知道要开始另一个主题：a good moisturizer is still recommended。当广告告诉你 "... is recommended"（"我们建议你……"），通常这个建议都是重点信息！
>
> 广告的最后常是购买方式和最后促销："Find... products at your local pharmacy. Your best skin is yet to come"。

■ 超级实用句型

be yet to come 就是会来但尚未来临

not the same old... 不是老是那一套……

Simply... 只要……即可

■ 可活用的补充句型

David played a vital role in guiding the project.
大卫在这个专案中扮演了重要的角色。

It is vital that you follow all safety procedures.
你遵循所有的安全程序是很重要的。

I admire your direct approach to the problem.
我欣赏你在处理这个问题上的直接方式。

Some doctors are trying a new approach to cancer treatment.
有些医生正在尝试用一种新的方式来治疗癌症。

We are approaching our destination.
我们快到终点站了。

There's an additional charge for returning the car two hours late.
车子晚两个小时还需要额外收费。

■ 超级实用词汇

vital a. 重要的；必需的
radiant a. 有光泽的
approach n. 方式
scientifically tested phr. 经过科学测试的
efficacy n. 效果
clinically proven ability phr. 经过临床证明的能力
density n. 密度；紧实度
appearance n. 外观
tablet n. （药丸）颗粒
moisturizer n. 保湿乳液
recommen(d) v. 建议
additional a. 额外的
available a. 可以得到的
local a. 当地的

Unit 2 电视及广播的广告

提醒便条纸 Reminder 舒葳老师的小叮咛，提枪上阵也不怕。

- 广播与广告都有一定的习惯与模式。习惯这样的模式有助于听力的理解。

- 广播与广告一开始都会先说明主题与目的，因此听清楚开头很重要。知道了这篇广播／广告主题是什么，便对接下来会听到的东西有了心理准备，就会比较容易听懂。

- 广播与广告中一直重复的关键词，也能帮助我们抓到主题、目的、对象和场合。

- 听长篇听力时，若能辨别哪一类的语句后面会接重要信息，便能让你在信息出来前准备好集中你的注意力。比如说，以下的这些句型都是在提示我们说话者马上要进入重点，听到这些，就表示你得特别注意听了："You must..., Remember to..., Don't forget..., Simply..., It's recommended..., It's important..."等。

- 另外，一般的祈使句也常会接重点，例如"Send..., Complete..., Find..., Call..., Listen carefully..."等句型。既然说话者在请你做某些事情，这些事情就有可能是重点。

MEMO

Listening & Speaking

MEMO

Practice 4

听力实战练习 4
News and Weather Reports
新闻与天气预报

听力
Listening
口语
Speaking

Unit 1 新闻与天气预报

学习重点
Main Point

最后，我们要来练习听新闻与天气预报。这也是我们在生活中经常接触到的听力类型。因为同样也是长篇听力，因此除了一般的发音、重音及连音等技巧外，使用"语调"及"语意单位"来提升听力水平仍然是本课的重点。

另一个重点则是熟悉老外在报新闻及天气时的习惯模式。听多了，熟悉了一贯的模式，也会帮助你听懂。

Unit 1

新闻与天气预报

热身活动 Warm Up 学习英语前，先来做个热身吧！

请听 MP3，并选择适当的答案，每段文章有两道题目。

题目 Questions

A What is the speaker's purpose?

  A. To state the latest findings on Mars.

  B. To describe a space adventure.

  C. To compare life on Earth with that on Mars.

2 What did the speaker say about Mars?

  A. There was water on Mars.

  B. There wasn't water on Mars ever.

  C. There was life on Mars.

B 1 What's the point the speaker is trying to make?

  A. The importance of creativity at work.

  B. The relationship between creativity and the atmosphere of the workplace.

  C. Pressure at work brings effectiveness.

2 A playful atmosphere in the work place is particularly important for which type of company?

  A. An advertising company.

  B. A shoe-making factory.

  C. Real estate brokers.

C ❶ What isn't true about the robber?

   A. He is often in black.

   B. He rides a black motorbike.

   C. He has broken into more than ten houses.

❷ Why is he considered dangerous?

   A. People have been reported injured.

   B. He carries weapons with him.

   C. He has a previous criminal record.

D ❶ What's the purpose of the news?

   A. To tell upsetting news about a boy from a poor family.

   B. To explain how one can improve his English ability.

   C. To report the story about a boy who has won a competition.

❷ What is NOT true about the boy?

   A. He has just started going to English classes.

   B. He is self-motivated and diligent.

   C. He won the first prize of the contest.

E ❶ What is Saturday evening's weather forecast?

   A. Hot and humid all over the island.

   B. Heavy rain over the entire island.

   C. Light showers over the northern part.

❷ Some people are planning for a picnic on Sunday. When should they go?

   A. After around 10:00 a.m.

   B. After around 1:00 p.m.

   C. After around 3:00 p.m.

F **❶** What is the main problem with the typhoon?

A. Heavy rain.

B. Strong wind.

C. Both.

❷ What is said about people who work for private companies?

A. They can have a day off tomorrow.

B. They should ask their boss if they need to work tomorrow.

C. They should wait for farther information to be announced.

解答 Answers		
A ❶A ❷A		D ❶C ❷A
B ❶B ❷A		E ❶C ❷C
C ❶C ❷B		F ❶A ❷B

实际演练 Explanation

通过认真的解题练习打下扎实的基础。

题目 Question

A After months and even years waiting for an answer, we at the 6 p.m. evening news have finally brought you the answer. The American and European space agencies' rocket to Mars has successfully touched down on the northern surface of Mars. We have been receiving radio signals from the landing craft and are now awaiting a basic response to our first processing request sent from earth this morning. The most momentous news so far, is that the Martian Lander has confirmed reports indicating the presence of water on the surface of Mars. Now, we wait for the answer to the biggest question of all, is there any evidence of life on the surface of Mars? Tune in tomorrow for continuing reports on the space expedition.

在长久的等待之后，我们在六点钟晚间新闻为大家带来一个您期待已久的问题的答案。美国和欧洲宇航局送往火星的火箭已经成功地在火星北边的表面着陆了。我们已经陆续收到从着陆的火箭上传来的信号，现在在等待的是，它们对我们今天早上传过去的初步请求做出回应。目前对历史最有决定性意义的发现是火星登陆号已经证实火星表面有水存在过的迹象。现在我们只需要等待我们最重要的问题的答案：火星表面有没有生命的迹象？明天请准时收看，我们将有火星探险的后续报道。

1 What is the speaker's purpose?
这段话的目的、主旨为何？

☑ (A) To state the latest findings on Mars.
陈述火星上的最新发现。

☐ (B) To describe a space adventure.
形容一场太空探险的经过。

☐ (C) To compare life on Earth with that on Mars.
比较地球和火星上生命的不同。

❷ What did the speaker say about Mars?
说话者如何叙述火星？

☑ **(A) There was water on Mars.** ……… 火星上曾经有水。

☐ **(B) There wasn't water on Mars ever.**
火星上从来没有水过。

☐ **(C) There was life on Mars.** ……… 火星上曾经有生命。

解析
Resolution

善用"语意单位"及语气停顿和语调来帮助理解。以下"//"符号表示较长停顿，也就是语句结束；"/"则表示短暂停顿，表示同一个句子内一个较小的"语意单位"的完成。

After months/ and even years waiting for an answer,/ we/ at the 6 p.m. evening news/ can finally bring you part of the answer.// The American and European space agencies' rocket to Mars/ has successfully touched down/ on the northern surface of Mars.// We have been receiving radio signals from the landing craft/ and are now awaiting a basic response/ to our first processing request/ sent from earth this morning.// The most momentous news so far,/ is that the Martian lander has confirmed reports/ indicating the presence of water on the surface of Mars.// Now,/ we wait for the answer to the biggest question of all,/ is there any evidence of life on the surface of Mars?// Tune in tomorrow/ for continuing reports on the space expedition.//

> 新闻一开始"After months and even years of waiting for an answer, we at the 6 p.m. evening news have finally brought you an answer",
>
> 即说明这段新闻的主题:我们带来一个大家期待的问题的解答。后来当我们听到"The most momentous news so far is that..."就知道播报员要给我们一些重要的信息,也就是题目要问的重点。他接着说"the... has confirmed reports... presence of water... Mars",因此我们知道火星上有水。
>
> 最后一段他用疑问的句型说:Is there any evidence of life on the surface of Mars? 表示我们还不知道这个问题的答案,"Tune in tomorrow for continuing reports...",要看明天的报道了。

■ 超级实用句型

tune in tomorrow for...
明天请转到这个频道继续收看……

■ 可活用的补充句型

Please tune in to the news channel.
请转到新闻台。

The dentist's office called to confirm your appointment for tomorrow.
牙医打电话来确认你明天的预约。

■ 超级实用词汇

surface n. 表面

signal n. 信号

landing craft phr. 着陆的火箭

craft n. 座舱

momentous a. 非常重要的;对历史有决定性意义的

confirmed a. 确定的;证实了的

presence n. 存在

evidence n. 证据

expedition n. 探险

题目 | **B** Good evening. CCB News. I'm Mark Kory. A recent Gallup poll comparing working environments suggests improving the atmosphere in the workplace can create higher creative output. Many businesses reported that employees that truly enjoy their workplace are more creative in their problem solving and that employees that find work miserable have trouble solving simple problems that arise each day. So if you find your workplace isn't providing you and your employees with an enjoyable experience, get up and bring some levity to the workplace. Your improved productivity and the employees' creativity may just surprise you.

晚上好，**CBB** 新闻。我是马克・科里。最近一项盖洛普比较工作环境的民意调查，发现改善工作场所的气氛能提高工作的创意。很多公司表示，真正享受工作环境的员工在解决问题上有较多的创意；而觉得工作很痛苦的员工，则没办法解决每天工作上遇到的简单问题。所以如果你觉得你的工作环境不能给你和你的员工愉快的工作体验，那么你得想办法为你的公司注入一点轻松的气氛了。工作效率的提升和员工的创意可能会给你意想不到的惊喜。

1 What's the point the speaker is trying to make?
本篇报道的重点为何？

☐ **(A)** The importance of creativity at work.
创意在工作上的重要性。

☑ **(B)** The relationship between creativity and the atmosphere of the workplace.
工作表现与工作气氛的关联。

☐ **(C)** Pressure at work brings effectiveness.
工作压力带来工作效率。

Unit 1 新闻与天气预报

2 A playful atmosphere in the work place is particularly important for which type of company?
气氛欢愉的工作场合对哪一种公司特别重要?

☑ **(A) An advertising company.** ············ 广告公司。
☐ (B) A shoe-making factory. ············ 制鞋工厂。
☐ (C) Real estate brokers. ············ 房地产中介。

解析 Resolution

善用"语意单位"及语气停顿和语调来帮助理解。以下"//"符号表示较长停顿,也就是语句结束;"/"则表示短暂停顿,表示同一个句子内一个较小的"语意单位"的完成。

Good evening.// CCB News.// I'm Mark Kory.// A recent Gallup poll comparing working environments/ suggests improving the atmosphere in the workplace/ can improve creative output.// Many businesses reported that employees who truly enjoy their workplace/ are more creative in their problem solving/ and that employees that find work miserable/ have trouble solving simple problems that arise each day.// So,/ if you find your workplace isn't providing you/ and your employees with an enjoyable experience,/ get up and bring some levity/ to the workplace.// Your improved productivity/ and the employees' creativity/ may just surprise you.//

谈话开头都会先说明主题:"A recent Gallup poll comparing working environments suggests... atmosphere... workplace... improve... output",因此我们知道主题是工作环境,并且与职场气氛、工作表现有关。

> 整个新闻接下来就会谈到此份调查的细节：Many businesses reported that...
>
> (1) ... employees... enjoy their workplace... creative...
>
> (2) ... employees... find... miserable have trouble solving simple problems
>
> 上面两句中间的 and that 表示连接两个完整的"语意单位"，也就是说有两个重点。
>
> 最后他说 "So, ..." 表示要做结论或建议。祈使句 "get up and bring some levity to the workplace... improved productivity... creativity... surprise you" 中，如果 levity 这个单词不认识，应该也可以从前后文猜到与良好气氛有关。关键词告诉我们会提升创造力与创意。因此，以创意为导向的行业自然是最需要轻松愉悦的工作环境。

■ 超级实用句型

A recent... suggests that... 最新的……认为……

■ 你也可以这么说

A recent scientific study suggests that whiskey causes worse hangovers than vodka.
最新的科学研究认为威士忌比伏特加更容易造成宿醉。

Data from a recent study suggests that stressful life experiences may play a larger role in provoking depression in women than in men.
最新研究资料显示，高压的人生经验导致女性忧郁的概率可能性高于男性。

■ 超级实用词汇

Gallup poll *phr.* 盖洛普民意调查

atmosphere *n.* 气氛

miserable *a.* 令人痛苦的

levity *n.* 轻松的气氛

productivity *n.* 生产力；创造力

Unit 1 新闻与天气预报

题目 Question | C

In Sanchung recently there has been a series of amazing bank robberies. The suspected mastermind works alone, but those who have witnessed the crimes have dubbed him the Black Rider. This name comes from his tendency to wear all black leather riding gear as he zips away from the scene of the crime. His motorcycle is completely black also, and he often rides away without any safety lights or headlights after committing his armed robberies. The police consider him armed and dangerous. Please use extreme caution if you see this man, anyone matching these characteristics or any odd behavior around any Sanchung area banks. Make your way to the nearest phone or use your mobile phone to inform the police immediately.

最近在三重发生了一连串的不可思议的银行抢劫案。这个智慧型嫌疑犯独自作案，那些看见过他的人称之为"黑骑士"。这个名字的由来是因为他习惯穿一身黑色皮制骑士装，从犯案现场蛇行离去。他的摩托车也是全黑，而且他常在武装抢劫后，不开安全灯或大灯就骑着他的黑色摩托车扬长而去。他因携带武器而被警方视为危险人物。如果你看到这个人，请特别小心——任何符合以上特征，或在三重地区银行附近举止怪异之人，请就近拨打电话或用手机向警方报案。

❶ What isn't true about the robber?
哪一个选项不符合对此抢劫者的叙述？

☐ (A) He is often in black. ……… 他常穿一身黑衣。

☐ (B) He rides a black motorbike. ……… 他骑黑色摩托车。

☑ (C) He has broken into more than ten houses.
……… 他已闯入了十户以上民宅。

② Why is he considered dangerous?
他为什么被视为危险人物？

☐ (A) People have been reported injured. ········ 据报道有人受伤。

☑ (B) He carries weapons with him. ········ 他身上携带武器。

☐ (C) He has previous criminal records. ········ 他有犯罪前科。

解析
Resolution

善用"语意单位"及语气停顿和语调来帮助理解。以下"//"符号表示较长停顿，也就是语句结束；"/"则表示短暂停顿，表示同一个句子内一个较小的"语意单位"的完成。

In Sanchung recently/ there has been a series of amazing bank robberies.// The suspected mastermind works alone,/ but those who have witnessed the crimes/ have dubbed him/ the Black Rider.// This name comes from his tendency/ to wear all black leather riding gear/ as he zips away from the scene of the crimes.// His motorcycle is completely black,/ and he often rides away/ without any safety lights or headlights/ after committing his armed robberies.// The police consider him/ armed and dangerous.// Use extreme caution if you see this man,/ anyone matching these characteristics/ or if you witness any odd behavior/ around any Sanchung area banks.// Make your way to the nearest phone/ or use your mobile phone/ to inform the police immediately.//

Unit 1 新闻与天气预报

> 新闻报道一开始即说明 "In Sanchung recently... bank robberies"，我们知道这篇报道是关于 "三重的银行抢劫"。
>
> 接着 "The suspected..., but those... the Black Rider"，我们知道接下去是关于嫌疑犯的信息。从重音抓关键词，我们听到 "Black Rider... tendency... all black leather riding gear... motorcycle... black... rides away" 等，我们可以推测他身穿黑衣并骑摩托车。从 "...committing his armed robberies ...police... armed dangerous"，关键词 armed 出现两次，因此我们可以推知他有武器。

■ 超级实用句型

consider him... 认为他……

those who have witnessed the crimes 那些犯罪的目击者

■ 你也可以这么说

Everyone considered Daniel is a very smart kid.
大家都认为丹尼尔是一个非常聪明的小孩。

Daniel was considered one of the smartest kids in the class.
丹尼尔被认为是班上最聪明的小孩之一。

■ 超级实用词汇

robbery n. 抢劫

suspect n. 嫌疑犯

dub v. 称某人为；为某人取绰号

tendency n. 倾向

riding gear ph. 骑士装

zip away phr. 蛇行离开

the scene of the crime phr. 犯罪现场

commit v. 犯案

armed a. 武装的

characteristics n. 特征

题目 **D** Although much of the news tends towards the negative these days, we are proud now to bring you this human-interest story. In the recent English Spelling Bee for high school children all over Taiwan, there was a young boy who consistently proved better than the rest. Not only was his incredible accuracy in spelling English words remarkable, but also his background. He never attended an English cram school. He does not come from a rich family and never had any tutoring. It was through his own interest and incredible work ethic that he managed to study the English language all by himself. He learned by reading the paper, listening to the radio, TV and books he bought for himself. Just to let you know how amazing this feat was, the winning word, that he alone spelled correctly, was antidisestablishmentarianism, the longest word in most English language dictionaries. Tonight on SWW TV's evening news program, we will proudly recognize this boy's feat and award him the Spelling Bee's million-dollar prize. Congratulations John, you make us all proud!

虽然最近的新闻都倾向负面内容的报道，但今天我们很高兴为您带来一则人文趣闻。在最近举办的高中英语拼字比赛中，有一个男孩表现出众。令人赞赏的，他不只是他在拼字上有令人无法置信的正确度，还有他的背景。他从未上过英语补习班、并非出生于富裕家庭、也没请过家教。他凭着自己的兴趣和异常的认真态度，自己苦读英语。他通过读报纸、听广播、看电视、和阅读他自己买的书来自学。你知道他的成就有多么让人惊叹吗？他拿下最难的字获得冠军，他也是唯一一个拼出这个词的参赛者，是"反对国家政府和教堂之间应该有官方正式关系的主张"（**antidisestablishmentarianism**）。这是英语字典中最长的一个字。今晚，在 SWW 电视新闻中，我们将荣幸地肯定这个男孩的成就，并且颁发这个拼词比赛的百万元奖金。恭喜你约翰，我们都很为你感到骄傲！

Unit 1 新闻与天气预报

① What's the purpose of the news?
新闻主旨是什么？

☐ **(A) To tell upsetting news about a boy from a poor family.** 叙述一个来自贫苦家庭的男孩令人难过的故事。

☐ **(B) To explain how one can improve his English ability.** 解释人如何能改进自己的英语能力。

☑ **(C) To report the story about a boy who has won a competition.** 报道一个男孩赢得比赛的故事。

② What is NOT true about the boy?
关于这个男孩，以下的哪一个叙述不正确？

☑ **(A) He has just started going to English classes.** 他才刚开始去补习班上课。

☐ **(B) He is self-motivated and diligent.** 他自己有高度的学习动机，并且很用功。

☐ **(C) He won the first prize of the context.** 他赢得比赛冠军。

解析 Resolution

善用"语意单位"及语气停顿和语调来帮助理解。以下"//"符号表示较长停顿，也就是语句结束；"/"则表示短暂停顿，表示同一个句子内一个较小的"语意单位"的完成。

Although much of the news tends towards the negative these days,/ we are proud/ to bring you this human-interest story.// In the recent English Spelling Bee/ for high school children all over Taiwan,/ there was a young boy/ who consistently proved better than the rest.// Not only was his incredible accuracy/

in spelling English words remarkable,/ but also his background.// He never attended an English cram school.// He does not come from a rich family/ and never had any tutoring.// It was through his own interest/ and incredible work ethic/ that he managed to study the English language/ all by himself.// Just to let you know how amazing this feat was,/ the winning word,/ that he alone/ spelled correctly,/ was antidisestablishmentarianism,/ the longest word in most English language dictionaries.// Tonight/ on SWW TV's evening news program,/ we will proudly recognize this boy's feat/ and award him the Spelling Bee's/ million-dollar prize.// Congratulations John,// you make us all proud!//

第一句话，当我们听到"Although... news tends... negative, ..."（"虽然通常是负面的，……"），我们就知道接下去会听到的，会是一个令人高兴的新闻。因为 although 后面接的句子都会是跟前面的 idea 是相反的。也就是说 Although A, B，中文为：虽然 A，但是 B（A 子句和 B 子句会表达相反的意念）。

当我们听到"Not only was his incredible accuracy in spelling English words remarkable..."我们就知道除了比赛成绩优异，还有其他故事，果然他说：... but also his background. 他的背景也很值得一听。所以我们也可以推知接下去应该会介绍他的背景。

接下去的几个重点：

(1) He never attended an English cram school.

(2) He does not... a rich family and never... tutoring.

(3) It was... his own interest and incredible work ethic... study the English language all by himself.

> (4) He learned by reading the paper, listening to the radio, TV and books...
>
> 都是在介绍他的背景，之后的较长的停顿告诉我们这个主题已经结束了。
>
> 当我们听到语调提高 Just to let you know how amazing this feat was...，我们知道这又是一个新的 idea 的开始。详细说明他的表现。停顿之后的"Tonight on SWW TV's evening news..."语调提高，又是一个新的"语意单位"。最后的"million-dollar prize Congratulations..."重新强调他赢了大奖的这件事。

■ 超级实用句型

Not only was..., but also... 不仅……，而且……

It was through... that he... 通过……他……

■ 可活用的补充句型

Not only is it a comfortable and stylish hotel, it's also a popular conference venue.
这不仅是一间舒服时尚的饭店，也是很受欢迎的会议场地。

Not only can Jason make people laugh, he can make them cry as well.
杰生不仅能使人捧腹大笑，他也能使人痛哭流涕。

Through hard work, perseverance, Stanly made sure he was noticed.
经努力与坚持，史丹利让别人看见了他的表现。

People could make a good life for themselves and their families through hard work and determination.
人们可以经努力与意志力，为他们自己以及他们的家庭创造好的生活。

My mom is constantly changing her mind.
我妈妈总是改变主意。

My dad suffers from constant headaches.
我父亲有持续性头痛的毛病。

Her contribution to the country has been generally recognized.
她的贡献是受到多数人的肯定的。

I didn't recognize you at first with your new haircut.
你换发型了，我一开始没认出你来。

■ 超级实用词汇

English Spelling Bee phr. 英语拼词比赛

negative a. 负面的

consistently a. 持续地；一再不断地

constant a. 固定的

proved a. 被证明的

incredible a. 令人不可置信的

accuracy n. 正确度

remarkable a. 非常优异的

attend(ed) v. 出席

feat n. 某人做的某件令人赞赏的事

recognize v. 认可；肯定

prize n. 奖金；奖品

Unit 1 新闻与天气预报

题目 Question **E** For those of you planning outdoor activities this weekend, you can expect fair skies for most of the day Saturday with temperatures in the high 30's. However, things may change by Saturday evening with a storm front moving in. We can expect light, scattered showers over the northern part of the island bringing slightly cooler temperatures in the 20's throughout Saturday evening. This rain should taper off by mid-Sunday morning. The partly cloudy skies will persist for the rest of the morning, and move out by mid-afternoon on Sunday, when things will improve dramatically. The sun will come out and the skies should be clear for the rest of the day on Sunday and through the night. And that's all for today's weekend weather report.

计划这个周末要从事户外活动的人，预计星期六几乎整天都是晴天，气温大约是三十七到三十九摄氏度。但是星期六晚上暴风雨云团接近，可能会变天。轻度阵雨会散布整个本岛北部，带来星期六晚上微凉的二十几摄氏度的气温。雨势在星期天早上中间时段就会变小。几乎整个早上都是多云的天气，但是在下午的中间时段云层会散去，天气会放晴，并且一直持续到晚上。以上是今天的周末气象预报。

1 What is Saturday evening's weather forecast?
星期六晚上的气象预告如何？

☐ (A) Hot and humid all over the island. 全岛炎热潮湿。

☐ (B) Heavy rain over the entire island. ⋯⋯北部有豪雨。

☑ (C) Light showers over the northern part.
岛上某些地方有些雨。

Practice **4**

② Some people are planning for a picnic on Sunday. When should they go?
有一群人计划星期天要野餐,他们应该什么时候能去?

- ☐ (A) After around 10:00 a.m. ……… 大约早上十点以后。
- ☑ (B) After around 1:00 p.m. ……… 大约下午一点以后。
- ☐ (C) After around 3:00 p.m. ……… 大约下午三点以后。

解析 Resolution

善用"语意单位"及语气停顿和语调来帮助理解。以下"//"符号表示较长停顿,也就是语句结束;"/"则表示短暂停顿,表示同一个句子内一个较小的"语意单位"的完成。

For those of you planning outdoor activities this weekend,/ you can expect fair skies/ for most of the day Saturday/ with temperatures in the high 30's.// However,/ things may change by Saturday evening/ with a storm front moving in.// We can expect light,/ scattered showers/ over the northern part of the island/ bringing slightly cooler temperatures/ in the 20's/ throughout Saturday evening.// This rain should taper off/ by mid-Sunday morning.// The partly cloudy skies will persist/ for the rest of the morning,/ and move out/ by mid-afternoon on Sunday,/ when things will improve dramatically.// The sun will come out/ and the skies should be clear/ for the rest of the day on Sunday/ and through the night.// And/ that's all for today's/ weekend weather report.//

Unit 1 新闻与天气预报

开头听重音，我们听到"weekend，fair skies，Saturday，temperatures，high 30's"，告诉我们周六会有好天气。但接下去当我们听到"However..."（"但是……"），就知道应该要说坏消息了，果然他说："Saturday evening... a storm front"，"周六晚会有暴风雨云团"。接下来听到"We can expect..."就表示他要开始叙述接下来的天气变化：

(1) scattered showers，the northern part... island，cooler temperatures... 20's
我们知道北部会有轻微的阵雨。

(2) ... rain... taper off by mid-Sunday morning.
星期天早上雨量减小。

(3) ... partly cloudy... persist... rest... morning, and move out... mid-afternoon... Sunday, ... improve dramatically.
几乎整个早上都是多云，云层在下午的中间时段以前散去，天气立即转好。

(4) ... sun... come out... skies... clear... rest of Sunday... through the night.
天气会放晴，并且一直持续到晚上。

■ 超级实用句型

temperatures in the high 30's 近四十摄氏度的气温
└ high 30's 大约是三十七到三十九摄氏度

■ 超级实用词汇

expect `v.` 预期
fair skies `phr.` 晴空
a storm front `phr.` 暴风雨云团
scattered `a.` 散布
taper off `phr.` 变小；变少
persist `v.` 持续
clear `a.` 放晴
mid Sunday morning `phr.` 星期天早上中间时段，约十点左右
mid afternoon `phr.` 下午中间时段，两三点左右

题目 **F**

As of 8 p.m. this evening, due to the continuing effects of the typhoon pummeling northern Taiwan with record rainfalls, we have to report the official closings of many schools and government offices for tomorrow. The flooding has so far caused an estimated 1 million dollars in property damage and flooding over much of Taipei with more flooding expected tomorrow. The official list of closings consists of all elementary and secondary schools, Taipei University, Taiwan Normal University, and National Taiwan University. In addition, all government offices not directly involved with disaster prevention and recovery will also be closed. The decision to close individual businesses will be left up to the owners of each business, but we expect many stores and offices to be closed tomorrow. Please stay tuned for more information.

今晚八点钟，由于台风带来的暴雨对台湾北部的持续影响，明天许多学校及公共机构停止上课上班。目前为止，大暴雨所导致的洪水估计已经造成了一百万美元的财物损失。台北市到处是洪水，并且预期洪水区域明天会继续扩大。已公布停止上课的学校包括：所有中小学、台北大学、台湾师范大学和台湾大学。另外，所有不涉及灾害防治及重建的公共机构也都停止上班一天。私人公司是否上班上课，将由公司自行决定，但我们可以预见许多商家及公司明天会停止营业。请不要转台，我们还会有陆续的报道。

① What is the main problem with the typhoon?
这个台风最大的威胁是什么？

☑ **(A) Heavy rain.** .... 暴雨。

☐ **(B) Strong wind.** .... 强风。

☐ **(C) Both.** .... 两者皆是。

② What is said about people who work for private companies?

报道怎么说私人公司的员工？

☐ (A) They can have a day off tomorrow. 他们明天放假一天。

☑ (B) They should ask their boss if they need to work tomorrow. 他们应该问老板是否要上班。

☐ (C) They should wait for further information to be announced. 他们应该等更多信息的公告。

解析
Resolution

善用"语意单位"及语气停顿和语调来帮助理解。以下"//"符号表示较长停顿，也就是语句结束；"/"则表示短暂停顿，表示同一个句子内一个较小的"语意单位"的完成。

As of 8 p.m. this evening,/ due to the continuing effects of the typhoon/ pummeling northern Taiwan with record rainfalls,/ we have to report the official closings of many schools/ and government offices for tomorrow.// The flooding has/ so far caused an estimated/ 1 million dollars/ in property damage,/ and we expect the water to keep rising over much of Taipei/ throughout the day tomorrow.// The official list of closings consists of all elementary and secondary schools,/ Taipei University,/ Taiwan Normal University,/ and National Taiwan University.// In addition,/ all government offices/ not directly involved with disaster prevention and recovery/ will also be closed.// The decision to close individual businesses/ will be left up to the owners of each business,/ but we expect many stores/ and offices to be closed tomorrow.// Please stay tuned for more information.//

报道的一开始即说明主题，听重音："... effects... typhoon... northern Taiwan... record rainfalls... official closings... schools... government offices"，表示因台风及暴雨之故，宣布停止上班上课。

接着的 "... flooding... 1 million dollars in property damage... flooding... Taipei... more flooding expected..."，让我们了解到大家深受淹水之苦。

当我们听到 "The official list of closings consists of..." 表示要开始宣布停止上班上课的学校机构：elementary and secondary schools, Taipei University, Taiwan Normal University, and National Taiwan University。注意音调到全部说完时才下降，因此当他语调仍上扬时我们应该知道还要继续注意听。听到 "In addition..."，表示这个主题还没结束："... all government offices... not involve disaster prevention... also... closed" 说明公家机关的状况。最后一个 item 则谈到私人公司："The decision... individual businesses... left up... the owners... business"，表示由老板自行决定。

■ 超级实用句型

Please stay tuned... 不要转台（留在这个频道上）

as of（时间）起、截至（时间）

■ 可活用的补充句型

The project was terminated as of January 1.
这个项目到 1 月 1 日终止。

The report remains unfinished as of yet.
这个报告到目前为止尚未完成。

It is impossible to estimate how many of the residents were affected. 很难估算有多少居民被影响。

One conservative estimate is that the damage is worth five million dollars. 保守估计，损失达到了五百万美元。

They lost all their property in the fire.
他们在火灾中失去了所有的财物。

If you want to make things better, you need to get involved.
如果你想要让事情更好，你需要身体力行地参与进来。

■ 超级实用词汇

pummel v. 冲击；造成灾害
rainfall n. 雨量
flood n. 洪水；水灾
estimate v. 估计
property n. 财物
damage n. 伤害；损失
involve v. 参与；牵涉
disaster n. 灾害
prevention n. 防止；防范
recovery n. 复原；重建
tune v. 转到某电视台或广播频道

> **提醒便条纸 Reminder** 舒葳老师的小叮咛，提枪上阵也不怕。

- 在新闻播报中，新闻主题通常在第一句话就会出现。有时候第一句话则是用来转承及连接上一则新闻的开场白，即便如此，主题也一定在第二句话出现。听清楚主题句才能帮助我们听懂细节。

- 新闻播报通常以主题句先概述重点，再叙述细节；气象预报则会开宗明义地进入正题，讲天气，并依天气出现的时间顺序播报。了解播报员说话的架构或顺序，能帮助我们轻松抓到重点。

- 听长篇听力时，熟悉特定转承语的用法和语意，能帮助我们预测接下来的内容，让你的听力大大加分。以下是一些例子：

    (1) 表示接下去是相反或对比的语意：however, ...（然而……）；on the other hand, ...（另一方面……）；...having said that, ...（……虽然这么说，但是……）；although A, B（虽然 A，但是 B，A 子句与 B 子句意义相反）；despite A, B（尽管 A，但是 B，A 子句与 B 子句意义相反）；等等。

    (2) 表示接下去是相同概念的补充说明：in addition, ...（除此之外……）；on top of that, ...（不仅如此……）；besides, ...（除此之外……）；moreover, ...（还有……）；what is more, ...（还有……）；等等。

    (3) 表示要举例说明：for instance, ...（例如……）；to give you an example, ...（譬如说……）；take... as an example, ...（例如……）；consider...（想想……）；等等。

    (4) 表示原因或影响：due to the...（由于……）；owing to the...（由于……）；since...（既然……）；in consequence, ...（因此……）；hence, ...（因此……）；therefore, ...（因此……）；等等。

- 最后，无论是句子还是对话，短篇或者长篇，一定要多听。在重复听时可以边听边看录音稿，用这本书学到的东西诊断自己听不懂的原因，是单词不认识？是自己发音不正确？是听不懂连音？是不了解惯用语的意思吗？是语调会错意吗？找到原因后对症下药，不会什么就学什么。学会了自己不懂的东西后，再持续多听几次，你的听力一定会有提高！

版权专有 侵权必究

图书在版编目（CIP）数据

英语听力、口语技巧大全 / 王舒葳著. —北京：北京理工大学出版社，2019.7
ISBN 978-7-5682-4596-8

Ⅰ.①英… Ⅱ.①王… Ⅲ.①英语—听说教学—自学参考资料 ②英语—口语—自学参考资料 Ⅳ.①H319.9

中国版本图书馆CIP数据核字（2017）第197707号

北京市版权局著作权合同登记号图字：01-2017-2396
简体中文版由我识出版社有限公司授权出版发行
61亿人都在学的听力、口说技巧：王舒葳老师英文听力、口说特训班，王舒葳著，2016年，初版
ISBN：9789865785888

出版发行 / 北京理工大学出版社有限责任公司
社　　址 / 北京市海淀区中关村南大街5号
邮　　编 / 100081
电　　话 / （010）68914775（总编室）
　　　　　（010）82562903（教材售后服务热线）
　　　　　（010）68948351（其他图书服务热线）
网　　址 / http://www.bitpress.com.cn
经　　销 / 全国各地新华书店
印　　刷 / 天津久佳雅创印刷有限公司
开　　本 / 710毫米×1000毫米　1/16
印　　张 / 21.75　　　　　　　　　　　　　　　责任编辑 / 李慧智
字　　数 / 500千字　　　　　　　　　　　　　　文案编辑 / 李慧智
版　　次 / 2019年7月第1版　2019年7月第1次印刷　责任校对 / 周瑞红
定　　价 / 66.00元　　　　　　　　　　　　　　责任印制 / 李志强

图书出现印装质量问题，请拨打售后服务热线，本社负责调换